D0794253

Analysis of
Financial
Statements

Second Edition

THE FRANK J. FABOZZI SERIES

Analysis of
Financial
Statements

Second Edition

PAMELA P. PETERSON

FRANK J. FABOZZI

WILEY

John Wiley & Sons, Inc.

Copyright © 2006 by John Wiley & Sons, Inc. All rights reserved

Published by John Wiley & Sons, Inc., Hoboken, New Jersey
Published simultaneously in Canada

No part of this publication may be reproduced, stored in a retrieval system, or transmitted in
any form or by any means, electronic, mechanical, photocopying, recording, scanning, or otherwise, except as permitted under Section 107 or 108 of the 1976 United States Copyright
Act, without either the prior written permission of the Publisher, or authorization through
payment of the appropriate per-copy fee to the Copyright Clearance Center, Inc., 222 Rose-
wood Drive, Danvers, MA 01923, (978) 750-8400, fax (978) 750-4470, or on the web at
www.copyright.com. Requests to the Publisher for permission should be addressed to the Per-
missions Department, John Wiley & Sons, Inc., 111 River Street, Hoboken, NJ 07030, (201)
748-6011, fax (201) 748-6008, or online at http://www.wiley.com/go/permissions.

Limit of Liability/Disclaimer of Warranty: While the publisher and author have used their best
efforts in preparing this book, they make no representations or warranties with respect to the
accuracy or completeness of the contents of this book and specifically disclaim any implied
warranties of merchantability or fitness for a particular purpose. No warranty may be created
or extended by sales representatives or written sales materials. The advice and strategies con-
tained herein may not be suitable for your situation. You should consult with a professional
where appropriate. Neither the publisher nor author shall be liable for any loss of profit or
any other commercial damages, including but not limited to special, incidental, consequential,
or other damages.

For general information on our other products and services or for technical support, please
contact our Customer Care Department within the United States at (800) 762-2974, outside
the United States at (317) 572-3993 or fax (317) 572-4002.

Wiley also publishes its books in a variety of electronic formats. Some content that appears in
print may not be available in electronic books. For more information about Wiley products,
visit our web site at www.wiley.com.

ISBN-13 978-0-471-71964-9
ISBN-10 0-471-71964-1

Printed in the United States of America

10 9 8 7 6 5 4 3 2 1

PPP
To my husband Randy and my children Erica and Ken

FJF
To my daughter Karly, my little Pumpkin Pie

Contents

PART TWO

Analysis of Financial Statements   93

PART THREE

Applying Financial Analysis   195

Preface

In *Analysis of Financial Statements*, we introduce you to the tools and techniques of financial analysis. We also provide a foundation for financial analysis with the goal of assisting you in the analysis of the financial condition and operating performance of a company.

This book is the second edition of *Analysis of Financial Statements*, which was first published in 1999. The most significant difference between this book and the previous edition is the role of the Sarbanes-Oxley (SOX) Act of 2002, which affects disclosures, the role of auditors, the role of financial analysts, and even the information set with which analysts have to work. We have incorporated the changes from the SOX Act throughout this book and discuss the key events that inspired the SOX Act.

You will notice throughout this book that we emphasize the importance of assessing the quality of the financial data. Though it is important to understand how to calculate financial ratios and measures, look at trends, use credit models, and the like, it is even more important to understand the data with which you are working. The recent corporate scandals, in which the managers of some high profile companies had manipulated financial data, have brought to the forefront the need to understand the quality of the data that we work with in financial analysis. Though the SOX Act has enhanced disclosures and, through significant penalties, discouraged financial data misdeeds, the financial analyst must continue to be diligent in assessing the quality of the data that is available for analysis.

We structure the book into three parts. In Part One, we introduce you to financial analysis, discuss the available financial information, and then focus on the quality of the information. In Part Two, we present different ways of analyzing financial data, including financial ratios and cash flow analysis. We also discuss the pitfalls that you may encounter in analysis, citing numerous actual cases to illustrate these pitfalls. In Part Three, we apply these financial analysis tools developed in Part Two to valuation, credit analysis, and fundamental factor models. We close the book with a recap of the lessons that we have learned.

Pamela P. Peterson
Frank J. Fabozzi

About the Authors

Pamela P. Peterson is an Associate Dean of the College of Business and Professor of Finance at Florida Atlantic University, where she teaches financial management and investments. She received her Ph.D. from the University of North Carolina at Chapel Hill in 1981 and taught at Florida State University for 24 years. She earned the designation of Chartered Financial Analyst in 1992.

Frank J. Fabozzi is the Frederick Frank Adjunct Professor of Finance in the School of Management at Yale University and a Fellow of the International Center for Finance. Prior to joining the Yale faculty, he was a Visiting Professor of Finance in the Sloan School at MIT. Professor Fabozzi is the editor of the *Journal of Portfolio Management*. He earned a doctorate in economics from the City University of New York in 1972. In 2002 he was inducted into the Fixed Income Analysts Society's Hall of Fame. He earned the designation of Chartered Financial Analyst and Certified Public Accountant.

Analysis of Financial Statements

Second Edition

The Basics

CHAPTER 1

Introduction

The investments arena is large, complex, and dynamic. These characteristics make it interesting to study, but also make it challenging to keep up with. What changes? Laws and regulations, the introduction of new types of securities and derivatives, innovations in markets and trading, an economy that is persistently changing, and company events, to name a few. Add to this mix the political, technological, and environmental changes that occur throughout the world every day, and you have quite a task to understand investment opportunities and investment management.

There is a wealth of financial information about companies available to financial analysts and investors. The Internet has made vast amounts of information available to everyone, displacing print as a means of communication. Consider the amount of information available about Microsoft Corporation. Not only can investors find annual reports, quarterly reports, press releases and links to the companies' filings with regulators on Microsoft's web site, anyone can download data for analysis in spreadsheet form and can listen in on Microsoft's management's conversations with analysts.

Availability and convenience has eased the data-gathering task of financial analysis. What remains, however, is the more challenging task of analyzing this information in a meaningful way. Recent scandals involving financial disclosures increase the importance of knowing just how to interpret financial information. In response to these scandals, Congress passed the Sarbanes-Oxley (SOX) Act of 2002, which increases the responsibility of publicly traded corporations, accounting firms performing audits, companies' management, and financial analysts. And while this Act is an attempt to restore faith in financial disclosures, investors and analysts must still be diligent in interpreting financial data in a meaningful way. The purpose of this book is to assist the analyst and investor in understanding financial information and using this information in an effective manner.

WHAT IS FINANCIAL ANALYSIS?

We focus on *financial analysis* in this book, which is the selection, evaluation, and interpretation of financial data and other pertinent information to assist in evaluating the operating performance and financial condition of a company. The operating performance of a company is a measure of how well a company has used its resources—its assets, both tangible and intangible—to produce a return on its investment. The financial condition of a company is a measure of its ability to satisfy its obligations, such as the payment of interest on its debt in a timely manner.

Financial reporting is the collection and presentation of current and historical financial information of a company. This reporting includes the annual reports sent to shareholders, the filings with the Securities and Exchange Commission for publicly traded companies, and press releases and other reports made by the company. Financial analysis takes that information—and much more—and makes sense out of in terms of what it says about the company's past performance and condition and—more importantly—what it says about the company's future performance and condition.

The financial analyst must determine what information to analyze (e.g., financial reports, market information, economic information) and how much information (Five years? Ten years?). The analyst must sift through the vast amount of information, selecting the information that is most important in assessing the company's current and future performance and condition. A part of this analysis requires the analyst to assess the quality of the information. Though publicly traded companies must report their financial information according to generally accepted accounting principles (GAAP), there is still some leeway that the reporting company has within these principles. The analyst must understand the extent of this leeway and what this implies for the company's future performance.

The analyst has many tools available in the analysis of financial information. These tools include financial ratio analysis and quantitative analysis. The analyst must understand how to use these tools in the most effective manner.

WHAT HAPPENS IF WE ARE NOT LOOKING CLOSELY AT FINANCIAL INFORMATION?

Several of the scandals that arose in the past few years were actually detectable using basic financial analysis and common sense. It is not possible to spot all cases of fraud and manipulation, but there are some telltale signs that should raise caution flags in analysis. Examples of these signs:

- Revenue growth that is out of line with others in the same industry or not reasonable given the current economic climate
- Profits that are increasing at a much faster rate than cash flows generated from operations
- Debt disappearing from the balance sheet

Consider Enron Corporation, Enron's revenues grew from a little over $13.5 billion to over $100 billion in the 10-year period from 1991 through 2000 as shown in Exhibit 1.1; in other words, its revenues grew at an average rate of over 25% per year. During this period, Enron's debts grew too, from 76% of its assets to over 82% of its assets. Enron experienced significant growth and reported significant debt, becoming one of the largest corporations in the United States within 15 years of becoming a publicly traded corporation.

Since 2001 Enron has been embroiled in a financial scandal that involved removing debt from its balance sheet into special purpose enti-

EXHIBIT 1.1   Enron's Revenues, 1991–2000

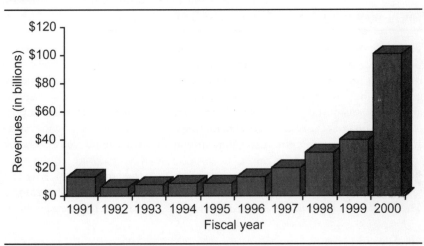

Source: Enron, Inc. 10-K filings, various years.

ties. While the scandal was shocking, Enron had actually provided information in its financial disclosures that hinted at the problems.

Enron disclosed in footnotes to its 2000 10-K filing that it had formed wholly owned and majority-owned limited partnerships "for the purpose of holding $1.6 billion of assets contribute by Enron." [Enron 10-K, 2000] The result?

1. Assets and liabilities of Enron did not appear directly in its balance sheet.
2. Gains on Enron stock invested in by these partnerships found their way to Enron's income statement.

The most notorious deal involved Joint Energy Development Investment Limited Partnership II (JEDI II). Enron executives created this partnership using Enron funds and loans fed through Chewco Investments. Though accounted for as a special purpose entity, with its assets and liabilities removed from Enron's balance sheet, there was insufficient *independent* ownership of the entity to qualify JEDI II as a special purpose entity because Chewco was essentially Enron.

In all of this, keep in mind that Enron left a trail for the analyst to find in the filings of Enron and these entities. The limited partnerships and their relation to Enron were reported in the footnotes to Enron's filings and in other filings with the SEC. Not all the pieces were there, but enough to raise concerns.

WHERE DO WE FIND THE FINANCIAL INFORMATION?

There are many sources of information available to analysts and investors. One source of information is the company itself, preparing documents for regulators and distribution to shareholders. Another source is information prepared by government agencies that compile and report information about industries and the economy. Still another source is information prepared by financial service firms that compile, analyze, and report financial and other information about the company, the industry, and the economy.

The basic information about a company can be gleaned from publication (both print and Internet), annual reports, and sources such as the federal government and commercial financial information providers. The basic information about a company consists of the following:

■ Type of business (e.g., manufacturer, retailer, service, utility)
■ Primary products

- Strategic objectives
- Financial condition and operating performance
- Major competitors (domestic and foreign)
- Degree of competitiveness of the industry (domestic and foreign)
- Position of the company in the industry (e.g., market share)
- Industry trends (domestic and foreign)
- Regulatory issues (if applicable)
- Economic environment
- Recent and planned acquisitions and divestitures

A thorough financial analysis of a company requires examining events that help explain the firm's present condition and affect on its future prospects. For example, did the firm recently incur some extraordinary losses? Is the firm developing a new product, or acquiring another firm? Current events can provide useful information to the financial analyst. A good place to start is with the company itself and the disclosures that it makes—both financial and otherwise.

Most of the company-specific information can be picked up through company annual reports, press releases, and other information that the company provides to inform investors and customers about itself. Information about competitors and the markets for the company's products must be determined through familiarity with the products of the company and its competitors. Information about the economic environment can be found in many available sources. We take a brief look at the different types of information in the remainder of this chapter.

WHO GETS WHAT TYPE OF INFORMATION AND WHEN?

Disclosures Required by Regulatory Authorities

Companies whose stock is traded in public markets are subject to a number of securities laws that require specific disclosures. Several of these securities laws are described briefly in Exhibit 1.2. Publicly traded companies are required by these securities laws to disclose information through filings with the Securities and Exchange Commission (SEC). The SEC is a federal agency that administers federal securities laws.

The SEC, established by the Securities and Exchange Act of 1934, carries out the following activities:

- Issues rules that clarify securities laws or trading procedure issues
- Requires disclosure of specific information

EXHIBIT 1.2   Federal Regulations of Securities and Markets in the United States

Law	Description
Securities Act of 1933	Regulates new offerings of securities to the public; requires the filing of a registration statement containing specific information about the issuing corporation and prohibits fraudulent and deceptive practices related to security offers
Securities and Exchange Act of 1934	Establishes the Securities and Exchange Commission (SEC) to enforce securities regulations and extends regulation to the secondary markets
Investment Company Act of 1940	Gives the SEC regulatory authority over publicly held companies that are in the business of investing and trading in securities
Investment Advisers Act of 1940	Requires registration of investment advisors and regulates their activities
Federal Securities Act of 1964	Extends the regulatory authority of the SEC to include the over-the-counter securities markets
Sarbanes-Oxley Act of 2002	Wide-ranging law that creates the Public Accounting Oversight Board, requires auditor independence, increases corporate responsibility for financial disclosures, enhances financial disclosures, and extends the authority of the SEC

- Makes public statements on current issues
- Oversees self-regulation of the securities industry by the stock exchanges and professional groups such as the National Association of Securities Dealers

A publicly traded company must make a number of periodic and occasional filings with the SEC. In addition, major shareholders and executives must make periodic and occasional filings. A number of these filings are described in Exhibit 1.3. Company filings to the Securities and Exchange Commission are available free, in real-time, from the SEC's EDGAR web site, at www.sec.gov.

By law the SEC has the authority to specify accounting principles for corporations under its jurisdiction. The SEC has largely delegated this responsibility to the Financial Accounting Standards Board (FASB). While recognizing FASB Statements of Financial Accounting Standards (SFAS) as authoritative, the SEC also issues accounting rules, often dealing with supplementary disclosures. Therefore, the financial information provided in the company's 10-K filing is more comprehensive than that provided in its annual report provided to shareholders.

EXHIBIT 1.3 Summary of Filings of Publicly Traded Companies, Their Owners, and Executives

Statement	Purpose	Information
10-K report	Annual disclosure of financial information required of all publicly traded companies; due 90 days following the company's fiscal year-end	Description of the company's business, financial statement data found in the company's annual report, notes to the financial statements, and additional disclosures including a management discussion and analysis
10-Q report	Quarterly disclosure by publicly traded companies; required 45 days following the end of each of the company's first three fiscal quarters	A brief presentation of quarterly financial statements, notes, and management's discussion and analysis
8-K filing	Filed to report unscheduled, material events or events that may be considered of importance to shareholders of the SEC	Description of significant events that are of interest to investors and are filed as these events occur
Prospectus	Filing made by a company intending to issue securities; registration statement complying with the Securities Act of 1933	Basic company and financial information of the issuing company
Proxy statement (Schedule 14A)[a]	Issued by the company pertaining to issues to be put to a vote by shareholders; complies with Regulation 14A; circumstances that are required for a vote are determined by state law	Description of issues to be put to a vote; management's recommendations regarding these issues; compensation of senior management; shareholdings of officers and directors

[a] There are different types of proxy: preliminary, confidential, and definitive. The most common is the definitive proxy, generally indicated with the abbreviation DEF (e.g., DEF 14A).

EXHIBIT 1.3 (Continued)

Statement	Purpose	Information
Registration statements (e.g., S-1, S-2, F-1)	A registration statement is a filing made by a company issuing securities to the public; required by the 1933 Act	Financial statement information as well as information that describes the business and management of the firm
Schedule 13D	Filing made by a person reporting beneficial ownership of shares of common stock of a publicly traded company such that the filer's beneficial ownership is more than 5% of a class of registered stock; filed within 10 days of the shares' acquisition	Report of an acquisition of shares, including information on the identity of the acquiring party, the source and amount of funds used to make the purchase, and the purpose of the purchase
Schedule 14D-1	Filing for a tender offer by someone other then the issuer such that the filer's beneficial ownership is more than 5% of a class of registered stock	Report of an offer to buy shares including information on the identity of the acquiring party, the source and amount of funds used to make the purchase, and the purpose of the purchase, and the terms of the offer

Form 10-K

The *Form 10-K* filing contains the information provided in the annual report (that is, balance sheet, income statement, statement of cash flows, statement of stockholders' equity, and footnotes), plus additional disclosures, such as the *management discussion and analysis* (MDA). For most large corporations, the 10-K must be filed within 60 days after close of corporation's fiscal year.[1] We provide a list of the required disclosures for Form 10-K in Exhibit 1.4, as identified using the SEC's numbering system of requirements.

EXHIBIT 1.4   Required Disclosures of the Form 10-K Filing

Part I
1. Business
2. Properties
3. Legal proceedings
4. Submission of matters to a vote of security holders

Part II
5. Market for registrants common equity, related stockholder matters and issue purchases of equity securities
6. Selected financial data
7. Management's discussion and analysis of financial conditions and results of operations
7A. Quantitative and qualitative disclosures about market risk
8. Financial statements, and supplementary data
9. Changes in and disagreement with accountants on accounting and financial disclosure
9A. Controls and procedures
9B. Other information

Part III
10. Directors and executive officers
11. Executive compensation
12. Security ownership of certain beneficial owners and management and related stockholder matters
13. Certain relationships and related transactions
14. Principal accounting fees and services
15. Exhibits and financial statement schedules

---

[1] The deadline was 90 days after the fiscal year prior to the SEC's RIN 3235-AI33, "Acceleration of Periodic Report Filing Dates and Disclosure Concerning Website Access to Reports," (Effective November 15, 2002). The revised deadline of sixty days was phased in over three years and applies to issuers with a public float of at least $75 million.

The disclosure requirements in the 10-K have changed over time as the SEC seeks additional information from companies regarding risk, internal controls, and the company's auditing firm.

The MDA is generally viewed as an important disclosure, providing additional transparency of financial statements. In the MDA, the company's management provides a discussion of risks, trends, unusual or infrequent events, and uncertainties that pertain to the company and is a useful device for management to explain the financial results in terms of the company's strategies, recent actions (e.g., mergers) and the company's competitors.

In addition, the company's management must provide a discussion of significant components of revenues and expenses that are important in understanding the company's results of operations. The MDA also provides information that may help reconcile previous years' financial results with the current year's results. Effective in 2003, the MDA must also provide additional information about off-balance sheet arrangements, as well as a table that discloses contractual obligations.[2]

Form 10-Q

A similar form, *Form 10-Q*, must be filed within 35 days after close of corporation's fiscal quarter.[3] This filing is similar to the 10-K, yet there is much less detailed information. We list the required contents of the Form 10-Q in Exhibit 1.5.

8-K Statement

The *8-K statement* is an occasional filing that provides useful information about the company that is not generally found in the financial statements. A company files the 8-K statement within four business days of the event. There are currently 22 specific events for which a company is required to file the 8-K statement, as detailed in Exhibit 1.6.[4] Previous to the SOX Act and the resulting SEC rules, the company was required to file an 8-K for any of eight events. The SOX Act shifted four additional requirements from the 10-K disclosures and added eight additional events.

---

[2] Securities and Exchange Commission, RIN3235-AI170, "Disclosure in Management's Discussion and Analysis about Off-Balance Sheet Arrangements and Aggregate Contractual Obligations," effective April 7, 2003.

[3] SEC's RIN 3235-AI33.

[4] Securities and Exchange Commission, RIN3235-AI46, "Additional form 8-K Disclosure Requirements and Acceleration of Filing Date," (August 23, 2004). Under the previous rule, the SEC required 8-K filings for disclosure of nine different events. The 2002 rule added eight additional events that require 8-K disclosure and shifted four disclosure requirements from the 10-K and 10-Q disclosures.

EXHIBIT 1.5   Required Disclosures of the Form 10-Q Filing

Part I

1. Financial statements
2. Management's discussion and analysis of financial conditions and results of operations
3. Quantitative and qualitative disclosures about market risk legal proceedings
4. Controls and procedures

Part II

1. Legal proceedings
2. Unregistered sales of equity securities and use of proceeds
3. Defaults upon senior securities
4. Submission of matters to a vote of security holders
5. Other information
6. Exhibits

EXHIBIT 1.6   Events Requiring Disclosure of 8-K

	Pre-SOX Act Requirement for 8-K Filings	Previous Requirement for 10-K and 10-Q Filings	Post-SOX Act Require- ments
1. Bankruptcy or receivership	✓		
2. Completion of an acquisition or disposition of assets	✓		
3. Changes in registrant's certifying accountant	✓		
4. Changes in the control of the registrant.	✓		
5. Change in fiscal year	✓		
6. Temporary suspension of trading under registrants employee benefit plans	✓		
7. Amendments to the registrant's code of ethics or the waiver of a provision of the code of ethics.	✓		
8. Regulation FD disclosure	✓		
9. Departure of directors or principal officers, election of directors, or appointment of principal officers.		✓	
10. Unregistered sales of equity securities		✓	
11. Material modifications to rights of security holders		✓	
12. Amendments to articles of incorporation or bylaws		✓	

EXHIBIT 1.6   (Continued)

	Pre-SOX Act Requirement for 8-K Filings	Previous Requirement for 10-K and 10-Q Filings	Post-SOX Act Require- ments
13. Entry into a material definitive agreement			✓
14. Termination of a material definitive agreement			✓
15. Creation of a direct financial obligation or an obligation under an off-balance sheet arrangement			✓
16. Events that accelerate or increase a direct financial obligation of an obligation under an off-balance sheet arrangement			✓
17. Costs associated with exit or disposal activities			✓
18. Material impairments			✓
19. Notice of delisting or failure to satisfy a continued listing rule or standard, or a transfer of listing			✓
20. Unregistered sales of equity securities			✓
21. Material modifications to rights of security holders			✓
22. Nonreliance on previous issued financial statements or a related audit report or completed interim review			✓

In addition, any other event that the company deems important to shareholders may be reported using an 8-K filing. Because 8-K filings are triggered by major company events, it is useful for the analyst to keep abreast of any such filings for the companies that they follow.

Proxy Statement

In addition to the financial statement and management discussion information available in the periodic 10-Q and 10-K filings, companies provide useful nonfinancial information in proxy statements. The *proxy statement* is the company's notification to the shareholders of matters to be voted upon at a shareholders' meeting. The proxy statement provides an array of information on issues such as:

- The reappointment of the independent auditor
- Compensation (salary, bonus, and options) of the top five executives and the stock ownership of executives and directors

■ Detailed information about proposals subject to a vote by the shareholders

Other Filings

In addition, when a corporation offers a new security to the public, the
SEC requires that the corporation prepare and file a registration statement. The registration statement presents financial statement data,
along with detailed information about the new security. A condensed
version of this statement, referred to as a *prospectus*, is made available
to potential investors.

Documents Distributed to Shareholders

The objective of financial reporting is to

> provide information that is useful to present and potential
> investors and creditors and other users in making rational
> investment, credit, and similar decisions.[5]

With that objective in mind, the financial reports prepared and distributed by the company should help users in assessing "the amounts,
timing and uncertainty of prospective net cash inflows of the enterprise."[6] Therefore, the financial reports to shareholders are not simply a
presentation of the basic financial statements—the balance sheet, the
income statement, the statement of cash flows, and the statement of
stockholders' equity—but also a devise to communicate additional nonfinancial information, such as information about the relevant risks and
uncertainties of the company. To that end, recent changes in accounting
standards have broadened the extent and type of the information presented within the financial statements and in notes to the financial statements. For example, companies are now required to disclose risks and
uncertainties related to their operations, how they use estimates in the
preparation of financial statements, and the vulnerability of the company to geographic and customer concentrations.[7]

---

[5] Financial Accounting Concept 1, *Objectives of Financial Reporting by Business Enterprises* (Stamford: Financial Accounting Standards Board, November 1978).
[6] Financial Accounting Concept 1, *Objectives of Financial Reporting by Business Enterprises*.
[7] Statement of Position 94-6 *Disclosure of Significant Risks and Uncertainties* (Accounting Standards Executive Committee, 1994), effective for fiscal years beginning
after December 15, 1995.

The annual report is the principal document used by corporations to communicate with shareholders. It is not an official Securities and Exchange Commission (SEC) filing; consequently, companies have significant discretion in deciding on what types of information is reported and the way it is presented. The annual report presents the financial statements, notes to these statements, a discussion of the company by management, the report of the independent accountants, and financial information on operating segments, product and services, geographical areas, and major customers.[8] Along with this basic information, annual reports may present five or ten-year summaries of key financial data, quarterly data, and other descriptions of the business or its products.

Quarterly reports to shareholders provide limited financial information on operations. These reports are simpler and more compact in presentation than their annual counterpart. In addition to the annual and quarterly reports, companies provide information through press releases using the services of commercial wire services such as Reuters (www.reuters.com), PR Newswire (www.prnewswire.com), Business Wire (www.business-wire.com), First Call (www.firstcall.com), or Dow Jones (www.dow-jones.com). The wire services then distribute this information to print and Internet mediums. The information provided in press releases includes earnings, dividend, new product, and acquisition announcements.

Issues

There are a number of issues that should be considered in using the financial statement data provided in company annual and quarterly reports. We will discuss many of these issues in later chapters that focus on financial analysis, cash flow analysis, and earnings quality.

For example, consider the following examples:

- The restatement of prior years' data
- The different accounting standards used by non-U.S. companies
- There may be "off-balance sheet" activity

The Restatement of Prior Years' Data   When a company reports financial data for more than one year, which is often the case, previous years' financial data is restated to reflect any changes in accounting methods or acquisitions that have taken place since the previous data had been reported. Consider the case of J. C. Penney, shown in Exhibit 1.7. The originally reported data for 2002 is shown alongside the restated data. Therefore,

---

[8] Statement of Financial Accounting Standards, No. 131 *Disclosures about Segments of an Enterprise and Related Information* (Stamford: Financial Accounting Standards Board, June 1997).

EXHIBIT 1.7   Selected Data for J.C. Penney

	2002 As Originally Reported (in millions)	2002 As Restated to Reflect the Sale of Eckerd (in millions)
Sales	$32,347	$17,633
Net profit	$405	$120
Total assets	$18,300	$17,787
Shareholders' equity	$5,425	$6,370

Source: Form 10-K filings with the Securities and Exchange Commission

the analyst must consider which data is most appropriate to use in the analysis.[9] If, for example, the analyst were looking at J. C. Penney and its competitive position in 2002, the analyst would want to use the as-reported 2002 data. If, on the other hand, the analyst is looking at trends in some of the data in an effort to forecast future performance or condition, the restated 2002 data is more appropriate.

The Different Accounting Standards Used by Non-U.S. Companies   Another concern is dealing with financial statements of non-U.S. reporting entities. There are several reasons for this concern. First, as of this writing, there are no internationally acceptable standards of financial reporting. This includes not only the accounting methods that are acceptable for handling certain economic transactions and the degree of disclosure, but other issues. Specifically, there is no uniform treatment of the frequency of disclosure. Some countries require only annual or semiannual reporting rather than quarterly as in the United States.

There is an effort to harmonize accounting standards around the world. The International Accounting Standards Board (IASB) and the Financial Accounting Standards Board (FASB) are working toward the development of international accounting standards. In addition, the IASB and the FASB have agreed to produce joint pronouncement regarding new accounting standards. Beginning January 1, 2005, most companies listed in the European Union are required to prepare their financial

---

[9] In academic studies that examine the relation between stock prices and accounting information, the "as originally reported" data is most often the relevant data to use because the researcher is examining the market's reaction to the accounting information as it is released. It is reasonable to assume that investors use all currently available information, but it is not reasonable to assume that investors are psychic and, therefore, know what the information will be restated as in future years.

statements according to the International Financial Reporting Standards (IFRS), which are promulgated by the IASB. The adoption of IFRS, along with the convergence of the standards of IASB and FASB, are significant strides toward consistent international accounting standards.[10]

There May Be "Off-Balance Sheet" Activity   There is always some investment or financing activity that simply does not show up in financial statements. Though there have been improvements in accounting standards that have moved much of this activity to the financial statements (e.g., leases, pension benefits, postretirement benefits, asset retirement obligations), opportunities remain to conduct business that is not represented adequately in the financial statements. An example is the case of joint ventures. As long as the investing corporation does not have a controlling interest in the joint venture, the assets and financing of the venture can remain off of the balance sheet. Limited information is provided in notes to the statements, but this information is insufficient to adjudge the performance and risks of the joint venture.

The opportunity to keep some information from the financial statements places a greater burden on the financial analyst to dig deep into the company's notes to the financial statements, filings with the SEC, and the financial press.

Interviewing Company Representatives

Interviewing representatives of a company may produce additional information and insight into the company's business. The starting place for the interview is the company's investors' relations (IR) office, which is generally well prepared to address the analyst's questions.

The key is for the analyst to do their homework before meeting with the IR officer so that the interview questions can be well focused. This preparation includes understanding the company's business, its products, the industry in which it operates, and its recent financial disclosures. The analyst must understand the industry-specific terminology and any industry-specific accounting methods. In the telecommunications industry, for example, the analyst must understand measures such as *gigahertz* and *minutes-in-use*, and such terms as *bandwidth*, *point-of-presence*, and *spectrum*.[11] As another example, an analyst for the oil and gas industry should understand that a *degree-day* is a measure of temperature variation from a reference temperature.

---

[10] We discuss the IFRS and compare it with U.S. GAAP in Chapter 2.
[11] *The Telecommunications Industry* (Charlottesville: Association for Investment Management and Research, 1994), pp. 108–110.

The analyst must keep in mind that the IR officer has an obligation to treat all investors in a fair manner, which means that the IR officer cannot give a financial analyst material information that is not also available to others. There is also information that the IR officer *cannot* give the analyst. For example, in a very competitive industry it may not be appropriate to give monthly sales figures for specific products. The analyst must understand the competitive nature of the industry and understand what information is typically not revealed in the industry.

Because the analyst comes armed with knowledge of the company's financial statements, the questions should focus on taking a closer look at the information provided by these disclosures:

- Extraordinary or unusual revenues and expenses
- Large differences between earnings and cash flows
- Changes in how data is reported
- Explanations for deviations from consensus earnings expectations
- How the company values itself versus the market's valuation
- Sales to major customers

An analyst that uses a statistical model to develop forecasts for the company or its industry may, of course, require very specific data that may not be readily available in the financial statements.

It is sometimes useful to determine what the company expects to earn in the future. Though companies may be reluctant to provide a specific earnings forecast, they will sometimes respond to a query regarding analysts' consensus earnings forecasts. In their response about analysts' forecasts, the company may reveal their own forecast. If a company provides a forecast of its earnings, the analyst must consider the forecast in light of the company's previous forecasting; for example, some companies may consistently underestimate future earnings in order to avoid a negative earnings surprise. Further, the company's forecast or response to a consensus forecast might be accompanied by significant defensive disclosures that concern the risks that the company may not meet projected earnings.

Regulation FD

In an attempt to "level the playing field", the Securities and Exchange Commission in 2000 adopted new rules regarding selective disclosure.[12] These rules, in the form of the Fair Disclosure regulation, are referred to

---

[12] Securities and Exchange Commission, RIN 3235-AH82, "Selective disclosure and Insider Trading," effective October 23, 2000.

as Regulation FD. Basically, if a publicly traded company or anyone act-ing on its behalf makes a material, nonpublic information available to certain persons, the company must make a *public* disclosure of this information. All intentional disclosures must be made simultaneously to the public. If someone makes an *un*intentional disclosure, the company is required to make a prompt, public disclosure of the information.

Information Prepared by Government Agencies

Federal and state governmental agencies provide a wealth of informa-tion that may be useful in analyzing a company, its industry, or the eco-nomic environment.

Company-Specific Information

One the most prominent innovations in the delivery of company infor-mation is the Securities and Exchange Commission's Electronic Data Gathering and Retrieval (EDGAR) system that is available on the Inter-net (www.sec.gov). The EDGAR system provides online access to most SEC filings for all public domestic companies from 1994 forward. The EDGAR system provides real-time access to filings, providing up-to-date information accessible to everyone.

In addition to the EDGAR system at the SEC site, several financial service companies provide free or fee access to the information in the EDGAR system in different data base forms that assist in searching or data base creation tasks.[13]

Industry Data

The analysis of a company requires that the analyst look at the other firms that operate in the same line of business. The purpose of examining these other companies is to get an idea of the market in which the com-pany's products are sold: What is the degree of competition? What are the trends? What is the financial condition of the company's competitors?

Several government agencies provide information that is useful in an analysis of an industry. The primary governmental providers of industry data are the U. S. Bureau of the Census and the Bureau of Economic Analysis, an agency of the U. S. Department of Commerce. A recent inno-vation is the creation of Stat-USA, a fee-based collection of governmental data. Stat-USA is an electronic provider of industry and sector data that is produced by the U.S. Department of Commerce. The available data pro-

---

[13] These services include EDGAR Online (www.edgar-online.com) and EDGAR from Compustat (www.compustat.com)

vided for different industries includes gross domestic product, shipments of products, inventories, orders, and plant capacity utilization.[14]

The government classification of businesses into industries is based on the *North American Industry Classification System* (NAICS).[15] NAICS is a recently adopted system of industry identification, replacing the Standard Industrial Classification (SIC) system in 1997.[16] The NAICS is a six-digit system that classifies businesses using 350 different classes. The broadest classification comprises the first two digits of the six-digit code and is listed in Exhibit 1.8. The NAICS is now the basis for the classification of industry-specific data produced by governmental agencies. Like the SIC system before it, the NAICS will, over time, become the basis for the classification of companies for industry-specific data used by nongovernmental information providers as well.

EXHIBIT 1.8 North American Industry Classification System Sector Codes

Code	NAICS Sectors
11	Agriculture, Forestry, Fishing and Hunting
21	Mining
22	Utilities
23	Construction
31–33	Manufacturing
42	Wholesale Trade
44–45	Retail Trade
48–49	Transportation and Warehousing
51	Information
52	Finance and Insurance
53	Real Estate and Rental and Leasing
54	Professional, Scientific, and Technical Services
55	Management of Companies and Enterprises
56	Administrative and Support, Waste Management and Remediation Services

[14] Web access to this data is available through the Department of Commerce site (www.doc.gov), Stat-USA (www.stat-usa.gov) and the Census Bureau (www.census.gov).

[15] This classification system is the result of the joint efforts of the U.S. Bureau of Economic Analysis (BEA), the U.S. Bureau of Labor Statistics, the U.S. Census Bureau, Statistics Canada, and Mexico's Instituto Nacional de Estadistica, Geografia e Informatica (INEGI).

[16] The SIC system was developed by the Office of Management and Budget and had been in use since the 1930s.

EXHIBIT 1.8   (Continued)

Code	NAICS Sectors
61	Education Services
62	Health Care and Social Assistance
71	Arts, Entertainment, and Recreation
72	Accommodation and Foodservices
81	Other Services (except Public Administration)
92	Public Administration

Source: http://www.census.gov/epcd/www/naics.html

EXHIBIT 1.9   Examples of Government Sources of Economic Data

Publisher	Web Sources	Print or CD-ROM Product
Board of Governors of the Federal Reserve System	www.bog.frb.fed.us	Federal Reserve Bulletin
Bureau of Economic Analysis	www.bea.doc.gov	National Product Accounts Business Inventories Gross Product by Industry
Federal Reserve Bank of St. Louis, FRED II	research.stlouisfed.org/ fred2/	
Stat-USA	www.stat-usa.gov	National Trade Data Bank
U.S. Census Bureau	www.census.gov	CenStats
U.S. Department of Commerce	www.doc.gov	Survey of Current Business

Economic Data

Another source of information for financial analysis is economic data, such as the gross domestic product and consumer price index, which may be useful in assessing the recent performance or future prospects of a firm or industry. For example, suppose you are evaluating a firm that owns a chain of retail outlets. What information do you need to judge the firm's performance and financial condition? You need financial data, but they do not tell the whole story. You also need information on consumer spending, producer prices, and consumer prices. These economic data are readily available from government sources, a few of which are listed in Exhibit 1.9.

Information Prepared by Financial Service Companies

A whole industry exists to provide financial and related information about individual companies, industries, and the economy. The ease and low cost of providing such data on the Internet has fostered a proliferation of information providers. However, the prominent providers in today's Internet-based world are some of the same providers that were prominent in print medium.

Company-Specific Information

Information about an individual company is available from a vast number of sources, including the company itself through its own web pages. In addition to relaying the company's financial information that is presented by the company through its communication with shareholders and regulators, there are many financial service firms that compile the financial data and present analyses.

Several sources of data on individual companies are listed in Exhibit 1.10. This is by no means an exhaustive listing because of the large and ever-growing number of information providers. The providers distinguish themselves in the market for information through the breadth of coverage (in terms of the number of companies in their data base), the depth of coverage (in terms of the extensive nature of their data for individual companies), or their specialty (e.g., the collection of analyst recommendations and forecasts).

Just what data is used to analyze an industry depends on the particular industry. We provide examples of industry-specific data in Exhibit 1.11.

A number of financial information providers offer industry-specific data and compile financial data by industry. Some services, such as Standard & Poor's Compustat and Value Line, provide industry data based on their large universe of stocks covered in their database of individual company financial data.

Economic Data

Much of the economic data that is used in financial analysis is taken from government sources, though some information is independently produced through surveys and research. There are many commercial services that collect and disseminate this and other information. These services include AP Business News (www.ap.org), Bridge (www.bridge.com), and Business Wire (www.businesswire.com). Financial publications, such as the *Wall Street Journal* (www.wsj.com), *Investors Business Daily* (www.investors.com) and the *Financial Times* (www.ft.com), provide economic data in both in print and electronic forms. In addition, databases such as the DRI U.S. Central database (USCEN) offer an historical series of U.S. economic and financial data.

EXHIBIT 1.10 Sources of Individual Company Financial Data

Provider	URL	Products
Dun & Bradstreet	www.dnb.com	*Principal International Businesses*. Electronic data base of selected information on 50,000 companies in 140 countries
Fitch IBCA	www.fitchibca.com	*BankScope*. Comprehensive database of financials on 10,000 international banks *CreditDisk*. International bank rating service on CD-ROM *FitchResearch*. In-depth research on U.S. corporations
Mergent	www.mergentonline.com	*Mergent Online*. U.S. and International Company data (formerly, Moody's® Manual)
Microsoft's MSN Money	moneycentral.msn.com	Company profiles, SEC filings, daily stock price data
Moody's Investor Services	www.moodys.com	*Company Data Direct*. An online database of information on companies' history, financial statements, and long-term debt. *Company Data with EDGAR*. An electronic database consisting of company SEC filings
Standard and Poor's, McGraw-Hill, Inc.	www.standardandpoors.com	*Compustat*. Electronic database of annual and quarterly financial statement and market data coverage for over 18,000 North American and 11,000 global companies. *Market Insight*. Web-based access to individual company financial statement data on the Standard & Poor's universe of companies.
Thomson	thomson.com/financial/	*Thomson Research*. Electronic database of companies' financial statements and financial analyst forecasts (formerly Disclosure Global Access).
Value Line, Inc.	www.valueline.com	*Value Line DataFile*. Electronic database with annual and quarterly financial statement and monthly market price data for over 5,000 securities on an "as reported" basis since 1955. *Estimates & Projections File*. Electronic data with Value Line's proprietary estimates of earnings and dividends for the 1,700 companies.
Yahoo! Finance	Finance.yahoo.com	Company profiles, company links, three years of annual financial statement data, and daily stock price data.
Zack's Investment Research	www.zackspro.com	*Zacks Historical Data*. Electronic database comprised of financial statement data, analyst forecasts, earnings surprise and stock recommendations. *Zacks Research System (ZRA)*. An electronic database that includes financial statement, price, and earnings data for over 6,000 companies.

EXHIBIT 1.11 Examples of Industry-Specific Factors

Industry	Factor	Explanation
Advertising	Gross billings	Total dollar amount of revenues from advertising
Air transport	Load factor	Percentage of seats sold
Aircraft manufacturer	Backlog	Number of aircraft ordered for production not completed
Banking/Credit	Loan origination	Dollar amount of loans made
	Loan loss provision	Percentage of loans considered being bad debt
	Cards in force	Number of credit cards outstanding
Electric Utility	Load factor	Average of the percentage of total capacity used
Retail	Same-store sales	Revenues of the same store in a previous period
Savings and Loan	Interest cost to gross income	Percentage of interest paid on deposits to total gross income
Semiconductor	Book-to-bill ratio	Ratio of orders to completed orders
Telecommunications	Cost per access line	Ratio of operating cost to number of lines of service

WHAT DOES SARBANES-OXLEY MEAN TO COMPANIES AND INVESTORS?

The financial scandals that arose recently created problems in terms of the public's confidence in the capital markets, companies' financial disclosures, and the reliance on the auditing by public accounting firms. In response to this lack of confidence, the Sarbanes Oxley Act of 2002 was passed in mid-2002.[17] The Sarbanes-Oxley Act of 2002 has changed the landscape with respect to financial disclosures, corporate governance, auditing, and penalties for financial misdeeds. A list of key provisions that affect financial analysis of companies is provided in Exhibit 1.12.

EXHIBIT 1.12   Key Provisions of the Sarbanes-Oxley Act of 2002

Title I   Public Company Accounting Oversight Board
- Establishes the oversight board, as well as provide policies and procedures for registration of accounting firms. The purpose of the board is to provide oversight of auditing firms and develop standards for auditors, auditing, and auditing reports, as well as to inspect accounting firms for compliance [Sec. 101].

Title II   Auditor Independence
- Prohibits most types of nonaudit services of client by auditing accounting firm [Sec. 201]. Any nonaudit service by an auditor must be approved by the audit committee of the client [Sec. 202].

Title III   Corporate Responsibility
- Requires that members of the client's audit committee be independent (i.e., not an employee of the client or consultant or advisor other than in capacity as a member of the board of directors) [Sec. 301]
- Requires certification of the annual and quarterly filings with the SEC by the chief financial officer and the chief executive officer, attesting to the internal controls of the firms [Sec. 302]
- Prohibits improper influence on audits [Sec. 303]
- Specifies forfeiture of bonuses and profits on securities in the event of financial restatements [Sec. 304]
- Prohibits insider trading during pension fund blackouts and requires sufficient communication to fund participants and beneficiaries in the event of a blackout period [Sec. 306]

---

[17] Public Law 107-204, July 30, 2002 116 stat.745.

EXHIBIT 1.12 (Continued)

Title IV   Enhanced Financial Disclosures
- Enhances disclosure of off-balance sheet transactions [Sec 401]
- Requires reconciliation of pro forma financial information with results according to generally accepted accounting principles [Sec. 401]
- Prohibits many types of personal loans to directors or executives [Sec. 402]
- Increases disclosure requirements for transactions with directors, executives and principal shareholders [Sec. 403]
- Requires disclosure of whether the firm has a code of ethics for financial officers [Sec. 406]
- Requires disclosure whether there is at least one financial expert on the audit committee [Sec. 407]

Title V   Analyst Conflicts of Interest
- Increase the independence of analysts and investment banking activities and requires disclosure of potential conflicts of interest of analysts [Sec. 501]

Title VIII   Corporate and Criminal Fraud Accountability
- Imposes criminal penalties for destruction of documents [Sec. 802]
- Provides whistleblower protection in fraud actions. [Sec. 806]
- Provides criminal penalties for defrauding shareholders. [Sec. 807]

Title IX   White-Collar Crime Penalty Enhancements
- Provides increased criminal penalties for white-collar crimes, such as mail and wire fraud [Sec. 902]
- Imposes criminal penalties for false certification of financial reports [Sec. 906]

Title XI   Corporate Fraud and Accountability
- Imposes fines and possible imprisonment for tampering with documents in an investigation [Sec. 1102]
- Provides the SEC with authority to freeze payments in the event of an investigation [Sec. 1103]

Auditors

The role of the auditing accounting firm is to attest to whether the client company is providing financial statements that are prepared consistent with generally accepted accounting principles. Consider the Supreme Court of the United States opinion in the case of United States v. Arthur Young:[18]

> This 'public watchdog' function demands that the accountant maintain total independence from the client

---

[18] United States v. Arthur Young & Co., Et. Al 465 U. S. 805 (1984).

at all times and requires complete fidelity to the public
trust. . . . Public faith in the reliability of a corporation's
financial statements depends upon the public perception
of the outside auditor as an independent professional. . . .
If investors were to view the auditor as an advocate for
the corporate client, the value of the audit function itself
might well be lost.

The establishment of a the oversight board for accounting firms and
the requirements pertaining to auditor independence are in response to
the problems encountered when the relationship between the auditor
and the audit client becomes too close, inhibiting the audit firm from
being the "public watchdog" of the client's compliance with generally
accepted accounting principles. Consider the case of Enron Corporation. In 2000, the year before the scandal erupted, Enron paid its auditing accounting firm a total of $52 million in fees: $25 million for audit
services and $27 million for consulting services.[19]

Corporate Responsibility

There are a number of provisions in the SOX Act that affect the responsibilities of publicly traded corporations and build upon previous
attempts to strengthen the role of the audit committee, which is a committee comprised of members of the company's board of directors.[20] The
SOX Act provisions affect the corporate governance with respect to the
composition of the audit committee that has responsibilities related to
financial reporting, monitoring choices of accounting policies, monitor
the internal control process, and oversee the hiring and performance of
the auditors.

In addition to the enhanced role of the audit committee, the SOX Act
and subsequently issued rules prohibit insider trading during a pension
blackout period.[21] A blackout period is the period of time in which participants in a participant-directed pension plan cannot trade employer
securities. This is, again, a response to problems observed at firms
involved in scandals in which the executives were able to sell their stock
in the company before the company's demise, but other employees were
not able to do so.[22]

---

[19] Enron Corporation's definitive proxy, DEF 14A, filed March 28, 2001, p. 11.

[20] Previous movements to strengthen the role of the audit committee include the
Treadway Commission, which was the National Commission on Fraudulent Financial Reporting.

[21] SEC RIN3235-AI171, "Insider Trades During Pension Fund Blackout Periods,"
effective January 23, 2003.

Financial Disclosures

Financial disclosures were enhanced in three ways with the SOX Act. First, more information must be disclosed regarding off-balance sheet transactions. Second, companies are required to reconcile pro forma financial information with financial information determined using generally accepted accounting principles. Pro forma results are financial statement information, such as earnings, that are calculated by the company using their own creative approach to accounting. For example, Trump Hotels & Casinos Resorts, Inc. released earnings results for 1999 that selectively included some information (a one-time gain), but excluded other information (a one-time charge):[23]

	As Reported October 25, 1999 (in millions)	Per GAAP (in millions)
Revenues before one-time gain		$385.9
One-time gain		17.2
Revenues	$403	$403.1
Net income before any one-time losses		
One-time charge		−81.4
Net income	$14.0	−$67.5

As you can see, investors get a different picture of Trump Hotels & Casinos Resorts' performance, depending on which results they focus on.

In addition, companies must now make disclosures regarding the corporation's governance, such as whether there is a financial expert on the audit committee, whether there is a code of ethics for financial officers. Further, there are greater restrictions on loans to executives.

---

[22] Many Enron employees had the majority of their retirement savings in Enron stock prior to the scandal. Making matters worse was the while Enron's stock fell, the 401(k) plan was "locked down" during an pension "blackout period," prohibiting those over 50 years of age from selling their shares. However, this prohibition did not apply to the company's executives. As the stock was falling from around $90 per share to less than $1 a share following the news of the scandal, most Enron employees had lost the vast majority of their retirement savings. The executives, many of whom sold their stock prior to the stock's bottom price, took home millions of dollars.

[23] Accounting and Auditing Enforcement Release No. 1499, January 16, 2002, Administrative Proceeding File No. 3-10680.

Analysts

There is a potential for a conflict of interest in the case of financial analysts that are employed by firms that perform investment banking functions. One of the important functions of an investment banking firm is to help companies bring stock and bond issues to the market, providing capital for corporations. If the investment banking part of the company is not sufficiently independent of the financial analysts of the same company, who may be making stock or bond recommendations, there is a potential for biased ratings on the stock or bond issue.

The goal of the analyst provisions in the SOX Act, among other actions taken by the SEC, is to insure that there is no link between the investment banking and the financial analyst functions within a company.[24]

Accountability

There are a number of deterrents to financial fraud included in the SOX Act. There are criminal penalties included for defrauding shareholders, destroying documents, false certification of financial reports, and mail fraud. There is also increased protection of whistleblowers. Many of the expanded criminal penalties are the direct result of recent scandals.

SUMMARY

Financial analysis is the selection, evaluation and interpretation of financial data and other information with the objective of formulating forecasts of future cash flows of a company. Financial analysis is different from financial reporting; financial reporting conveys past and current financial information, whereas financial analysis is forward-looking. A challenge of financial analysis is to sort through the wealth of information and develop a meaningful analysis of a company.

Companies prepare and distribute information for regulators and shareholders. This information includes annual and quarterly financial reports (e.g., 10-K, 10-Q). Additional information may be gathered from 8-K filings, company press releases, proxy statements, and through interviewing a company's representatives. Government agencies and commercial services prepare and disseminate information about individual companies, industries, and the economy.

---

[24] An example is the Merrill Lynch, which settled with the SEC, paying $100 million in 2002, in a case that involved an analyst who gave high ratings to a stock of a company that was an investment banking client of the firm. However, in private emails that same analyst did not believe that the stock was of high quality.

The Sarbanes-Oxley Act of 2002 has changed financial reporting and disclosures through additional disclosure requirements and through enhanced penalties for financial misconduct. This Act has also changed the responsibilities of the company's audit committee, as well as the relation with the auditor. In addition, the Act has provisions that require the independence of the financial analyst from any investment banking functions of the analyst's employer.

CHAPTER 2

Financial Statements

Financial statements are summaries of the operating, financing, and investment activities of a business. Financial statements should provide information useful to both investors and creditors in making credit, investment, and other business decisions. And this usefulness means that investors and creditors can use these statements to predict, compare, and evaluate the amount, timing, and uncertainty of future cash flows.[1] In other words, financial statements provide the information needed to assess a company's future earnings and, therefore, the cash flows expected to result from those earnings. In this chapter, we discuss the four basic financial statements: the balance sheet, the income statement, the statement of cash flows, and the statement of shareholders' equity.

ACCOUNTING PRINCIPLES: WHAT ARE THEY?

The accounting data in financial statements are prepared by the firm's management according to a set of standards, referred to as *generally accepted accounting principles* (GAAP). Generally accepted accounting principles are not one set of standards, but rather a hierarchy of accounting principles that are promulgated from a number of sources. In order of importance, these sources include:[2]

---

[1] The purpose, focus, and objectives of financial statements are detailed in "Objectives of Financial reporting by Business Enterprises," *Statement of Financial Accounting Concepts No. 1* (Stamford: Financial Accounting Standards Board, 1978); and "Qualitative Characteristics of Accounting Information," *Statement of Financial Accounting Concepts No. 2* (Stamford: Financial Accounting Standards Board, 1980).

    a. AICPA Accounting Research Bulletins and Accounting
       Principles Board Opinions that are superseded by
       action of the FASB, Financial Accounting Standards
       Board (FASB) Statements and Interpretations, FASB
       Statement 133 Implementation Issues, and FASB Staff
       Positions.
    b. FASB Technical Bulletins and, if cleared by the FASB,
       AICPA Industry Audit and Accounting Guides and
       Statement of Positions.
    c. AICPA Accounting Standards Executive Committee
       Practice Bulletins that have been cleared by the FASB
       and consensus positions of the FASB Emerging Issues
       Task Force (EITF).
    d. Implementation guides (Q&As) published by the FASB
       staff, AICPA accounting interpretations, and practices
       that are widely recognized and prevalent either gener-
       ally or in the industry.

The financial statements of a company whose stock is publicly traded must, by law, be audited at least annually by independent public accountants (i.e., accountants who are not employees of the firm). In such an audit, the accountants examine the financial statements and the data from which these statements are prepared and attest—through the published auditor's opinion—that these statements have been prepared according to GAAP. The auditor's opinion focuses whether the statements conform to GAAP and that there is adequate disclosure of any material change in accounting principles.

    The financial statements are created using several assumptions that affect how we use and interpret the financial data:

■ *Transactions are recorded at historical cost.* Therefore, the values shown in the statements are not market or replacement values, but rather reflect the original cost (adjusted for depreciation in the case of a depreciable assets).

■ *The appropriate unit of measurement is the dollar.* While this seems logical, the effects of inflation, combined with the practice of recording values at historical cost, may cause problems in using and interpreting these values.

---

[2] Proposed Statement of Financial Accounting Standards, *The Hierarchy of General-ly Accepted Accounting Principles*, (April 28, 2005), which is a restatement of AIC-PA Statement of Auditing Standards No. 69, *The Meaning of Present Fairly in Conformity with Generally Accepted Accounting Principles*.

■ *The statements are recorded for predefined periods of time.* Generally, statements are produced to cover a chosen fiscal year or quarter, with the income statement and the statement of cash flows spanning a period's time and the balance sheet and statement of shareholders' equity as of the end of the specified period. But because the end of the fiscal year is generally chosen to coincide with the low point of activity in the operating cycle, the annual balance sheet and statement of shareholders' equity may not be representative of values for the year.

■ *Statements are prepared using accrual accounting and the matching principle.* Most businesses use the *accrual accounting*, where income and revenues are matched in timing such that income is recorded in the period in which it is earned and expenses are reported in the period in which they are incurred *in an attempt to generate revenues*. The result of the use of accrual accounting is that reported income does not necessarily coincide with cash flows. Because the financial analyst is concerned ultimately with cash flows, he or she often must understand how reported income relates to a company's cash flows.

■ *It is assumed that the business will continue as a going concern.* The assumption that the business enterprise will continue indefinitely justifies the appropriateness of using historical costs instead of current market values because these assets are expected to be used up over time instead of sold.

■ *Full disclosure requires providing information beyond the financial statements.* The requirement that there be full disclosure means that, in addition to the accounting numbers for such accounting items as revenues, expenses, and assets, narrative and additional numerical disclosures are provided in notes accompanying the financial statements. An analysis of financial statements is, therefore, not complete without this additional information.

■ *Statements are prepared assuming conservatism.* In cases in which more than one interpretation of an event is possible, statements are prepared using the most conservative interpretation.

The financial statements and the auditors' findings are published in the firm's annual and quarterly reports sent to shareholders and the 10-K and 10-Q filings with the Securities and Exchange Commission (SEC). Also included in the reports, among other items, is a discussion by management, providing an overview of company events. The annual reports are much more detailed and disclose more financial information than the quarterly reports.

WHAT DO THE BASIC FINANCIAL STATEMENTS TELL US?

The Balance Sheet

The *balance sheet* is a report of the assets, liabilities, and equity of a firm at a point in time, generally at the end of a fiscal quarter or fiscal year. *Assets* are resources of the business enterprise, which are comprised of current or long-lived assets. How did the company finance these resources? It did so with liabilities and equity. *Liabilities* are obligations of the business enterprise that must be repaid at a future point in time, whereas *equity* is the ownership interest of the business enterprise. The relation between assets, liabilities and equity is simple, as reflected in the balance of what is owned and how it is financed, referred to as the *accounting identity*:

$$\text{Assets} = \text{Liabilities} + \text{Equity}$$

Assets

Assets are anything that the company owns that has a value. These assets may have a physical in existence or not. Examples of physical assets include inventory items held for sale, office furniture, and production equipment. If an asset does not have a physical existence, we refer to it as an intangible asset, such as a trademark or a patent. You cannot see or touch an intangible asset, but it still contributes value to the company.

Assets may also be current or long-term, depending on how fast the company would be able to convert them into cash. Assets are generally reported in the balance sheet in order of liquidity, with the most liquid asset listed first and the least liquid listed last.

The most liquid assets of the company are the current assets. *Current assets* are assets that can be turned into cash in one operating cycle or one year, whichever is longer. This contrasts with the noncurrent assets, which cannot be liquidated quickly.

There are different types of current assets. The typical set of current assets is the following:

- Cash, bills, and currency are assets that are equivalent to cash (e.g., bank account).
- *Marketable securities*, which are securities that can be readily sold.
- *Accounts receivable*, which are amounts due from customers arising from trade credit.
- *Inventories*, which are investments in raw materials, work-in-process, and finished goods for sale.

A company's need for current assets is dictated, in part, by its operating cycle. The *operating cycle* is the length of time it takes to turn the investment of cash into goods and services for sale back into cash in the form of collections from customers. The longer the operating cycle, the greater a company's need for liquidity. Most firms' operating cycle is less than or equal to one year.

Noncurrent assets comprise both physical and nonphysical assets. Plant assets are physical assets, such as buildings and equipment and are reflected in the balance sheet as gross plant and equipment and net plant and equipment. *Gross plant and equipment*, or *gross property, plant, and equipment*, is the total cost of investment in physical assets; that is, what the company originally paid for the property, plant, and equipment that it currently owns. *Net plant and equipment*, or *net property, plant, and equipment*, is the difference between gross plant and equipment and accumulated depreciation, and represents the book value of the plant and equipment assets. *Accumulated depreciation* is the sum of depreciation taken for physical assets in the firm's possession. Therefore,

$$
\begin{array}{r}
\text{Gross plant and equipment} \\
- \text{ Accumulated depreciation} \\
\hline
= \text{ Net plant and equipment}
\end{array}
$$

Companies may present just the net plant and equipment figure on the balance sheet, placing the detail with respect to accumulated depreciation in a footnote. Interpreting financial statements requires knowing a bit about how assets are depreciated for financial reporting purposes. *Depreciation* is the allocation of the cost of an asset over its useful life (or economic life). In the case of the fictitious Sample Company, whose balance sheet is shown in Exhibit 2.1, the original cost of the fixed assets (i.e., plant, property, and equipment)—less any write-downs for impairment—for the year 2006 is $900 million. The accumulated depreciation for Sample in 2006 is $250 million; this means that the total depreciation taken on existing fixed assets over time is $270 milion. The net property, plant, and equipment account balance is $630 million. This is also referred to as the *book value* or *carrying value* of these assets.

Intangible assets are assets that are not financial instruments, yet no physical existence, such as patents, trademarks, copyrights, franchises, and formulae. Intangible assets may be amortized over some period, which is akin to depreciation. Keep in mind that a company may own a number of intangible assets that are not reported on the balance sheet. A company may only include an intangible asset's value on its balance sheet if (1) there are likely future benefits attributable specifically to the asset, and (2) the cost of the intangible asset can be measured.

EXHIBIT 2.1   The Sample Company Balance Sheet, as of December 31, 2006 (in millions)

	2006	2005
Cash	$40	$30
Accounts receivable	100	90
Inventory	180	200
Other current assets	10	10
TOTAL CURRENT ASSETS	$350	$330
Property, plant, and equipment	$900	$800
Less accumulated depreciation	270	200
Net property, plant, and equipment	630	600
Intangible assets	20	20
TOTAL ASSETS	$1,000	$950
Accounts payable	$150	$140
Current maturities of long-term debt	60	40
TOTAL CURRENT LIABILITIES	$180	$165
Long-term debt	300	250
TOTAL LIABILITIES	$380	$325
Minority interest	30	15
Common stock	50	50
Additional paid-in capital	100	100
Retained earnings	500	400
TOTAL SHAREHOLDERS' EQUITY	650	550
TOTAL LIABILITIES AND SHAREHOLDERS' EQUITY	$1,000	$950

Suppose a company has an active, ongoing investment in research and development to develop new products. It must expense what is spent on research and development each year because for a given investment in R&D does not likely meet the two criteria because it is not until much later, after the R&D expense is made, that the economic viability of the investment is determined. If, on the other hand, a company buys a patent from another company, this cost may be capitalized and then amortized over the remaining life of the patent. So when you look at a company's assets on its balance sheet, you may not be getting the complete picture of what it owns.

Liabilities

We generally use the terms "liability" and "debt" as synonymous terms, though "liability" is actually a broader term, encompassing not only the explicit contracts that a company has, in terms of short-term and long-term debt obligations, but also includes obligations that are not specified in a contract, such as environmental obligations or asset retirement obligations. Liabilities may be interest-bearing, such as a bond issue, or noninterest bearing, such as amounts due to suppliers.

In the balance sheet, liabilities are presented in order of their due date and are often presented in two categories, current liabilities and long-term liabilities. *Current liabilities* are obligations due within one year or one operating cycle (whichever is longer). Current liabilities consist of:

■ *Accounts payable* are amounts due to suppliers for purchases on credit
■ Wages and salaries payable are amounts due employees
■ Current portion of long-term indebtedness
■ Short term bank loans

Long-term liabilities are obligations that are due beyond one year. There are different types of long-term liabilities, including:

■ *Notes payables* and *bonds*, which are indebtedness (loans) in the form of securities
■ *Capital leases*, which are rental obligations that are long-term, fixed commitments
■ *Asset retirement liability*, which is the contractual or statutory obligation to retire or decommission the asset and restore the site to required standards at the end of the asset's life
■ *Deferred taxes*, which are taxes that may have to be paid in the future that are currently not due, though they are expensed for financial reporting purposes. Deferred taxes arise from differences between accounting and tax methods (e.g., depreciation methods).[3]

Equity

The equity of a company is the ownership interest. The book value of equity, which for a corporation is often referred to as shareholders' equity or stockholders' equity, is basically the amount that investors

---

[3] Though deferred income taxes are often referred to as liabilities, some analysts will classify them as equity if the deferral is perceived to be perpetual. For example, a company that buys new depreciable assets each year will always have some level of deferred taxes; in that case, an analyst will classify deferred taxes as equity.

paid the company for their ownership interest, plus any earnings (or less any losses), and minus any distributions to owners. For a corporation, equity is the amount that investors paid the corporation for the stock when it was initially sold, plus or minus any earnings or losses, less any dividends paid. Keep in mind that for any company, the reported amount of equity is an accumulation over time since the company's inception (or incorporation, in the case of a corporation).

Shareholders equity is the carrying or book value of the ownership of a company. Shareholders' equity is comprised of:

+ Par value	A nominal amount per share of stock (sometimes prescribed by law), or the **stated value**, which is a nominal amount per share of stock assigned for accounting purposes if the stock has no par value.
+ Additional paid-in-capital	Also referred to as **capital surplus**, the amount paid for shares of stock by investors in excess of par or stated value.
− Treasury stock	The accounting value of shares of the firm's own stock bought by the firm.
+ Retained earnings	The accumulation of prior and current periods' earnings and losses, less any prior or current periods' dividends.
± Accumulated comprehensive income or loss	The total amount of income or loss that arises from transactions that result in income or losses, yet are not reported through the income statement. Items giving rise to this income include foreign currency translation adjustments and unrealized gains or losses on available-for-sale investments.

= Shareholders' equity

As an example, consider The Coca-Cola Company reported on its 2004 balance sheet:[4]

	Year Ended December 31, 2004 (in millions)
Common stock, $0.25 par value	$875
Capital surplus	4,928
Reinvested earnings	29,105
Accumulated other comprehensive income (loss)	−1,348
Less treasury stock	−17,625
Shareowners' equity	$15,935

[4] The Coca-Cola Company Annual Report, 2004, page 62.

The book value of equity for Coca-Cola at the end of 2004 is $15.935 billion. With 2.209 billion shares outstanding, Coca-Cola's book value of equity per share of stock is $15.935/2.209 = $7.214 per share. This differs from its market value, which was $100.3 billion, or $41.64 per share.

A Note on Minority Interest

On many companies' consolidated financial statements, you will notice a balance sheet account entitled "Minority Interest." When a company owns a substantial portion of another company, the accounting principles require that the company consolidate that company's financial statements into its own. Basically what happens in consolidating the financial statements is that the parent company will add the accounts of the subsidiary to its accounts (i.e., subsidiary inventory + parent inventory = consolidated inventory).[5] If the parent does not own 100% of the subsidiary's ownership interest, an account is created, referred to as **minority interest**, which reflects the amount of the subsidiary's assets *not* owned by the parent. This account will be presented between liabilities and equity on the consolidated balance sheet. Is it a liability or an equity account? It is neither.

A similar adjustment takes place on the income statement. The minority interest account on the income statement reflects the income (or loss) in proportion to the equity in the subsidiary *not* owned by the parent.

Structure of the Balance Sheet

Consider a simple balance sheet for the Sample Company shown in Exhibit 2.1 for fiscal years ending 2005 and 2006, with the most recent fiscal year's data is presented in the left-most column of data. You will notice that the accounting identity holds; that is, total assets are equal to the sum of the total liabilities and the total shareholders' equity.

The Income Statement

The **income statement** is a summary of operating performance over a period of time (e.g., a fiscal quarter or a fiscal year). We start with the revenue of the company over a period of time and then subtract the costs and expenses related to that revenue. The bottom line of the income statement consists of the owners' earnings for the period. To

---

[5] There are other adjustments made for intercorporate transactions, but we will not go into these at this time.

arrive at this "bottom line," we need to compare revenues and expenses. The basic structure of the income statement includes the following:

Sales or revenues	⇦ Represent the amount of goods or services sold, in terms of price paid by customers
Less: Cost of goods sold (or cost of sales)	⇦ The amount of goods or services sold, in terms of cost to the firm
Gross profit	⇦ The difference between sales and cost of goods sold
Less: Selling and general expenditures	⇦ Salaries, administrative, marketing expenditures, etc.
Operating profit	⇦ Income from operations (ignores effects of financing decisions and taxes); earnings before interest and taxes (EBIT), operating income, and operating earnings
Less: Interest expense	⇦ Interest paid on debt
Net income before taxes	⇦ Earnings before taxes
Less: Taxes	⇦ Taxes expense for the current period
Net income	⇦ Operating profit less financing expenses (e.g., interest) and taxes
Less: Preferred stock dividends	⇦ Dividends paid to preferred shareholders
Earnings available to common shareholders	⇦ Net income less preferred stock dividends; residual income

Though the structure of the income statement varies by company, the basic idea is to present the operating results first, followed by non-operating results. The *cost of sales*, also referred to as the *cost of goods sold*, is deducted from revenues, producing a gross profit; that is, a profit without considering all other, general operating costs. These general operating expenses are those expenses related to the support of the general operations of the company, which includes salaries, marketing costs, and research and development. Depreciation, which is the amortized cost of physical assets, is also deducted from gross profit. The amount of the depreciation expense represents the cost of the wear and tear on the property, plant, and equipment of the company.

Once we have the operating income, we have summarized the company's performance with respect to the operations of the business. But there is generally more to company's performance. From operating income, we deduct interest expense and add any interest income. Further, adjustments are made for any other income or cost that is not a part of the company's core business.

There are a number of other items that may appear as adjustments to arrive at net income. One of these is extraordinary items, which are defined as unusual and infrequent gains or losses. Another adjustment would be for the expense related to the write-down of an asset's value.

In the case of the Sample Company, whose income statement is presented in Exhibit 2.2, the income from operations—its core business—is $190 million, whereas the net income (i.e., the "bottom line") is $100 million.

Earnings Per Share

Companies provide information on *earnings per share* (EPS) in their annual and quarterly financial statement information, as well as in their periodic press releases. Generally, EPS is calculated as net income, divided by the number of shares outstanding. Companies must report both basic and diluted earnings per share.[6]

Basic earnings per share is net income (minus preferred dividends), divided by the average number of shares outstanding. *Diluted earnings per share* is net income (minus preferred dividends), divided by the number of shares outstanding considering all dilutive securities (e.g., convertible debt, options). Diluted earnings per share, therefore, gives the shareholder information about the *potential* dilution of earnings. For companies with a large number of dilutive securities (e.g., stock options, convertible preferred stock or convertible bonds), there can be a significant difference between basic and diluted EPS. You can see the effect of dilution by comparing the basic and diluted EPS.

EXHIBIT 2.2   The Sample Company Income Statement for the Period Ending December 31, 2006 (in millions)

Sales	$1,000
Cost of goods sold	600
Gross profit	$400
Depreciation	50
Selling, general, and administrative expenses	160
Operating profit	$190
Interest expense	23
Income before taxes	$167
Taxes	67
Net income	$100

[6] This replaces the previous requirement of simple, primary, and fully diluted EPS that was used prior to 1998.

EXHIBIT 2.3 Adobe Systems, Inc., Earnings per Share, 1998–2004

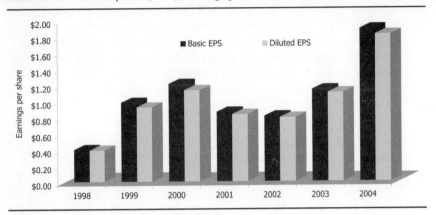

Source: Adobe Systems, Inc., 10-K filings, various years.

Consider Adobe Systems. We provide its basic and diluted earnings per share in Exhibit 2.3. These two per share amounts differ slightly, primarily due to restricted stock options.

More on Depreciation

There are different methods that can be used to allocate an asset's cost over its life. Generally, if the asset is expected to have value at the end of its economic life, the expected value, referred to as a *salvage value* (or *residual value*), is not depreciated; rather, the asset is depreciated down to its salvage value. There are different methods of depreciation that we classify as either straight-line or accelerated. *Straight-line depreciation* allocates the cost (less salvage value) in a uniform manner (equal amount per period) throughout the asset's life. *Accelerated depreciation* allocates the asset's cost (less salvage value) such that more depreciation is taken in the earlier years of the asset's life. There are alternative accelerated methods available, including:[7]

- *Declining balance method*, in which a *constant* rate applied to a *declining* amount (the undepreciated cost)
- *Sum-of-the-years' digits method*, in which a *declining* rate applied to the asset's *depreciable basis*

---

[7] Another method is the units-of-activity method, in which the useful life is defined in terms of a measure of units of production or some other metric or use (e.g., hours, miles). The depreciation expense in any period is determined as the usage in that period.

A common declining balance method is the *double-declining balance method* (DDB), which applies the rate that is twice that of the straight-line rate. In this case, the straight-line rate is 10% per year; therefore, the declining balance rate is 20% per year. We apply this rate of 20% against the original cost of $1,000,000, resulting in a depreciation expense in the first year of $200,000. In the second year, we apply this 20% against the un-depreciated balance of $1,000,000 − 200,000 = $800,000, resulting in a depreciation of $160,000.[8,9]

For this same asset, the *sum-of-the-years' digits* (SYD) depreciation for the first year is the rate of 10/55, or 18.18%, applied against the depreciable basis of $1,000,000 − 100,000 = $900,000:

$$\text{SYD first year} = \$900,000 \ (^{10}/_{55}) = \$163,636.$$

We calculate the denominator as the "sum of the years": $10 + 9 + 8 + 7 + 6 + 5 + 4 + 3 + 2 + 1 = 55$. In the second year, the rate is 9/55 applied against the $900,000, and so on.

Accelerated methods result in higher depreciation expenses in earlier years, relative to straight-line, as you can see in Exhibit 2.4. As a result, accelerated methods result in lower reported earnings in earlier years, relative to straight-line. When comparing companies, it is important to understand whether the companies use different methods of depreciation because the choice of depreciation method affects both the balance sheet (through the carrying value of the asset) and the income statement (through the depreciation expense).

A major source of deferred income taxes and deferred tax assets is the accounting methods used for financial reporting purposes and tax purposes. In the case of financial accounting purposes, the company chooses the method that best reflects how its assets lose value over time, though most companies use the straight-line method. However, for tax purposes the company has no choice but to use the prescribed rates of depreciation, using the *Modified Accelerated Cost Recovery System* (MACRS). For tax purposes, a company does not have discretion over the asset's depreciable life or the rate of depreciation—they must use the MACRS system.

---

[8] Because the declining balance methods result in more depreciation sooner, relative to straight-line, and lower depreciation in the later years, companies may switch straight-line in these later years. The same amount is depreciated over the life of the asset, but the pattern—and depreciation's impact on earnings—is modified slightly.
[9] In the case of the declining balance method, salvage value is not considered in the calculation of depreciation until the undepreciated balance reaches the salvage value.

EXHIBIT 2.4   Comparison of Depreciation Expense and Book Value
Depreciation expense each year for an asset with an original cost of $1,000,000, a
salvage value of $10,000, and a 10-year useful life

Panel A: Depreciation Expense

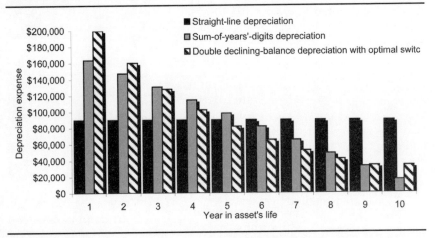

Panel B: Book Value of the Asset

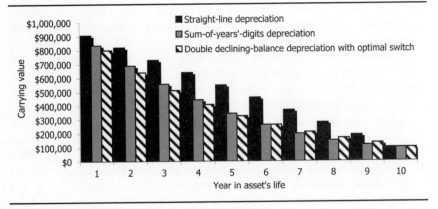

The MACRS system does not incorporate salvage value and is based
on a declining balance system. The depreciable life for tax purposes may
be longer than or shorter than that used for financial reporting purposes.
For example, the MACRS rate for a 3- and 5-year assets are as follows:

Year	3-year	5-year
1	33.33%	20.00%
2	44.45%	32.00%
3	14.81%	19.20%
4	7.41%	11.52%
5		11.52%
6		5.76%

You'll notice the fact that a 3-year asset is depreciated over 4 years and a 5-year asset is depreciated over six years. That is the result of using what is referred to as a half-year convention—using only half a year's worth of depreciation in the first year of an asset's life. This system results in a leftover amount that must still be depreciated in the last year (i.e., the fourth year in the case of a 3-year asset and the sixth year in the case of a 5-year asset). We provide a comparison of straight-line and MACRS depreciation in Exhibit 2.5. You can see that the methods produce different depreciation expenses, which result in the different income amounts for tax and financial reporting purposes.

The Statement of Cash Flows

The *statement of cash flows* is the summary of a firm's cash flows, summarized by operations, investment activities, and financing activities. A simplified cash flow statement is provided in Exhibit 2.5 for the fictitious Sample Company. *Cash flow from operations* is cash flow from day-to-day operations. Cash flow from operating activities is basically net income adjusted for (1) noncash expenditures, and (2) changes in working capital accounts. The adjustment for changes in working capital accounts is necessary to adjust net income that is determined using the accrual method to a cash flow amount. Increases in current assets and decreases in current liabilities are positive adjustments to arrive at the cash flow; decreases in current assets and increases in current liabilities are negative adjustments to arrive at the cash flow.

Cash flow for/from investing is the cash flows related to the acquisition (purchase) of plant, equipment, and other assets, as well as the proceeds from the sale of assets. *Cash flow for/from financing activities* is the cash flow from activities related to the sources of capital funds (e.g., buyback common stock, pay dividends, issue bonds).

Not all of the classifications required by accounting principles are consistent with the true flow for the three types of activities. For example, interest expense is a financing cash flow, yet it affects the cash flow from operating activities because it is a deduction to arrive at net income. This

EXHIBIT 2.5 Depreciation for Financial Accounting Purposes versus Tax Purposes Consider an asset that costs $200,000 and has a salvage value of $20,000. If the asset has a useful life of 8 years, but is classified as a 5-year asset for tax purposes, the depreciation and book value of the asset will be different between the financial accounting records and the tax records.

Panel A: Depreciation Expense

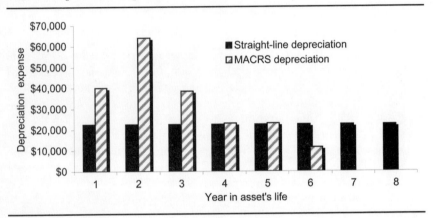

Panel B: Carrying Value

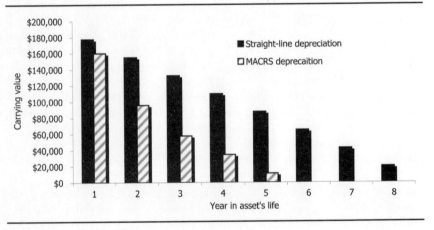

inconsistency is also the case for interest income and dividend income, both of which result from investing activities, but show up in the cash flow from operating activities through their contribution to net income.

The sources of a company's cash flows can reveal a great deal about the company and its prospects. For example, a financially healthy company tends to consistently generate cash flows from operations (that is, positive operating cash flows) and invests cash flows (that is, negative investing cash flows). To remain viable, a company must be able to generate funds from its operations; to grow, a company must be continually make capital investments.

The change in cash flow—also called net cash flow—is the bottom line in the statement of cash flows and is equal to the change in the cash account as reported on the balance sheet. For the Sample Company, shown in Exhibit 2.6, the net change in cash flow is a positive $10 million; this is equal to the change in the cash account from $50 million in 2005 to $60 million in 2006.

By studying the cash flows of a company over time, we can gauge a company's financial health. For example, if a company relies on external financing to support its operations (that is, reliant on cash flows from financing and not from operations) for an extended period of time, this is a warning sign of financial trouble up ahead.

We provide two examples of patterns in Exhibit 2.7: Microsoft Corporation and Toys "R" Us. Both companies have healthy cash flows, yet as you can see, Toys "R" Us experienced some difficulties 2000, prior to its extensive store remodeling/remerchandising.

EXHIBIT 2.6   The Sample Company Statement of Cash Flows, for the period ending December 31, 2006 (in millions)

Net income	$100	
Add depreciation	50	
Subtract increase in accounts receivable	–10	
Add decrease in inventory	20	
Add increase in accounts payable	50	
Cash flow from operations		$210
Retire debt	–$100	
Cash flow for financing		–100
Purchase of equipment	–$100	
Cash flow for investment		–100
Change in cash flow		$10

EXHIBIT 2.7   Examples of Cash Flow Patterns
Panel A: Microsoft

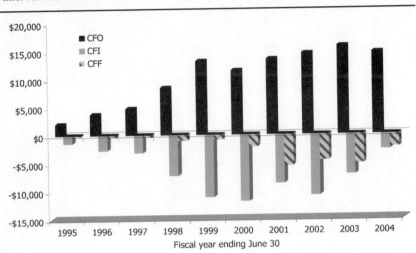

Panel B: Toys "R" Us

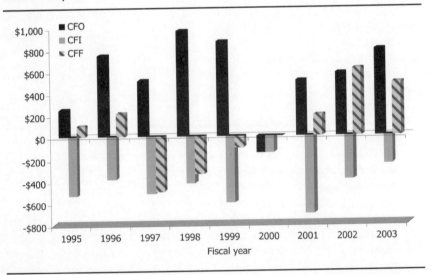

Source: 10-K filings, various years.

The Statement of Stockholders' Equity

The *statement of stockholders' equity* (also referred to as the *statement of shareholders' equity*) is a summary of the changes in the equity accounts, including information on stock options exercised, repurchases of shares, and Treasury shares. The basic structure is to include a reconciliation of the balance in each component of equity from the beginning of the fiscal year with the end of the fiscal year, detailing changes attributed to net income, dividends, purchases or sales of Treasury stock. The components are common stock, additional paid-in capital, retained earnings, and Treasury stock. For each of these components, the statement begins with the balance of each at the end of the previous fiscal period and then adjustments are shown to produce the balance at the end of the current fiscal period.

In addition, there is a reconciliation of any gains or losses that affect stockholders' equity but which do not flow through the income statement, such as foreign-currency translation adjustments and unrealized gains on investments. These items are of interest because they are part of comprehensive income, and hence income to owners, but they are not represented on the company's income statement.

Why Bother About the Footnotes?

Footnotes to the financial statements contain additional information, supplementing or explaining financial statement data. These notes are presented in both the annual report and the 10-K filing (with the SEC), though the latter usually provides a greater depth of information.

The footnotes to the financial statements provide information pertaining to:

- *The significant accounting policies and practices that the company uses.* This helps the analyst with the interpretation of the results, comparability of the results to other companies and to other years for the same company, and in assessing the quality of the reported information.
- *Income taxes.* The footnotes tell us about the company's current and deferred income taxes, breakdowns by the type of tax (e.g., federal versus state), and the effective tax rate that the company is paying.
- *Pension plans.* The detail about pension plans, including the pension assets and the pension liability, is important in determining whether a company's pension plan is overfunded or underfunded.
- *Leases.* You can learn about both the capital leases, which are the long-term lease obligations that are reported on the balance sheet, and about the future commitments under operating leases, which are not reflected on the balance sheet.

■ *Long-term debt.* You can find detailed information about the maturity dates and interest rates on the company's debt obligations.

The phrase "the devil is in the details" applies aptly to the footnotes of a company's financial statement. Through the footnotes, a company is providing information that is crucial in analyzing a company's financial health and performance. If footnotes are vague or confusing, as they were in the case of Enron prior to the break in the scandal, the analyst must ask questions to help understand this information.

ACCOUNTING FLEXIBILITY

The generally accepted accounting principles provide some choices in the manner in which some transactions and assets are accounted. For example, a company may choose to account for inventory, and hence costs of sales, using *Last-in, First-out* (LIFO) or *First-in, First-out* (FIFO) This is intentional because these principles are applied to a broad set of companies and no single set of methods offers the best representation of a company's condition or performance for all companies. Ideally, a company's management, in consultation with the accountants, chooses those accounting methods and presentations that are most appropriate for the company.

A company's management has always had the ability to manage earnings through the judicious choice of accounting methods within the GAAP framework. The company's "watchdogs" (i.e., the accountants) should keep the company's management in check. However, recent scandals have revealed that the watchdog function of the accounting firms was not working well. Additionally, some companies' management used manipulation of financial results and out-right fraud to distort the financial picture.

The Sarbanes-Oxley Act of 2002 offers some comfort in terms of creating the oversight board for the auditing accounting firms. In addition, the Securities and Exchange Commission, the Financial Accounting Standards Board, and the International Accounting Standards Board are tightening some of the flexibility that companies had in the past.

Pro Forma Financial Data

Pro forma financial information is really a misnomer—the information is neither pro forma (that is, forward looking), nor reliable financial data. What is it? Creative accounting. It started during the Internet-Tech boom in the 1990s and persists today: Companies release financial information that is prepared according to its own liking, using accounting methods that they create.

Why did companies start doing this? What is wrong with generally accepted accounting principles (GAAP)? During the Internet-Tech stock boom, many startup companies quickly went public and then felt the pressures to generate profits. However, profits in that industry were hard to come by during that period of time. What some companies did is generate financial data that they included in company releases that reported earnings not calculated using GAAP—but rather by methods of their own. In some cases, these alternative methods hid a lot of the ills of these companies. We show a couple of examples of the differences between a company's pro forma net income and net income per GAAP in Exhibit 2.8. As you can see in these examples, the pro forma amounts may differ substantially from the amounts according to GAAP.

The use of pro forma financial data may be helpful, but also may be misleading to investors. Analysts routinely adjust published financial statement data to remove unusual, non-recurring items. This can give the analyst a better predictor of the continued performance of the company. So what is wrong with the company itself doing this? Nothing, unless it becomes misleading, such as a company including its non-recurring gains, but not including its nonrecurring losses. In concern for the possibility of misleading information being given to investors, the Securities and Exchange Commission now requires that if companies release pro forma financial data, they must also reconcile this data with GAAP.[10]

EXHIBIT 2.8 Examples of Pro Forma versus GAAP Earnings (in millions)

	Net Income for 2001	
	Pro Forma	IAS or U.S. GAAP
Nokia (EUR)	€3,789	€2,220
Cisco (USD)	$3,086	−$1,014

IAS = International accounting standards
U.S. GAAP = U.S. Generally accepted accounting standards
EUR = Euro
USD = U.S. Dollar
Source: Yahoo! Finance

---

[10] Securities and Exchange Commission RIN3235-A169, "Conditions for Use of Non-GAAP Financial Measures," effective March 28, 2003.

HOW DOES ACCOUNTING IN THE UNITED STATES DIFFER FROM ACCOUNTING OUTSIDE OF THE UNITED STATES?

The generally accepted accounting standards in the United States (U.S. GAAP) differ from those used in other countries around the world. But not for long. What is happening is an international convergence of accounting standards. The first major step was the agreement in 2002 between two major standard setting bodies—the U.S.'s Financial Accounting Standards Board (FASB) and the International Accounting Standards Board (IASB)—to work together for eventual convergence of accounting principles. The second major step was the requirement of International Financial Reporting Standards (IFRS) by the European Commission, effective in 2005. IFRS are promulgated by the IASB and must be used by all publicly traded and private companies in the European Union. IFRS are also used, in varying degrees, by companies in Australia, Hong Kong, Russia, and China.

IFRS, like GAAP, uses historical cost as the main accounting convention. However, IFRS permits the revaluation of intangible assets, property, plant and equipment (PPE) and investment property. IFRS also requires fair valuation of certain categories of financial instruments and certain biological assets. U.S. GAAP, on the other hand, prohibits revaluations except for certain categories of financial instruments, which must be carried at fair value. We summarize a comparison of the differences between U.S. GAAP and IFRS in Exhibit 2.9.[11]

SUMMARY

Much of the financial data that is used in financial analysis is drawn from the company's financial statements. It is important to understand this data so that we can interpret this information and use it in analysis of a company's past financial condition and performance so that we have an idea of what to expect the future.

There are four basic financial statements: the balance sheet, the income statement, the statement of cash flows, and the statement of stockholders' equity. The balance sheet and the statement of shareholders' equity are statements with values of accounts at a point in time. In the case of the balance sheet, the company presents data as of the end of the most recent two years. In the case of the statement of shareholders' equity, the balances in accounts are reconciled from the beginning of the

---

[11] This table is based on *Similarities and Differences—IFRS, US GAAP and Belgian GAAP* (January 2005), PriceWaterhouseCooper.

EXHIBIT 2.9   Comparison of U. S. GAAP and IFRS

Issue	U.S. GAAP	IFRS
Historical costs	Use historical costs, except for the valuation of securities and derivatives at fair value	Use historical costs generally, but allow revaluations for property plant and equipment, intangibles, and investment property Require revaluation to fair value in the case of derivatives, biological assets, and specified securities
Number of years of presentation	Three years for statements other than the balance sheet, in which two years are required	Two years for all statements
Balance sheet classifications	Decreasing order of liquidity	May use liquidity presentation or current/noncurrent presentation
Income statement	Single-step or multiple-step presentation Expenses are classified by function Extraordinary items are both unusual and infrequent, and identified as extraordinary	No standard format Expenses may be classified either by function or nature
Cash flow statement	Interest paid and interest received are classified as operating cash flows Dividends paid are classified as financing cash flows Dividends received are classified as operating cash flows	Interest paid may be classified as operating or financing cash flows Interest received may be classified as operating or investment cash flows Dividends paid may be classified as operating or financing cash flows Dividends received may be classified as operating or investment cash flows
Statement of recognized gains and losses	Information included in comprehensive income presentation	Required

EXHIBIT 2.9 (Continued)

Issue	U.S. GAAP	IFRS
Special purpose entities (SPEs)	If SPE satisfies requirements of a qualifying SPE, no consolidation	Consolidate in cases in which the company has control
Joint ventures	Requires equity method	Allows proportional consolidation or equity method
Construction contracts	Allows both the percentage-of-completion method and the completed contracts method, but the former is preferred	Allows for the use of only the percentage-of-completion method
Employee compensation in the form of company shares	Fair value at issue using an option pricing model	Expense is fair value of shares or share options when granted
	Cost recognized over the option's vesting period	Liability or equity, depending on whether shares are provided for cash or as new shares
	Changes in the value of the options recorded as compensation expense, determined annually	
Impairment of assets	If impaired, write down value to higher of fair value less sales cost and fair value based on discounted cash flows	Impairment test determined using undiscounted cash flows
		Write-down value to market value or discounted cash flows
	May reverse impairment, writing up asset	Reversals prohibited
Inventories	Permit use of FIFO, LIFO or weighted average method	Permit use of FIFO or weighted average method
	Permit write-downs of impaired value	Permit write-downs of impaired value
		Reversals of write-downs required if value has increased
Convertible debt	Generally recognized as a liability	Some proceeds allocated as a liability, some proceeds allocated as equity

56

latest fiscal year to the end. The income statement and the statement of cash flows provide data on earnings and cash flows over the period, whether that period is a fiscal quarter or year.

The information conveyed in the footnotes is essential to the understanding of these financial statements. There is detail in these footnotes that gives us a better idea of the financial health of the company.

In addition to being able to read the financial statements and the accompanying footnotes, an analyst must understand the accounting principles that guide companies in the preparation of these financial statements. Not only must the analyst understand the accounting methods that a company uses, but the choices that a company has made among the available accounting methods.

There is an intent among regulatory bodies around the world to develop one set of accounting principles to be used by companies worldwide. The International Financial Reporting Standards and the coordination of FASB and IASB in an effort to move toward convergence are significant steps toward this goal.

CHAPTER 3

The Quality of Financial Information

Shareholders and creditors depend on the financial statements of companies that are prepared according to generally accepted accounting standards (GAAP). These financial statements have important economic consequences that include determining management compensation, the credit quality of the company's debt obligations, and compliance with loan covenants. Yet despite the important economic consequences of these financial statements, a company's management has considerable flexibility in the choice of accounting methods and estimates. This flexibility, however, creates a situation in which the accounting choices that a company makes affects reported financial information.

The Sarbanes-Oxley Act of 2002 and the regulations and changes in accounting standards that followed increase the transparency of financial statements. Financial reporting by companies is considered *transparent* when it is easy for investors to understand the company's performance and financial condition. We associate transparency with a high quality of financial information. In terms of valuing companies, those companies with more transparent financial information will be associated with higher values than companies with nontransparent information, if everything else is the same. This is because the opaqueness of the financial information in the latter company increases the uncertainty with respect to the current and future performance of the company and thereby reduces the company's value.

Aside from the lack of comparability that it presents, the wide latitude that management has in making choices and estimates allows for earnings management. *Earnings management* is the judicious choice of accounting methods for financial reporting to produce results that are in the best interests of the company or its management. This is different from earnings manipulation, which has a more sinister connotation, though it is admittedly sometimes difficult to distinguish management from manipulation. Earnings management involves working within the bounds of GAAP, whereas earnings manipulation involves violating GAAP.

Do companies manage earnings? There is sufficient academic research that suggests that companies do manage earnings, whether for managers' self-interest or for some other reasons (e.g., to comply with debt covenant compliance or to minimize political costs).[1] The risk of this type of management is great when management's compensation depends on reported financial data, such as earnings.[2] The risk is also great when management is overly concerned with achieving analyst earnings forecasts or the company is near financial-data-based constraints, such as debt covenant restrictions.

The financial analyst must be able to detect earnings management, earnings manipulation, or any other type of management or manipulation of financial data. Financial data may be managed in many ways and it is a challenge of financial analysis to detect such management. The purpose of this chapter is to discuss the quality of financial information that companies report. There are many ways that companies can obscure the view of their financial performance and we will point out some of the devises that companies may use—either intentionally or unintentionally.

In this chapter, we discuss several avenues for financial information management and discuss what to look for in a financial data. In particular, we discuss:

- Accruals management
- Revenue and expense recognition
- Nonoperating and nonrecurring items
- Goodwill impairment
- Inventory accounting

---

[1] See, for example, R. Watts and J. Zimmerman, "Positive Accounting Theory: A Ten-Year Perspective," *Accounting Review* 65 (January 1990), pp. 131–156; and Katherine Shipper, "Commentary on Earnings Management," *Accounting Horizons* 15, no. 4 (December 1989), pp. 91–102.

[2] Practice Alert 95-1 CPA Letter No. 1, "Revenue Recognition Issues," AICPA *CPA Letter* (January 1995). Management of earnings for compensation purposes may result in (1) not recognizing income in periods of high earnings because of maximums in bonus plans; (2) large write-offs in years in which performance targets are not met because no bonus would be forthcoming for the period; and (3) speeding up recognition of revenues or delaying expenses to meet performance targets.

■ Depreciation
■ Income and expenses related to segments

After discussing the detective work that can reveal earnings management, we discuss some of the tell-tale signs to look for in an analysis of financial statements.

IT IS ALL IN THE TIMING

Accruals Management

Accruals are the accounting adjustments that relate earnings to cash flows. We typically classify accruals into two types: *discretionary accruals* and *nondiscretionary accruals*. A large part of earnings management deals with accruals and, in particular, discretionary accruals.

We expect that working capital accounts will move in accordance with revenues and that depreciation is proportionate to plant, property, and equipment. Therefore, we expect that accruals will increase as revenues increase and depreciation will increase as the company increases its investment in plant and equipment. Consider the sales of goods on credit. A sale on credit does not generate a cash flow, but rather increases accounts receivable (an accrual) and income. The accruals arising from sales on credit are part of the normal course of business and fall into the class of nondiscretionary accruals; as sales increase, the balance in the accounts receivable account should increase as well.

Aside from these nondiscretionary accruals that arise from the normal course of business there are also discretionary accruals, which should catch the attention of the financial analyst. The problem that the financial analyst faces is that accruals are not conveniently disclosed on the financial statements as discretionary or nondiscretionary. Therefore, the analyst must pay attention to particular aspects of accruals that may signal earnings management.[3]

An example of a discretionary accrual that bears watching is the allowance for doubtful accounts. The allowance for doubtful accounts is an estimate of the uncollectible accounts receivable and serves to reduce the value of accounts receivable on the balance sheet. The

---

[3] In academic research on earnings management, discretionary accruals are estimated from an examination of the historical difference between cash flows and net income; large deviations from the normal or typical relation between cash flows and net income are interpreted as use of discretionary accruals.

amount of receivables that are uncollectible is determined by management's judgment, considering past experience, the quality of the current customer accounts, the economy, and the company's collection policies. But because the allowance is an estimate, there is some flexibility for management to determine in any given period the change in the value of doubtful accounts.

Determining whether earnings are managed by varying the allowance is not possible, yet there are some tell-tale signs: the relation between the allowance and the balance in accounts receivable—that is, the percentage of uncollectible accounts—should be relatively constant unless there is a change in the economy overall or a change in customer base (i.e., extending credit to a broader range of credit quality). And for most companies, the allowance rate (allowance for doubtful accounts divided by the gross accounts receivable) is relatively constant. Further, because of similarities in customers within an industry, we should also find similar (but not identical) rates of uncollectible accounts within an industry.

There are companies that appear to change the rate of uncollectible accounts as their fortunes change. The ratio of the allowance of uncollectible accounts should be rather constant over time, varying primarily when there is change in product mix, a downturn in the economy, or a change in credit policies.

Consider Gateway's allowances for the years 1995 to 2004, as shown in Exhibit 3.1. In years in which revenues began to decline and profitability changed dramatically, as shown in Panel A, the allowance rate decreased, as shown in Panel B. The ratio of the allowance for uncollectible accounts to accounts receivable for Gateway is less than that of its closest competitor, Hewlett Packard, whose 2003 and 2004 ratios are 3.74% and 2.72% respectively.

Aside from looking at the relation between specific accounts and reserves, another screen that is useful is to compare the trend in net income to that of cash flows from operations. The two trends should be moving in the same direction at the same time. We expect that the amount of cash flow from operations will be different from that of net earnings, but we expect that the changes in each series should follow a similar path. A misalignment may suggest a problem with accruals.

Let us compare two companies using this method over the 15-year period 1990 to 2004. First, consider Wal-Mart Stores, Inc. The cash flow from operations and net income follow similar paths, as we show in Panel A of Exhibit 3.2. The correlation between these two series is 0.97, which indicates that these series are similar in terms of trends.[4]

---

[4] A correlation ranges from −1 (perfect negative correlation) and +1 (perfect positive correlation). A correlation of zero indicates no linear relation between the series.

EXHIBIT 3.1   Gateway, Inc., 1995–2004
Panel A: Revenues, in thousands

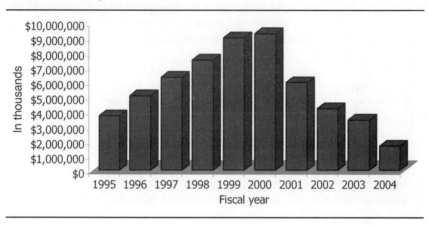

Panel B: Ratio of Allowance for Uncollectible Accounts to Gross Accounts
Receivable

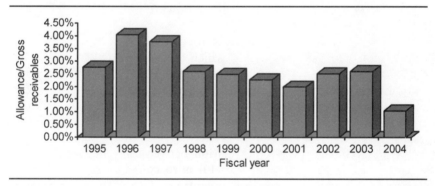

Source of data: 10-K filings of Gateway, Inc., various years.

This is not the same conclusion we draw from looking at the paths of
cash flow from operations and net income for Eastman Kodak, as
shown in Panel B. In this case, the correlation of the two series is –0.18.
The paths of these series are similar in the case of the earlier years for
Kodak, but beginning after 1996, the paths diverge.

Keep in mind that there may be reasons why a company's net
income and cash flow from operations differ, such as write-downs of
asset values. In performing a financial analysis of a company, however,
the analyst may want to identify the reasons why these two series
diverge.

EXHIBIT 3.2   Cash Flow from Operation and Net Income
Panel A: Wal-Mart Stores, Inc., 1990–2004

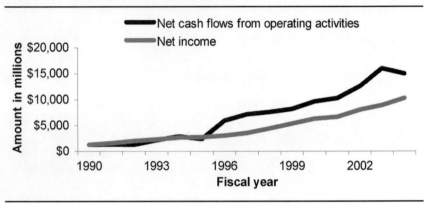

Source: Wal-Mart Stores, Inc. 10-K filings, various years.

Panel B: Eastman Kodak, 1990–2004

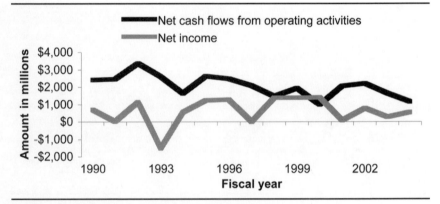

Source: Eastman Kodak, 10-K filings, various years.

Revenue and Expense Recognition

One of the basic guiding principles of accounting is that revenues and expenses are matched: Revenues are recognized (that is, included in income) in the period in which they are earned, and expenses are matched to coordinate with the corresponding revenue. Because most companies use the accrual method of accounting, revenues and expenses recognized in a period do not necessarily correspond with the cash inflows and outflows that are the basis of the revenues and expenses. The accrual basis of accounting relies on management's discretion in determining the timing of revenue and expense recognition. Along with management's discretion, however, is the potential to manipulate income through judicious timing of revenues and expenses.

The principle of conservatism in accounting suggests that if there is some flexibility in the recognition of revenues and expenses, the most conservative approach should be used. However, the recognition of revenues and expenses requires judgment and there are many cases in which the timing decisions have raised concern over the quality of a company's earnings.

Consider the case of Sunbeam Corporation.[5] The SEC alleged that Sunbeam executives provided false and misleading financial statements in the periods leading up to the merger with Coleman; the merger occurred in March 1998. Sunbeam's alleged illegal conduct included:

- The use of *cookie jar reserves*, which reduced the earnings in 1996, but then indicated a better turnaround performance in 1997[6]
- *Channel stuffing*, which resulted in better revenue growth in 1997 from inducements and discounts that would reduce future period's profitability[7]
- Improper accounting of revenues, recognizing revenues in period before permissible according to GAAP

Consider the conscientious attempt to shift earnings from the future into the past. In 1997, Sunbeam recorded transactions that required both the delivery and payment for goods in the *next* year. This practice is referred to as "bill and hold," which effectively increases revenues and income in 1997 and was described by the Company in its 1997 10-K filing:

> During 1997, the Company initiated early buy programs for highly seasonal products such as grills and warming blankets in order to more levelize production and distribution activities. [Sunbeam Corporation, 10-K, 1997, p. 6].

---

[5] Securities and Exchange Commission v. Albert Dunlap et al., Civil Action No. 01-8437-CIV.

[6] Cookie jar reserves are a method of income smoothing. In a typical cookie jar scheme, a company makes inappropriate assumptions about a liabilities (e.g., loan losses), often overstating them in good earnings years. Then, in a future period when earnings are not as good as expected, they reverse this transaction, hence reaching into the cookie jar.

[7] Channel stuffing is the practice of sending goods along its distribution channel (e.g., a manufacturer sending finished goods to retailers) that are knowingly in excess of what the receiving company requires. The company that is stuffing the channel is inflating sales and earnings in the period in which it is "stuffing."

This practice was revealed by a financial analyst, Andrew Shore, who detected an unusual pattern of inventory and accounts receivable, which we illustrate in Exhibit 3.3, Panel A. This graph covers the periods leading up to and including the merger with Coleman in the first quarter of 1998. You can see that accounts receivable and inventory increased in early 1997 without a corresponding increase in sales activity, with this pattern repeat-

EXHIBIT 3.3 Sunbeam's Accounts Receivable, Inventory and Revenues
Panel A: As Originally Reported

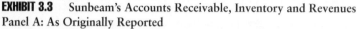
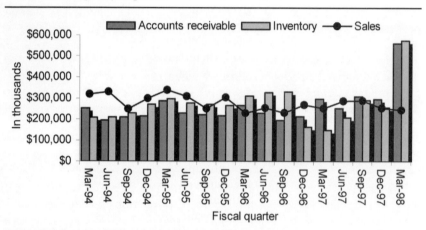

Panel B: Restated Revenues

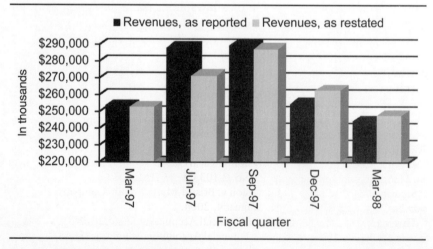

Source of data: Sunbeam 10-Q filings.

ing in a more dramatic fashion in the first quarter of 1998.[8] The SEC required, among other things, that Sunbeam restate its 1997 results. We present both the "as reported" and "as restated" revenues for Sunbeam in Panel B of Exhibit 3.3. You can see the shifting forward of revenues that took place in 1997, which moved the revenues forward in time.

Another example of channel stuffing is that alleged of ClearOne Communications, Inc. in 2001, in which the company forced distributors to take delivery of product that they did not want and then made verbal agreements for distributors to pay for the products as they sold them.[9] Still another example is the case of Bristol-Myers Squibb Company, which settled a civil action in 2004 regarding channel stuffing. In this case, the company was stuffing the channel near the end of each quarter in order to meet analysts' earnings estimates.[10] In these cases, there was an increase in revenues and net income that was a sacrifice of future years' revenues and net income.

Extraordinary and Nonrecurring Items

In general, a company's earnings and cash flows should be generated from the operations of its business, rather than through nonrecurring means. A close examination of the sources of revenues in the income statement and notes may reveal nonoperating gains and losses. These nonoperating items are presented under various names, including "special," "nonrecurring," and "unusual."

Nonrecurring items are the result of unusual events and are reported as part of operating expenses. For example, if a company that operates retail stores closes several of its stores, it would record a charge for the costs associated with these closings. As another example, a company that is on the losing side of a lawsuit would report the settlement or penalty as a nonrecurring charge against income. A special type of non-recurring item is the voluntary effect of a change in accounting principle. If the company changes an accounting principle in the current period, the company applies the change retrospectively, revising past earnings to reflect the effect in each period presented.[11] If it is not prac-

---

[8] John A. Byrne, "Al Dunlap Self-Destructed," *Business Week*, 6 July 1998, pp. 58–64, and Martha Brannigan, "Sunbeam Concedes 1997 Statements May be Off," *Wall Street Journal*, 1 July 1998, p. A4.

[9] Securities and Exchange Commission v. ClearOne Communications, Inc., Frances M. Flood, and Susie Strohm, Civil No. 2 103 CV 55 DAK.

[10] Securities and Exchange Commission v. Bristol-Myers Squibb Company, Civil Action No. 04-3680 (D.N.J.), filed August 4, 2004.

[11] This is prescribed by Statement of Financial Accounting Standards No. 154, which is in effect Previous to Statement of Financial Accounting Standards (SFAS) No. 154, a company would report the cumulative effect of the accounting change as a charge against earnings in the income statement.

tical to represent the cumulative effect of the change to earnings in the current or recent years (say, because the effect cannot be attributed to a particular year), the entire charge is presented in the balance sheet as an adjustment to shareholders' equity.[12]

Extraordinary items are defined as unusual and infrequent and are presented in the income statement after continuing operations and net of tax. There is a subtle distinction between nonrecurring items that are included in operating results and extraordinary items that are reported in the nonoperating portion of the income statement.

These nonrecurring items are unavoidable and, with recent changes in accounting standards, may become more frequent. From the point of view of the financial analyst, these items are important in at least two respects:

1. These items make the bottom line earnings more volatile and, hence, more difficult to use as a basis for predictions about future earnings.
2. These items may signal important company events, such as write-downs of inventory or fixed plant assets.

In the 1980s and 1990s, many companies had significant restructuring charges and may have used these to manage earnings. However, some companies, such as IBM, now consider restructuring charges part of their normal business and do not separate these changes as special.[13]

Further, many companies report nonrecurring and extraordinary items that have become quite ordinary, reporting gains and losses each year arising from these sources. This makes it difficult for the analyst to determine the result of the operations of the company and what is simply transitory.

Consider the example of Eastman Kodak. We show Eastman Kodak's operating earnings and net income in Exhibit 3.4 over the period 1990 to 2004. We calculated operating earnings for this example as the difference between revenues and the sum of cost of goods sold, selling, general and administrative expenses, and research and development costs. The difference between operating earnings and net income is largely the result of nonrecurring charges including:

■ Restructuring costs

---

[12] A retrospective change in earnings due to an accounting change is not the same thing as a restatement of earnings. Restatements are due to errors or fraud, not changes in accounting principle,

[13] Prior to 1994, IBM routinely reported substantial restructuring charges each year. Since 1994, however, they no longer break these items out separately.

EXHIBIT 3.4 Deviations Between Operating Earnings and Net Income, Eastman Kodak, 1990–2004

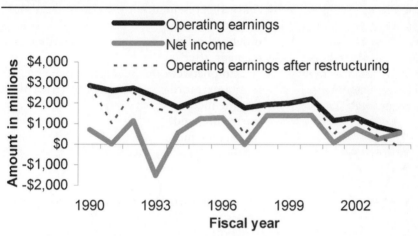

Source: Eastman Kodak 10-K filings, various years.

- Purchased in-process research and development[14]
- Cumulative effect of a change in accounting principle
- Other income and charges

There are, of course, recurring charges, including goodwill amortization (in those years in which permitted), interest expense, and taxes, that result in a difference in these two series. Eastman Kodak had restructuring charges in 10 of these 15 years and these charges made up the bulk of the difference between operating earnings and net income. We calculate operating earnings after the restructuring charges in Exhibit 3.4. As you can see, the restructuring costs introduced much of the fluctuation in the net income of Eastman Kodak over time.[15]

Deferred Taxes

A large difference between reported income and taxable income may suggest the inclusion of revenues or expenses in the reported income

---

[14] The charges for purchased research and development are the result of a write-off of a portion of the purchase price in an acquisition. When one company acquires another company, some of the purchase price may be allocated to the intangible asset of "in-process research and development." Then once the companies are combined, this purchased research and development is written off.

[15] The large deviation in 1993 between operating earnings and net income was due to a $2,168 million effect from a change in accounting principle.

that are not recognized for tax purposes in the current period. But examining the difference between accounting net income and taxable income is not possible because the tax returns are not made public. However, examining the sources and changes in deferred taxes—using notes to the financial statements—can provide some clues about how accounting and taxable income diverge.

Differences between income reported in the financial statements and taxable income arise from many sources, including differences in accounting for:

- Depreciation
- Installment sales
- Leases
- Warranties
- Pensions

It is quite common for companies to report a deferred tax liability or asset, and for this liability or asset to grow over time as the company's earnings and assets grow. What should catch the analyst's attention, however, is when the relation between reported earnings and taxable income diverges significantly, as indicated by a significant change in the deferred tax liability or asset.

Goodwill Hunting

The accounting for the combination of companies from mergers and acquisitions is carried out using the *purchase method*, whereby the acquired company's assets are valued at fair value and any excess of the purchase price of the acquired company over this fair value is goodwill, an intangible asset.[16]

The purchase method requires that assets of the acquired company be revalued, but this is not a straightforward process because many assets, such as intangibles, do not have discernible market price. The possible consequences of using the purchase method include:

- Increased cost of goods sold as revalued inventory of the acquired company is sold
- Goodwill created and reported as an asset on the balance sheet
- Depreciation expense may be increased because of increased value for depreciable assets of the acquired company

---

[16] Statement of Financial Accounting Standards No. 141, *Business Combinations*, effective for business combinations initiated after June 30, 2001.

■ Any debt discount resulting from a revaluation of debt must be amortized

What is goodwill? *Goodwill* is the difference between the purchase price of the acquired company and the fair value of the acquired company's assets. If the difference is positive, as it is most often, the amount is recorded as an intangible asset. Each year, the surviving company evaluates the current balance in goodwill to determine its value. If the value is less than the carrying amount (that is, the amount reported on the balance sheet), the asset is considered to have an impaired value and goodwill is written down to the current value.

For example, in 2003 and 2004, Yahoo! Paid $2.9 billion to acquire other companies, $2.1 of which was allocated to goodwill and the rest was allocated to tangible assets and amortizable intangible assets (e.g., patents). In other words, more than 72% of what it paid for in these acquisitions could not be attributed to identifiable tangible or intangible assets. One of acquisitions in 2003 was the $290 million paid for Inktomi, with only $49 million of these attributed to assets of Inktomi (Yahoo 2004 10-K filing, p. 64), in millions:

Cash acquired	$44.610
Other tangible assets acquired	27.522
Amortizable intangible assets	
Existing technology and related relationships	25.900
Customer contract and related relationships	23.500
Goodwill	217,425
Total assets acquired	$338.957
Liabilities assumed	50,638
Deferred stock-based compensation	1,387
Total	$289.606

The perplexing thing about goodwill is that it is really an intangible asset that is truly difficult to identify. If a company pays more for another company than what can identified as tangible or intangible assets, what type of asset is this? Is it simply the amount by what one company has *overpaid* to acquire another company?

Prior to 2002, companies amortized goodwill over a period not to exceed 40 years. The accounting principles changed with Statement of Financial Accounting Standard 142, effective January 1, 2002, that requires companies to test the goodwill annually for impairment.[17]

A write-down for impairment would hurt the earnings in the year of the write-down, but would result in improved returns on assets in the

---

[17] Statement of Financial Accounting Standards No. 142, *Goodwill and Other Intangible Assets*, effective for fiscal years after December 31, 2001.

future years. This is because the write-down would not effect earnings in years beyond the write-down, yet would result in lower assets in the future years. Many companies wrote off goodwill beginning in 2002, coinciding with a tough economic period, writing down goodwill during years in which earnings were low. For example, America Online, Inc., and Time Warner, Inc., merged in 2001, creating AOL-Time Warner Inc. With this merger, AOL Time Warner created goodwill of approximately $99 billion, and wrote down $54.235 billion of goodwill in 2002—the year after this goodwill was "created" through the merger. In subsequent years, the returns on assets are slightly higher than they would have been if there was no write-down (e.g., 2.73% with the write-down versus 1.89% without the write-down), as we show in Exhibit 3.5.

Of course, there are some companies that do not wish to take the earnings "hit" that a write-down in goodwill would entail. Enron did not write down impaired assets and it was found to have falsely represented the company's financial statements because of this.[18]

EXHIBIT 3.5   AOL Time Warner Return on Assets with and without the Write-Down of Goodwill

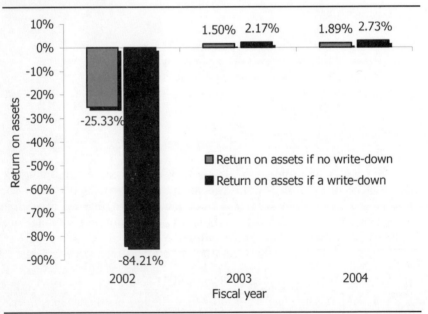

Source: AOL Time Warner 10-K filings, various years.

---

[18] United States Securities and Exchange Commission v. Kenneth Lay, Jeffrey K. Skilling, Richard A. Causey, Civil Action No. H-04-0284,

TOO MANY CHOICES?

Inventory Accounting

Choice of Method

The method chosen to account for inventory affects the value of inventory on the balance sheet, the cost of goods sold and earnings reported on the income statement, taxable income, and taxes. Therefore, the method affects not only the reported financial statements, but cash flows as well. There are three basic methods of accounting for inventory which differ in the assumptions regarding the cost flow of goods and cost of inventory remaining at the end of the period:

1. *FIFO (first in, first out)*, which assumes that the first items purchased are the first items sold
2. *LIFO (last in, first out)*, which assumes that the last items purchased are the first items sold
3. *Average cost*, which assumes that the cost of items sold is the cost of all items purchased

FIFO assumes that inventory items sold are the ones that have been in inventory the longest, so the cost of the older inventory items is recorded as the cost of goods sold, whereas LIFO assumes that any items sold are the ones that have been acquired recently, so the cost the newer inventory items is recorded as the cost of goods sold. During a period of rising prices, LIFO produces an estimate of profit that is closest to the true profit, whereas during a period of falling prices, FIFO produces the more accurate estimate of profit. Depending on whether prices are rising or falling, the choice of inventory method affects the values reported in the financial statements:

Comparing Amounts Reported Using FIFO and LIFO for:	During a Period of Rising Prices	During a Period of Falling Prices
Inventory on balance sheet	FIFO > LIFO	FIFO < LIFO
Cost of goods sold on income statement	FIFO < LIFO	FIFO > LIFO
Gross profit on income statement	FIFO > LIFO	FIFO < LIFO
Taxes	FIFO > LIFO	FIFO < LIFO

The average cost method produces estimates that fall somewhere between the values produced by FIFO and LIFO.

The financial analyst must understand also how the choice of inventory method affects the volatility of operating earnings. If selling prices are less flexible than prices of materials, a company's profits will be more volatile with the FIFO method as compared to the LIFO method. As a further note, if a company reduces its inventory substantially during a period and uses LIFO accounting, there will be artificial earnings boost from the sale of older, lower-priced inventory.

Because the method of inventory accounting affects the values shown in the financial statements, the financial analyst needs to know where to find the necessary information. In some cases, the company reports the method of inventory accounting in the balance sheet alongside the inventory account or, as is often the case, in the note that describes the company's accounting principles (usually Note 1). Additionally, if the company uses LIFO, an inventory note details the difference in inventory valuations if FIFO had been used if that difference is material. However, for companies using FIFO for inventory accounting, data necessary to convert FIFO into LIFO is not made available.

Companies in the same industry may use different methods of accounting for inventory, making comparisons among companies more difficult. Consider the household products industry. Colgate-Palmolive, Kimberly-Clark, and Procter & Gamble use both LIFO and FIFO in different proportions. Kimberly Clark, for example, uses LIFO for U.S. inventories, but FIFO for Non-U.S. inventories. Procter & Gamble, on the other hand, uses FIFO for most of their inventory, but use LIFO for the cosmetics and commodities inventories. The variety in the use of inventory methods makes it challenging for the analyst.

Write-Downs

Companies are permitted to write-down the value of inventory when the carrying value exceeds the fair value of the inventory. Though healthy companies may experience the need to write-down inventory because of shifts in customer demand, the questions arise:

- Is the company writing down inventory with the expectation of selling it at a higher profit in future periods?
- Is the company not writing down devalued inventory so that they do not dampen earnings?

Either of these cases would not be consistent with generally accepted accounting principles, but an analyst needs to ask the right questions in addressing the motive for the write-down.

Questions an analyst may ask about a write-down of inventory include the following:

- Is the company writing down its inventory on a timely basis?
- What changes in business have caused the loss in value of inventory?
- When the inventory is written down, does the company still have possession of the inventory? Will this inventory be sold in future periods?

There are cases of companies writing down inventory in one period and later selling this inventory at a higher profit margin in future periods. For example, the SEC alleges that Sunbeam Corporation wrote down the value of perfectly good inventory by $2.1 million on one year, only to sell this inventory in the next period for a $2.1 greater profit.[19] There are also cases in which a company did not write down inventory in a timely manner, resulting in an overstatement of earnings for the period.[20]

Depreciation

Methods of Depreciation

A company's depreciation expense can have an important effect on the firm's financial statements. Depreciation arises from the firm's investing activities, and it directly affects the firm's reported net income and asset values. The depreciation method and choice of useful life decisions affect the quality of earnings. For example, if assets are more productive in earlier years of their useful lives, the use of an accelerated method provides a higher quality of earnings relative to the use of the straight-line method.

Depreciation allocates the cost of the asset, less residual value, over the expected economic life of the asset. The *economic life*, also referred to as the *useful life*, is the number of years the asset is expected to be of use to the company. The *residual value*, also referred to as the *salvage value*, is the expected value of the asset at the end of its useful life. Depreciation thus provides a means for expensing the portion of the asset's cost that is expected to be used up during its life.

As we saw in Chapter 2, there are three classes of depreciation methods for financial reporting purposes. The first is *straight-line depreciation*, in which an equal amount of depreciation expense is taken each

---

[19] Securities and Exchange Commission, Accounting and Auditing Enforcement Release No. 1393, In the Matter of Sunbeam Corporation.
[20] In the Matter of Gerber Scientific, Inc., Respondent, Securities Exchange Act of 1934 Release No. 48441, April 8, 2004, Accounting and Auditing Enforcement Release No. 1987, April 8, 2004, Administrative Proceeding File No. 3-11455.

period of the asset's useful life. The second, referred to as *accelerated depreciation*, is more rapid depreciation than straight-line resulting in greater depreciation expense in the earlier years of an asset's life. The third class is *units of production*, whereby an estimate is made of the use of the asset (e.g., hours) and then the expense in any period reflects the usage in that period (i.e., number of hours used).

Over the life of the asset, the same amount of depreciation is expensed against income, no matter the method, as we demonstrated in Chapter 2. However, for any given period it makes a difference on the financial statements as to which method a company uses. Accelerated methods produce higher depreciation expense in the earlier years and lower earnings vis-à-vis the straight-line method. Accelerated methods also reduce the carrying value, shown on the company's balance sheet, faster in earlier years.

Most companies use straight-line depreciation for financial reporting purposes, though this does not mean that depreciation is directly comparable among companies because depreciable lives of assets may differ among companies. Limited information on depreciation methods and useful lives is provided in notes to the financial statements. The extent of this type of information varies widely. In Exhibit 3.6, we provide two examples of the typical statements that companies make regarding depreciation: Cisco Systems and Procter & Gamble.

Change in Estimates

The useful life and the salvage value of an asset are simply estimates. Companies review these estimates and occasionally change them— changing the depreciable life of an asset, whether lengthening or shortening the life, or changing the estimate of salvage value, affects the income statement and balance sheet, and hence the comparability of financial statements in different periods. A financial analyst must be aware of these changes and how they affect any comparisons overtime that are made for a given company.

When a company revises the depreciable life of an existing asset, for example, this is considered a change in accounting estimate. The company is required to account for the change in the period in which it occurs, but it is not permitted to restate prior period's financial accounts retroactively; in other words, the company makes a prospective disclosure, not a retrospective disclosure.[21] The company is required to disclose the effect on income from continuing operations, net income, and any per-share effect.

---

[21] Statement of Financial Accounting Standards, No. 154, *Accounting Changes and Error Corrections*, effective for fiscal years beginning after December 15, 2005.

EXHIBIT 3.6   Depreciable Lives Information

Cisco Systems, Inc., 2004 Annual Report, Note 1, p. 43:

Depreciation and amortization are computed using the straight-line method over the estimated useful lives of the assets. Estimated useful lives of 25 years are used for buildings. Estimated useful lives of 30 to 36 months are used for computer equipment and related software and five years for furniture and fixtures. Estimated useful lives of up to five years are used for production, engineering, and other equipment. Depreciation of operating lease assets is computed based on the respective lease terms, which range up to three years. Depreciation and amortization of leasehold improvements are computed using the shorter of the remaining lease terms or five years.

Procter & Gamble, Inc., 2004 Annual Report Note 1, p. 51:

Depreciation expense is recognized over the assets' estimated useful lives using the straight-line method. Machinery and equipment includes office furniture and equipment (15-year life), computer equipment and capitalized software (3 to 5-year lives) and manufacturing equipment (3 to 20-year lives). Buildings are depreciated over an estimated useful life of 40 years. Estimated useful lives are periodically reviewed and, where appropriate, changes are made prospectively. Where certain events or changes in operating conditions occur, asset lives may be adjusted and an impairment assessment may be performed on the recoverability of the carrying amounts.

Consider a company that is depreciating a $1 million asset, with a $100,000 salvage value, over 20 years. If the company revises the estimate of the useful life from 20 to 30 years in the 11th year of the asset's life, this will lower the depreciation expense from $45,000 per year to $22,500 per year in years eleven resulting in higher earnings (by $22,500) for the years 11 through 20 than with the original estimate. This revision also affects the carrying value of the asset (that is, cost, less accumulated depreciation), as we show in Exhibit 3.7.

The recent change in accounting standards with respect to accounting changes should increase the transparency of financial statements with respect to these types of changes, though the disclosures are made only in the year of the change, not the subsequent years. Therefore, the analyst must consider how these changes affect the company's future years' profitability.

EXHIBIT 3.7   Example of the Balance Sheet Effect of a Revision in the Useful Life of an Asset

$1 million asset, with a salvage value of $100,000, an original depreciable life of 20 years and a revised depreciable life of 30 years that is revised in the 11th year.

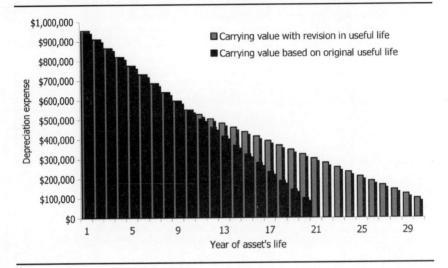

Pension Valuation Assumptions

A *pension plan* is an agreement under which an employer agrees to pay benefits to employees once the employee's period of service ends. A pension plan may either be a *defined contribution plan*, in which the employer makes only a specified contribution, or a *defined benefit plan*, in which a specific monetary benefit is promised. In the case of a defined benefit plan, these benefits depend on certain requirements specified by the employer, such as the employee's age and number of years of service.

The employer creates a pension fund, which is an intermediary used by the employer to meet the promised obligations. The employer makes payments to the fund and the fund invests these funds and makes pension payments to employees.

In terms of accounting for pension plans, defined contribution and defined benefit plans differ. In a defined contribution plan, accounting for the plan's obligation and assets is easy: The pension cost equals the contributions made and the employer reports an asset or liability reflecting the difference between actual payments made and the required payments.

In the case of a defined benefit, the promised payments are not known with certainty and represent a liability because benefits will be paid in the future. In this case, the employer invests in assets, the plan assets, which are intended to pay off the expected pension liability. The unknowns are:

1. *The expected return on plan assets.* This is a forecast of return on the assets set aside to meet the pension obligations.
2. *The discount rate.* The discount rate reflects the time value of money with respect to the pension liability.
3. *The rate of compensation increase.* For pension plans in which benefits are provided on the basis of compensation at a future point in time, the rate at which the employees' compensation will increase.

Companies report a pension expense on the income statement and a pension liability on the balance sheet. The pension expense is a result of a calculation that considers employees' earned pension benefits during the period, the time value of money, and the expected return on the pension plan's assets. In addition, companies are required to provide detail in a footnote to their financial statements with respect to the value of assets, the expected liability, and the assumptions used in these calculations, among other things. A recent change in accounting standards now requires companies to explain the basis for estimating the return on plan asset, the discount rate, and the rate of compensation increase (in the case of pay-related plans).[22] These assumptions are important because they affect both the expense and the liability.

It is important to understand just what a pension obligation is and how much of it shows up in the liabilities—and how much else there is that is *not* reported in liabilities. The pension liability that appears on the balance sheet may not be easy to find. To find the information we need, we must search the footnotes, but we have to know what we are looking for. Once in the footnotes, we have to sift through the various accounts. For example, there are three obligations that may be reported:

1. The *accumulated benefit obligation* (ABO) is the present value of pension benefits earned as of the balance sheet date based on current salaries
2. The *projected benefit obligation* (PBO) is the present value of pension benefits earned as of the balance sheet date based on projected salaries. This is relevant for plans with benefits that depend on career average or final pay.

---

[22] Statement of Financial Accounting Standards, No. 132, revised 2003, Employers' Disclosures about Pensions and Other Postretirement Benefits, effective for fiscal years beginning after December 15, 2003.

3. The *vested benefit obligation* (VBO) is the present value of the pension benefits for employees vested in the pension plan.

Our goal is to find the *funding status*, which is the difference between the projected benefit obligation (or accumulated benefit obligation if the pension obligation is not pay-related) and the fair value of plan assets (that is, the value of assets set aside to meet this obligation). Muddying the waters is the fact that when a company changes its plans, any change in costs is spread (i.e., amortized) over the remaining service life of employees. Therefore, the amount recognized as the liability—which makes its way to the balance sheet—is not the funding status but rather some other value.

For example, Ford's 2004 pension obligation for its U.S. plans is underfunded (that is, the value of the plan's assets are less than the obligation), but because of the smoothing process, we get a different picture looking at what is reflected, eventually, in the balance sheet. From the footnotes, we learn the following:[23]

Projected benefit obligation	$43,077
Fair value of plan assets	39,629
Funded status	−$3,449
Unamortized prior service costs	3,146
Unamortized net losses	4,838
Net amount recognized	$4,535

The funded status is negative (that is, it is *under*funded), yet there is, on net, no liability reported in the balance sheet, but rather an asset of $4,535 million. How did this happen? Because of the losses in the current year and prior years are deferred to future years, smoothing away the true picture of the pension obligation on the balance sheet. The "net amount recognized" actually appears on the balance sheet in four pieces that add up to the asset of $4,535:

Prepaid assets	$2,460
Accrued liabilities	−2,643
Intangible assets	2,517
Accumulated other comprehensive income	2,201

Companies may revise the assumptions that they make that they use in the calculation of the benefit obligation and the pension expense. These revisions, which are a change in an accounting estimate, affect the pension expense on the income statement and the liability (or asset) on

---

[23] Ford Motor Company, 2004 10-K filing, p. FS-39, Note. 22.

the balance sheet. The effect each assumption has on the obligation and expense is as follows:

	Change in Assumption	Effect on the Projected Benefit Obligation	Effect on the Pension Expense[a]
Discount rate	⇑	⇓	⇓
	⇓	⇑	⇑
Expected return on plan assets	⇑		⇓
	⇓		⇑
Expected compensation increase	⇑	⇑	⇑
	⇓	⇓	⇓

[a] Actually, the effect on the expense is mixed because it affects both the service cost and the interest cost. However, the effect on net is generally directly related to the direction of the discount rate change.

Therefore, if a company tends to use a low discount rate, a return on plan assets that is close to the discount rate, and uses a high rate of salary increase, it is conservative, an hence its earnings are of higher quality.

Looking at Ford's U.S. pension plan assumptions over time, as shown in Panel A of Exhibit 3.8, we see that the assumptions have changed over time, most notably the discount rate. We provide the funding status and pension expense for each of these years in Panel B of this exhibit. How do we interpret the effect of the change in the assumptions? Consider the discount rate, which was revised downward through the period 1999 through 2004. If nothing else was changed, this would reduce the funding status (that is, make it worse) and increase the pension expense. So why did the pension expense go down in 1999 through 2001? Because the expected return on plan assets increased during this same period. In the 2003–2004 fiscal years, however, the expected return on assets was kept the same, yet both the discount rate and the rate of compensation increase declined; the net result was an increase in the pension expense.

So what's an analyst to do? Dig through the pension and retirement benefits footnote, ferret out the funding status, examine any changes in assumptions and how these affect both the pension expense and the funding status, and examine closely the company's explanation of those changes.

EXHIBIT 3.8   Ford Motor Co. U.S. Pension Plan
Panel A: Rate Assumptions

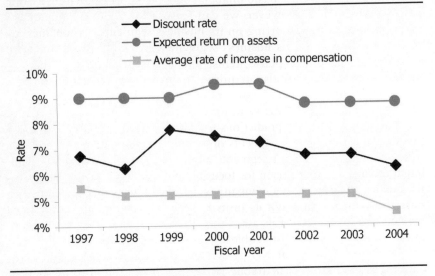

Panel B: Funding Status and Pension Expense

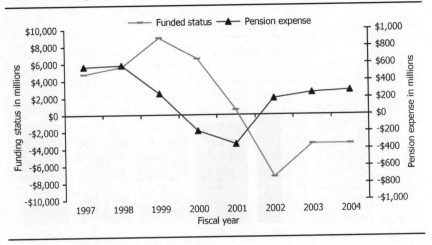

SO WHAT IS THEIR BUSINESS?

We tend to focus on the basic financial statements in evaluating a company's performance. However, we can learn a lot about a company by taking a look at the reporting on its business segments. Companies are required to report on its business segments, providing profit and loss, specific revenue and expense items, and assets attributed to the segment.[24] Companies are also required to provide a discussion of how they determined a business segment.

There are two primary reasons for focusing on business segment results. First, in terms of making predictions for future periods, it is easier to make predictions for individual segments of a company than for a company as a whole because a company's segments' performance may be affected by different factors. Another reason for focusing on business segments is to assess the quality of earnings. If a company is deriving much of its profits from a business segment that is not its primary segment in terms of the company mission and investment of its asset, then this may suggest that the earnings of the company are not sustainable and/or of lower quality.

Consider the case of Krispy Kreme, the donut retailer and franchiser. Krispy Kreme went public in 1999 and was the darling of Wall Street as its stock soared. But as its stock soared, its financial condition soured. As we show in Exhibit 3.9, Krispy Kreme derived less of its

EXHIBIT 3.9 Sources of Revenues for Krispy Kreme, 1999–2003

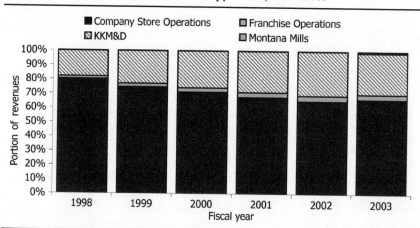

Source: Krispy Kreme 10-K filings, various years.

---

[24] Statement of Financial Accounting Standards, Statement No. 131, *Disclosures about Segment of an Enterprise and Related Information*, effective for fiscal years beginning after December 15, 1997.

income over time from its stores and franchise operations, and more
from a segment named "KKM&D." Taking a closer look at KKM&D in
the management discussion and company description, you can see that
KKM&D is the segment of Krispy Kreme that sells equipment to the
franchisors. By requiring franchisors to purchase the equipment at substantial margins, Krispy Kreme has increased its revenues and profit. In
fiscal year 2003, Krispy Kreme derived 32% of its operating income
from equipment sales. However, this is short-lived because once the
franchisors have purchased the equipment, this segment will not provide
future profit and growth unless additional franchises are sold.

RESTATEMENTS AND FINANCIAL ANALYSIS

Companies restate their financial results if there was an error in the previously reported results or the company is correcting financial results
because of detected fraudulent reporting.

For example, General Electric restated several years of financial
results because it had found errors in the method of accounting for
derivatives in its General Electric Capital Corporation (GECC) subsidiary, which resulted in an understatement of net earnings in the years
2001 through 2004. The restated results included a disclaimer:

> AS A RESULT OF GE'S RESTATEMENT OF ITS FINAN-
> CIAL INFORMATION IN ITS AMENDED 2004 FORM
> 10-K DATED MAY 6, 2005, READERS SHOULD NO
> LONGER RELY ON OUR PREVIOUSLY FILED FINAN-
> CIAL STATEMENTS AND OTHER FINANCIAL
> INFORMATION FOR THE YEARS AND FOR EACH
> OF THE QUARTERS IN THE YEARS 2004, 2003, 2002
> AND 2001. READERS SHOULD ALSO NO LONGER
> RELY ON OUR PREVIOUSLY ANNOUNCED RESULTS
> FOR THE FIRST QUARTER OF 2005.

We show the effect of this error in Exhibit 3.10 for the fiscal years 2001
through 2004.

So what is the importance of restatements to a financial analyst?
There are several reasons to take a close look at restatements:

The fact that there was an error should at least get the analyst's
attention. Some errors result from a misunderstanding of the application of accounting principles. Some errors results from intentional mis-
application of accounting principles. The analyst needs to take a close
look at SEC filings to determine the reasons behind the restatement.

EXHIBIT 3.10 General Electric's Restatement

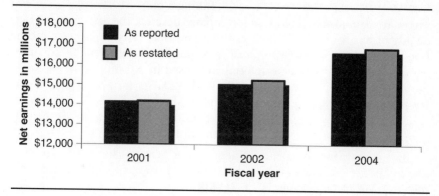

EXHIBIT 3.11 The Effect of Waste Management's Restatements

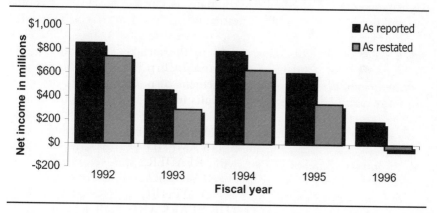

Another reason to look at restatements is when using data to make predictions of future performance. The restated data should be more useful in making such predictions.

Consider the restatements made by Waste Management, as we show in Exhibit 3.11.[25] Waste Management was charged with understating expenses, using one-time gains to reduce operating expenses, and "creative" (that is, non-GAAP) depreciation. These restatements resulted in a significant restatement of earnings and would effect any predictions beyond 1995.

---

[25] Securities and Exchange Commission vs. Dean L. Buntrock, Phillip B. Rooney, James E. Koenig, Thomas C. Hau, Herbert A. Getz, and Bruce D. Tobecksen, No. 02C 2180.

TELL-TALE SIGNS

There are a number of tell-tale signs that can alert the analyst to actual or potential problems. These signs may be obvious, such as a qualification in an auditor's report, or may require a bit of digging into the numbers, such as an analysis of deferred taxes.

The Independent Auditor's Opinion

There are many caution flags that financial analysts may heed with regard to the company's independent auditor.

In general, the independent accounting firm attests to the audit of the company's financial statements. There are several different possible results from the engagement of an auditor to review of the company's financial statements:

- *An unqualified opinion.* This is the good new. This means that the auditor believes that the financial statements are presented fairly in conformity with GAAP.
- *A qualified opinion.* This needs further research by the analyst. An auditor issues a qualified opinion when it believes that the financial statements present the company's financial position, results of operations, and cash flows in conformity with GAAP, except for some matter that remains qualified. This qualification will be spelled out in opinion and will relate to either the scope of the audit, a departure from GAAP, or doubt about the company continuing as a going concern.
- *An adverse opinion.* This is bad news. An auditor issues an adverse opinion when it believes that the financial statements do not present the company's financial position, results of operations, and cash flows in conformity with GAAP. This opinion is issued when there are significant departures from GAAP.
- *A disclaimer of opinion.* This is bad news too. The auditor issues this opinion when it is unable to form an opinion regarding the financial statements.
- *A withdrawal of opinion(s).* This is terrible news. In this case, the auditor is withdrawing previously issued opinions because of some egregious situation, such as suspected illegal activities by the audited company.

Most auditors' reports of publicly-traded companies' financial statements are unqualified, which means that the auditor is stating that the financial statements are prepared according to generally accepted accounting principles and that these statements present fairly the results of operations. Occasionally, as the need arises because of changes in accounting principles, an unqualified report may have some explanatory language added. This type of explanation is the result of the changes in accounting principles and is not a cause for concern. But any time there is a qualification or any other type of opinion, the analyst must pay close attention.

Another flag is an unjustified change in independent auditors or a change in auditor that is the result of a disagreement with the auditor. Companies may change auditors for a number of reasons. The requirements imposed by the Sarbanes-Oxley Act of 2002 limit the nonaudit engagements of accounting firms and a shuffling of companies among accounting firms to reduce the possible conflicts of interest related to nonaudit services is expected. However, auditor changes as a result of a disagreement are worth looking at.[26]

As a result of the Sarbanes-Oxley Act, the management of public companies must now include in its annual report a report on the company's internal control over financial reporting. The Public Company Accounting Oversight Board has added this additional responsibility of auditors. This additional requirement is to attest to the management's assessment of the company's internal control over financial reporting. In attesting to the internal controls, the auditor expresses an opinion whether and notes whether there is a control deficiency, a significant deficiency, or a material weakness with respect to the internal controls.

Other Signs

There are a number of other warning signs that the financial analyst can look for in the financial information. We list several of these signs in Exhibit 3.13, though each may not be applicable for every company. For example, examining inventory changes for a company with relatively little inventory (e.g., Walt Disney Company) or examining receivable balances for a company that does not typically extend customer credit (e.g., Wal-Mart Stores) would not be fruitful.

The financial analyst must consider the company's history, the industry in which it operates, and the effects of the economy on the company when analyzing potentially troubling signs. Understanding the company's revenue and expense cycle is important in detecting subtle

---

[26] There is evidence, both academic and anecdotal, that in the pre-Sarbanes-Oxley Act of 2002 world auditors may have bent under pressures from audit clients and may actually be complicit in the fraudulent acts of these audit clients. See, for example, "The Impact on the Market for Audit Services of Aggressive Competition by Auditors," by Debra Jeter, Paul Chaney, and Pam Shaw, *Journal of Accounting and Public Policy* (December 2003).

EXHIBIT 3.12 Examples of Auditor Opinions

Going concern qualification, expressed by Ernst & Young, LLP, in its report for O2Diesel Corporation, 10-KSB filing, p. F-1:

In our opinion, the financial statements referred to above present fairly, in all material respects, the consolidated financial position of O2Diesel Corporation at December 31, 2004 and the consolidated results of its operations and its cash flows for each of the two years in the period ended December 31, 2004 and for the period October 14, 2000 (inception) through December 31, 2004, in conformity with U.S. generally accepted accounting principles.

The accompanying financial statements have been prepared assuming the Company will continue as a going concern. As discussed in Note 1 to the consolidated financial statements, the Company's accumulated losses and working capital deficiency raise substantial doubt about the Company's ability to continue as a going concern. Management's plans with regard to these matters are also described in Note 1. The 2004 financial statements do not include any adjustments that might result from the outcome of this uncertainty."

Internal control issues, expressed in the BDO Seidman, LLP, report for Mastec, 10-K filing March 31, 2005, p. 76:

In our opinion, management's assessment that MasTec, Inc. did not maintain effective internal control over financial reporting as of December 31, 2004, is fairly stated, in all material respects, based on the criteria established in *Internal Control—Integrated Framework* issued by COSO. Also, in our opinion, because of the effect of the material weakness described above on the achievement of the objectives of the control criteria, MasTec, Inc. has not maintained effective internal control over financial reporting as of December 31, 2004, based on the criteria established in *Internal Control—Integrated Framework* issued by the COSO.

shifting of these items between periods. Understanding the changes in the company's industry is important for comparisons of the industry's conditions with those of the individual company (e.g., an industry-wide slow-down in customer payments). Understanding the economy and how the company may be affected by current conditions is important for detecting unusual changes in income or assets.

EXHIBIT 3.13 Warning Signs

Warning Sign	May Indicate:	Where to Look:
Change in auditor	Disagreements concerning the application of GAAP	Annual report's note to financial statements and auditor's opinion
Qualified auditor opinion	Company is not a going concern; auditor unable to examine all financial records	Auditor's opinion in annual report
Unexplained changes in accounting policies	Earnings management	Annual report's accounting principles' note; significant change in account (e.g. depreciation expense)
An increasing gap between reported income and cash flow from operations	Earnings management	Annual report: Comparison of balances in deferred taxes; income tax note
Unusual changes in inventories that do not coincide with changes in sales	Inflation of sales	Relationship of inventory (balance sheet) and sales (income statement) over time
Unusual changes in accounts receivable that do not coincide with changes in sales	Inflation of sales or understatement in allowance for doubtful accounts	Relationship of accounts receivable (balance sheet) and sales (income statement) over time
Large, unexpected asset write-offs	Earnings management or inflated asset accounts in prior years	Footnote on write-offs in annual report
Large changes in deferred taxes on the balance sheet	Changes in estimates of likelihood of reversals	Tax footnote, focusing on changes in the valuation allowance
Write-off of goodwill due to impairment	Managing earnings through timing of impairment	Write-off timing versus pattern of reported earnings
Tendency to use financing mechanisms such as research and development partnerships	Liabilities management (possible understatement of obligations) or asset management (possible overstatement of assets)	Management discussion in annual report

EXHIBTI 3.13   (Continued)

Warning Sign	May Indicate:	Where to Look:
Large change in discretionary expenses, such as advertising and research and development	Shifting expenses from one period to another	Income statement and comparison of discretionary expenses over time
Large fourth quarter adjustments	Earnings management	Quarterly income statement and balance sheet (e.g., comparison of fourth quarter results with prior year same quarter)
Related-party transactions	Inflation of revenues or understatement of expenses if transactions are not arms-length	Annual report's related-party note and any management discussion of major customers
Recurring non-recurring charges	Earnings management	Examine footnotes related to these charges
Changes in assumptions of pension plans	Management of pension liability and/or expense	Retirement benefit plans footnote

SUMMARY

The analysis of the financial condition and performance of a company requires understanding the quality of the financial data that is being analyzed. The management of a company has a great deal of room in selecting among accounting methods within the bounds of GAAP, though the recent changes resulting from the Sarbanes-Oxley Act of 2002 and the move toward convergence with Internal Financial Reporting Standards have resulted in fewer degrees of freedom. The analyst must understand the methods selected in order to make comparisons of financial data over time and among companies.

The many accounting choices that a company's management has available open up the possibility for management of earnings and make it more challenging to compare companies and to evaluate trends within a company over time. The devices that management may use include accruals management, revenue and expense recognition, and nonrecurring items. Financial results may also be affected by the impairment of goodwill, which results in a write-off of this intangible asset, reducing earnings in the period of the write-off and reducing total assets in future periods.

The different methods of accounting that a company's management may choose within generally accepted accounting principles creates opportunities to manage earnings, making the financial analyst job a bit more challenging. For example, different methods of accounting for inventory and depreciation may make a significant difference in reported asset values and earnings. A careful review of the company's accounting principles is useful in determining the types of adjustments the analyst must make to permit comparability.

Analysts need to examine the sources of a company's revenues and earnings. For example, a company that earns a large portion of its revenues from nonoperating sources or business segments that are not the primary lines of business may indicate potential problems in future earnings.

Analysts also need to be aware of companies' restatements of financial results. In the cases of errors and fraud, companies restate financial results for the periods affected. If we are assessing the market's reaction to financial reports, we would want to use the "as reported" information. On the other hand, as is often the case in financial analysis, we want to make forecasts concerning a company's future financial condition and performance, we should focus on the restated financial results.

An additional consideration for the financial analyst is the auditor's report. The independent accounting firm that audits a company's financial statements and reviews the management's reports on internal controls provides a statement regarding whether the financial statements are prepared according to generally accepted accounting statements and whether the internal controls for financial reporting are sufficient. Careful reading of these reports may reveal important information regarding the financial condition of the company.

Analysis of Financial Statements

CHAPTER 4

Financial Analysis

F *inancial analysis* is the selection, evaluation, and interpretation of financial data, along with other pertinent information, to assist in assessing the risk and return associated with an investment. Financial analysis may be used to evaluate the efficiency of operations, the effectiveness of credit policies, and the credit-worthiness of a company, among other things.

The analyst draws the financial data needed in financial analysis from many sources. As we discussed in Chapter 2, the primary source is the data provided by the company itself in its annual report and required disclosures. The annual report and the 10-K filing include the income statement, the balance sheet, and the statement of cash flows, as well as footnotes to these statements.

Besides information that companies are required to disclose through financial statements, other information is readily available for financial analysis. For example, you can find the market prices of publicly traded securities in the financial press and the electronic media daily. Similarly, information on stock price indices for industries and for the market as a whole are available in the financial press.

Another source of information is economic data, such as the Gross Domestic Product and Consumer Price Index, which may be useful in assessing the recent performance or future prospects of a company or industry. Suppose you are evaluating a company that owns a chain of retail outlets. What information do you need to judge the company's performance and financial condition? You need financial data, but it does not tell the whole story. You also need information on consumer spending, producer prices, consumer prices, and the competition. This is economic data that is readily available from government and private sources.

Besides financial statement data, market data, and economic data, you also need to examine events that may help explain the company's present condition and may have a bearing on its future prospects. For example, did the company recently incur some extraordinary losses? Is the company developing a new product? Or is it acquiring another company? Current events can provide information that may be incorporated into financial analysis.

The analyst must select the pertinent information, analyze it, and interpret the analysis, enabling judgments on the current and future financial condition and operating performance of the company. In this chapter, we introduce you to financial ratios—a tool of financial analysis. In financial ratio analysis we select the relevant information—primarily the financial statement data—and evaluate it. In this chapter, we show how to calculate and interpret financial ratios. And we also warn you of the pitfalls that occur when it's not used properly. We will use financial statements of Pfizer, Inc., for illustration purposes throughout this chapter. We provide Pfizer's 2004 and 2003 balance sheets in Exhibit 4.1 and Pfizer's 2004 and 2003 income statements in Exhibit 4.2.

WHAT ARE RATIOS AND HOW DO WE USE THEM?

Suppose we wish to evaluate the performance of Pfizer, Inc. And suppose we gather information about its earnings over time, as we show in Exhibit 4.3. What does this tell us? We learn that Pfizer's net income increased over time, with the exception of 2003. But does this tell us anything about whether these earnings are good, considering the capital that the company employs? Not at all. Though earnings are growing, is the profit margin constant or changing? We cannot tell this from just looking at earnings. This is why in financial analysis we need to examine relations between and among the different accounts and then consider trends over time, how the company fares relative to competitors, and how company specific events affect the performance and condition of the company.

A tool that we can use to help us examine relations between and among different financial accounts is *financial ratio analysis*. A *financial ratio* is simply an expression of the relation between two financial statement accounts and financial ratio analysis is the investigation of a company's condition and performance using one or more of these ratios. We use these ratios to get a measure of the relative value of one account to another. For example, we may want to know how much a company has invested in liquid assets. We can create a measure of this by comparing the current assets of the company—the liquid assets—to the total assets of the company. Or we could compare the current assets of the company with just the noncurrent assets of the company. Either way, we are getting a sense of the relative investment in liquid assets.

EXHIBIT 4.1   Pfizer, Inc., Balance Sheet (in millions)

	2004	2003
Cash and cash equivalents	$1,808	$1,520
Short-term investment	18,085	10,432
Accounts receivable, net	9,367	8,636
Short-term loans	653	391
Inventories	6,660	5,699
Prepared expenses and taxes	2,939	2,758
Assets of discontinued	182	1,241
Total current assets	$39,694	$30,677
Long-term investments and loans	$3,873	$6,142
Property plant and equipment, net	18,385	18,156
Goodwill	23,756	22,265
Identifiable intangible assets	33,251	35,591
Other assets	4,725	3,944
Total assets	$123,684	$116,775
Short-term borrowings and current portion of long-term debt	$11,266	$8,818
Accounts payable	2,672	2,587
Dividends payable	1,418	1,300
Income tax payable	1,963	1,910
Other current liabilities	9,075	8,992
Total current liabilities	$26,458	$23,909
Long-term debt	$7,279	$5,755
Pension and postretirement benefit obligation	4,271	4,312
Deferred taxes	12,632	13,012
Other noncurrent liabilities	4,766	4,413
Total liabilities	$55,406	$51,398
Preferred stock	$193	$219
Common stock	438	435
Additional paid-in capital	67,098	66,396
Less: Treasury stock and employee benefit trust	37,221	31,250
Retained earnings	35,492	29,382
Accumulated other comprehensive income	2,278	195
Total shareholders' equity	$68,278	$65,377
Total liabilities and shareholders' equity	$123,684	$116,775

Source: Pfizer, Inc., 2004 Annual Report, p. 31. For purposes of further analysis, the balance sheet as presented includes subtotals and summary items that are not part of the annual report presentation by Pfizer, Inc.

EXHIBIT 4.2   Pfizer, Inc., Income Statement (in millions)

	2004	2003
Revenues	$52,516	$44,736
Cost of sales	7,541	9,589
Gross income	$44,975	$35,147
Operating expenses:		
Selling, informational and administrative expenses	16,903	15,108
Research and development expenses	7,684	7,487
Amortization of intangible assets	3,364	2,187
Operating income	$17,024	$10,365
Nonoperating costs of expenses:		
Merger-related in-process research and development charges	1,071	5,052
Merger related costs	1,193	1,058
Interest income	346	346
Interest expense	347	270
Other income/(expenses), net	(752)	(1,085)
Income from continuing operations before taxes, minority interest, and cumulative effect of change in accounting principles	$14,007	$3,246
Provision for taxes on income	2,665	1,614
Minority interests	10	3
Income from continuing operations before cumulative effect of change in accounting principles	$11,332	$1,629
Discontinued operations, net of tax	29	2,311
Income before cumulative change in accounting principles	$11,361	$3,940
Cumulative effect of change in accounting principles, net of tax	0	(30)
Net income	$11,361	$3,910

Source: Pfizer, Inc., 2004 Annual Report, p. 31. For purposes of further analysis, the income statement as presented includes subtotals and summary items that are not part of the annual report presentation by Pfizer, Inc.

The value of a given ratio, however, is rarely informative. Financial ratios provide information when compared to other financial ratios and standards. For example, if we calculate the ratio of the company's current assets to its total assets and arrive at 20%, is this good or bad? Does this mean that the company has sufficient liquid assets? We cannot tell from this ratio alone. What else would we need to know to gauge whether this is sufficient liquidity for this company? We would want to know, for example, about the company's need for liquidity, whether the

EXHIBIT 4.3   Pfizer, Inc., Net Income, 1990–2004

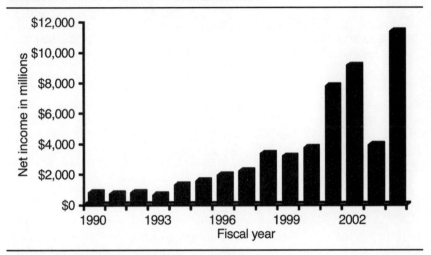

Source of data: Pfizer, Inc. 10-K filings, various years.

company is using its assets in the most effective manner, what is typical for a profitable company in this industry, how its investment in liquid assets has changed over time, and whether the company has debt covenants that require a specific minimum amount of liquid assets.

Once we calculate a financial ratio, we need to put it in perspective with the other aspects of the company's financial condition and performance, both over time and in comparison with other, leading companies in the same industry.

There are more financial ratios than there are different possible combinations of any two balance sheet, income statement, and statement of cash flow accounts. This means that there are too many to detail in this chapter. What we do in this chapter is focus on the most frequently used financial ratios that analysts use to capture the financial condition and performance of companies. Most of these ratios use balance sheet and income statement data, though a few require market data.

WHAT ARE THE DIFFERENT TYPES OF RATIOS?

We can use financial ratios to examine the different dimensions of a company's financial condition and performance:

- *Liquidity.* How able is the company to satisfy its immediate obligations?

■ *Activity.* Is the company getting the most use out of its asset deployment?

■ *Profitability.* Is the company efficient in managing its expenses?

■ *Financial leverage.* How reliant is the company on debt financing? Is the company expected to be able to satisfy its long-term obligations?

After looking at each of these dimensions, we take a look at return ratios, which bring these measures together in "bottom line" measures of a company's performance. In addition, we examine how we can use return ratios to evaluate how the different aspects of the company's financial condition and performance interact and affect the company's return on investment.

Liquidity Analysis

Liquidity in the context of financial analysis refers to a company's ability to satisfy its short-term obligations using assets that are most readily converted into cash. Assets that may be converted into cash in a short period of time are referred to as *liquid assets*. These assets are listed in financial statements as *current assets*. Current assets are often referred to as *working capital*, since they represent the resources needed for the day-to-day operations of the company's long-term, capital investments. Current assets are used to satisfy short-term obligations, or *current liabilities*. The amount by which current assets exceed current liabilities is referred to as the *net working capital*.

The Role of the Operating Cycle

How much liquidity a company needs depends on its operating cycle. The *operating cycle* is the duration between the time cash is invested in goods and services to the time that investment produces cash. For example, a company that produces and sells goods has an operating cycle comprising four phases, as we diagram in Exhibit 4.4.

The operating cycle is the length of time it takes to convert an investment of cash in inventory back into cash through the collections on sales. Considering that not all purchases a company makes are paid immediately with cash, we can use another cycle metric, the *net operating cycle*, to capture the length of time it takes to convert an investment of cash in inventory and back into cash considering that some purchases are made on credit.

The number of days a company ties up funds in inventory is determine by:

■ The total amount of money represented in inventory
■ The average day's cost of goods sold

EXHIBIT 4.4   The Operating Cycle

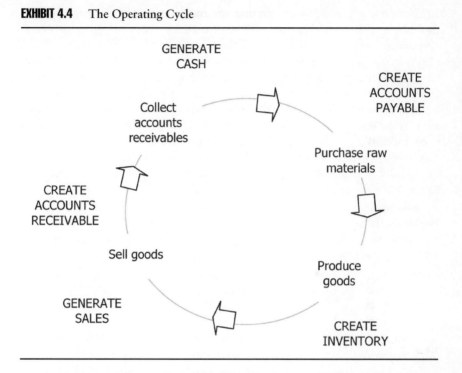

The current investment in inventory—that is, the money "tied up" in inventory—is the ending balance of inventory on the balance sheet. The average day's cost of goods sold is the cost of goods sold on an average day in the year, which can be estimated by dividing the *cost of goods sold* (COGS), found on the income statement, by the number of days in the year.

We compute the *number of days inventory* by calculating the ratio of the amount of inventory on hand (in dollars) to the average day's cost of goods sold (in dollars per day):[1]

$$\text{Number of days inventory} = \frac{\text{Inventory}}{\text{Average day's cost of goods sold}}$$

$$= \frac{\text{Inventory}}{\text{Cost of goods sold}/365}$$

If the ending inventory is representative of the inventory throughout the year, the number of days inventory tells us the length of time it takes

---

[1] The number of days inventory is also referred to as the inventory processing period.

to convert the investment in inventory into sold goods. Another way of looking at this metric is that it tells us how long the company can continue to generate sales with its existing inventory.

Why do we care about whether the year-end inventory is representative of inventory at any day throughout the year? Because if inventory at the end of the fiscal year is lower than on any other day of the year, we have understated the number of days inventory for the year. Most companies try to choose fiscal year-ends that coincide with the slower period of their business, which means that the ending balance of inventory is likely lower than the typical daily inventory of the year. To remedy this, we could look at quarterly financial statements and take averages of quarterly inventory balances to get a better idea of the typical inventory. However, for simplicity in this and other ratios, we make a note of this problem and deal with it later in the discussion of effective use of financial ratios.

You will notice a relation between the inventory turnover and the number of days inventory:

$$\frac{\text{Cost of goods sold}}{\text{Inventory}} \times \frac{\text{Inventory}}{\text{Cost of goods sold}/365} = 365$$

Suppose a company has cost of goods sold of $100, inventory of $10. Then,

- the inventory turnover is 10 times;
- the number of days inventory is $10/($100/365) = $10/$0.274 = 36.5 days; and
- inventory turnover x number of days inventory = 10 × 36.5 = 365.

We extend the same logic from the inventory turnover to estimate the number of days between a sale—when an account receivable is created—to the time it is collected in cash. If the ending balance of receivables at the end of the year is representative of the receivables on any day throughout the year, then it takes, on average, approximately the *number of days receivables* to collect the accounts receivable, or *number of days of credit*:[2]

$$\text{Number of days receivables} = \frac{\text{Accounts receivable}}{\text{Average day's sales on credit}}$$

$$= \frac{\text{Accounts receivable}}{\text{Sales on credit}/365}$$

---

[2] The number of days receivable is also referred to as the receivables processing period.

What does the number of days receivables tell us?

▪ Comparing the number of days receivables with the company's credit policy, we can draw conclusions about whether the company is collecting on accounts consistent with their policy.
▪ Comparing the number of days receivables of the company with that of its competitors can tell use about whether the credit policy of the company—with respect to both credit granting and collections—is more or less generous than its customers.

Adding the number of days inventory and the number of days receivables produces the operating cycle, which is the length of time it takes for the investment of cash in inventory to produce cash through collections of account. What does the operating cycle have to do with liquidity? The longer the operating cycle, the more current assets needed (relative to current liabilities) because it takes longer to convert inventories and receivables into cash. In other words, the longer the operating cycle, the more net working capital required.

We also need to look at the liabilities on the balance sheet to see how long it takes a company to pay its short-term obligations. We can apply the same logic to accounts payable as we did to accounts receivable and inventories. How long does it take a company, on average, to go from creating a payable (buying on credit) to paying for it in cash? The *number of days payables* does as follows:

$$\text{Number of days payables} = \frac{\text{Accounts payable}}{\text{Average day's purchases}}$$

$$= \frac{\text{Accounts payable}}{\text{Purchases}/365}$$

First, we need to determine the amount of an average day's purchases on credit. If we assume all purchases are made on credit, the total purchases for the year would be the cost of goods sold, less any amounts included in this cost of goods sold that are not purchases.[3]

The operating cycle tells us how long it takes to convert an investment in cash back into cash (by way of inventory and accounts receivable):

---

[3] For example, depreciation is included in the cost of goods sold, yet it not a purchase. However, as a quite proxy for purchases, we can use the accounting relationship: Beginning inventory + Purchases = COGS + Ending inventory.

$$\text{Operating cycle} = \text{Number of days inventory} \\ + \text{Number of days receivables}$$

The number of days payables tells us how long it takes use to pay on purchases made to create the inventory. If we put these two pieces of information together, we can see how long, on net, we tie up cash. The difference between the operating cycle and the number of days of payables is the net operating cycle:

$$\text{Net operating cycle} = \text{Operating cycle} - \text{Number of days payables}$$

or, substituting for the operating cycle,

$$\text{Net operating cycle} = \text{Number of days inventory} \\ + \text{Number of days receivables} \\ - \text{Number of days payables}$$

The net operating cycle is also referred to as the cash conversion cycle because it is an estimate of how long it takes for the company to get cash back from its investment in inventory and accounts receivable, considering that purchases may be made on credit. By not paying for purchases immediately (that is, using trade credit), the company reduces its liquidity needs. Therefore, the longer the net operating cycle, the greater the company's required liquidity.

The net operating cycle components for Pfizer in 2004 is computed in Exhibit 4.5.

Measures of Liquidity

Liquidity ratios provide a measure of a company's ability to generate cash to meet its immediate needs. The two most commonly used liquidity ratios are the current ratio and the quick ratio. The *current ratio* is the ratio of current assets to current liabilities. This ratio indicates a company's ability to satisfy its current liabilities with its current assets:

$$\text{Current ratio} = \frac{\text{Current assets}}{\text{Current liabilities}}$$

The *quick ratio* (also known as the *acid test ratio*) is the ratio of quick assets (generally current assets less inventory) to current liabilities This ratio indicates a company's ability to satisfy current liabilities with its most liquid assets:

EXHIBIT 4.5 Net Operating Cycle Components for Pfizer, Inc., 2004

$$\text{Number of days of inventory} = \frac{\text{Inventory}}{\text{Cost of goods sold}/365}$$

$$= \frac{\$6,600}{\$7,541/365} = \frac{\$6,600}{\$20.660} = 322.362 \text{ days}$$

$$\text{Number of days of receivables} = \frac{\text{Accounts receivable}}{\text{Sales on credit}/365}$$

$$= \frac{\$9,367}{\$52,516/365} = \frac{\$9,367}{\$143.879} = 65.103 \text{ days}$$

$$\text{Number of days of payables} = \frac{\text{Accounts payable}}{\text{Purchases}/365}$$

$$= \frac{\$2,672}{\$8,442/365} = \frac{\$2,672}{\$23.129} = 115.526 \text{ days}$$

$$\text{Operating cycle} = \text{Number of days of inventory}$$
$$+ \text{Number of days of receivables}$$
$$= 387.465 \text{ days}$$

$$\text{Net operating cycle} = \text{Operating cycle} - \text{Number of days of payables}$$
$$= 271.939 \text{ days}$$

* Estimated as COGS + Ending inventory – Beginning inventory = $7,541 + 6,600 – 5,699 = $8,442.

$$\text{Quick ratio} = \frac{\text{Current assets} - \text{Inventory}}{\text{Current liabilities}}$$

Generally, the larger these liquidity ratios the better the ability of the company to satisfy its immediate obligations. Is there a magic number that defines good or bad? Not really.

Consider the current ratio. A large amount of current assets relative to current liabilities provides assurance that the company will be able to satisfy its immediate obligations. However, if there are more current assets than the company needs to provide this assurance, the company may be investing too heavily in these non- or low-earning assets and therefore not putting the assets to the most productive use.

Another consideration is the operating cycle. A company with a long operating cycle may have more need to liquid assets than a company with a shorter operating cycle.

We provide the liquidity ratios for Pfizer in 2004 in Exhibit 4.6.

EXHIBIT 4.6   Liquidity Ratios for Pfizer, Inc., 2004

$$\text{Current ratio} = \frac{\text{Current assets}}{\text{Current liabilities}} = \frac{\$39,694}{\$26,458} = 1.500$$

$$\text{Quick ratio} = \frac{\text{Current assets} - \text{Inventory}}{\text{Current liabilities}} = \frac{\$33,034}{\$26,458} = 1.249$$

Activity Ratios

Activity ratios are measures of how well assets are used. Activity ratios can be used to evaluate the benefits produced by specific assets, such as inventory or accounts receivable. Or they can be use to evaluate the benefits produced by all a company's assets collectively. The most common turnover ratios are the inventory turnover, the total asset turnover, and the accounts receivable turnover.

Inventory turnover is the ratio of cost of goods sold to inventory. This ratio indicates how many times inventory is created and sold during the period:

$$\text{Inventory turnover} = \frac{\text{Cost of goods sold}}{\text{Inventory}}$$

Ideally, the inventory amount in the denominator reflects the average inventory during the period. Because many companies have seasonality in their sales and fiscal year ends are typically chosen to be at the lowest point of a company's operating cycle, the amount of inventory on a company's annual balance sheet is not representative of the inventory they tend to carry during the year. Therefore, we would want to use an average inventory amount in the calculation of this ratio.[4] However, when we are on the outside looking in, as is often the case in financial analysis, we must use annual inventory or the average of the quarterly inventory to estimate this turnover ratio.

The inventory turnover is an estimate of how many times during the period that inventory is created or purchased and sold. If we are using annual cost of goods sold and an average annual inventory, the ratio is a measure of the number of times inventory is created and sold during the year.

Is any particular number for an inventory turnover ratio good or bad? No, because the appropriate turnover varies by product line. What

---

[4] This is the case for most every ratio that involves the balance in an account that is seasonal, such as inventory and accounts receivable.

is important is the interaction of turnover and profitability, which then influence the returns on the company's or owners' investment.

Accounts receivable turnover is the ratio of net credit sales to accounts receivable. This ratio indicates how many times in the period credit sales have been created and collected:

$$\text{Accounts receivable turnover} = \frac{\text{Sales on credit}}{\text{Accounts receivable}}$$

The amount of sales on credit in the numerator is an estimate of the amount of sales that the company makes by on credit to customers. This amount is not reported on financial statements, though an analyst may estimate this by evaluating the customs of trade credit in the particular industry. The denominator should reflect the average accounts receivable throughout the period.

The accounts receivable turnover is a measure of the number of times accounts receivables have been created—through the sale of goods on credit—and extinguished through customer payments during the period. In other words, this estimate helps us gauge how long it takes customers to pay, on average, during the period. If the turnover is, say, 12 times, we know that it takes customers approximately 30 days to pay on their accounts. This ratio is therefore quite useful in assessing a company's credit policy.

Total asset turnover is the ratio of sales to total assets:

$$\text{Total asset turnover} = \frac{\text{Sales}}{\text{Total assets}}$$

This ratio indicates the extent that the investment in total assets results in sales. The resultant number is a multiplier of the sales that are generated for the investment in total assets. For example, if assets are £100 million and sales are £125 million, the total asset turnover is 1.25, meaning that £1.25 of sales are generated per £1 of asset investment.

As with any other ratio, the total asset turnover cannot be judged in isolation, but rather must be considered in conjunction with other dimensions of the company's condition and performance, the trend of the ratio over time, and industry norms.

A turnover ratio may be constructed to evaluate the use of any set of assets by comparing the gross benefit to the assets employed. For example, if you wish to focus on a company's fixed assets, you can construct a fixed asset turnover as the ratio of sales to net plant and equipment. We calculate several turnover ratios for Pfizer and provide these ratios in Exhibit 4.7.

EXHIBIT 4.7   Activity and Turnover Ratios for Pfizer, Inc., 2004

$$\text{Inventory turnover} = \frac{\text{Cost of goods sold}}{\text{Inventory}} = \frac{\$7,541}{\$6,660} = 1.132 \text{ times}$$

$$\text{Accounts receivable turnover} = \frac{\text{Sales on credit}}{\text{Accounts receivable}} = \frac{\$52,516}{\$9,367} = 5.606 \text{ times}$$

$$\text{Total asset turnover} = \frac{\text{Sales}}{\text{Total assets}} = \frac{\$52,516}{\$123,684} = 0.425 \text{ times}$$

* Assuming all sales on credit.

The actual values for a given point in time are not very meaningful. What we would want to do in a thorough analysis is compare these turnovers over time for Pfizer and compare these values with Pfizer's competitors.

Profitability Analysis

Profitability ratios (also referred to as *profit margin ratios*) compare components of income with sales. They give us an idea of what makes up a company's income and are usually expressed as a portion of each dollar of sales. The profit margin ratios we discuss here differ only by the numerator. It is in the numerator that we reflect and thus evaluate performance for different aspects of the business.

The *gross profit margin* is the ratio of gross income or profit to sales. This ratio is a measure of how much of every dollar of sales is left after costs of goods sold:

$$\text{Gross profit margin} = \frac{\text{Gross income}}{\text{Sales}}$$

The *operating profit margin* is the ratio of operating profit (also known as *earnings before interest and taxes* (EBIT), *operating income*, and *income before interest and taxes*) to sales. This is a ratio that indicates how much of each dollar of sales is left over after operating expenses:

$$\text{Operating profit margin} = \frac{\text{Operating income}}{\text{Sales}}$$

The *net profit margin* is the ratio of net income (also referred to as the *net profit*) to sales, and indicates how much of each dollar of sales is left over after all expenses:

$$\text{Net profit margin} = \frac{\text{Net income}}{\text{Sales}}$$

Profit margins alone do not tell us much about the company's performance or its ability to generate profits in the future. Additional information that we would need include the trend in these profit margins over time, the company's turnover ratios and the trends in these ratios, and the industry norms.

Consider Pfizer's profit margins, which we provide in Exhibit 4.8. The gross profit margin appears to be significant. However, Pfizer is a pharmaceutical company whose costs of its goods are spread primarily between two items: cost of sales and the research and development expenses. Therefore, it is more appropriate in the analysis of Pfizer is to focus on the operating profit margin, rather than the gross profit margin.

Financial Leverage

A company can finance its assets either with equity or debt. Financing through debt involves risk because debt legally obligates the company to pay interest and to repay the principal as promised. On the other hand, equity financing does not obligate the company to pay anything; dividends are paid at the discretion of the board of directors. There is always some risk, which we refer to as *business risk*, inherent in any operating segment of a business. But how a company chooses to finance its operations—the particular mix of debt and equity, its *capital structure*—may add financial risk on top of business risk. *Financial risk* is the extent that debt financing is used relative to equity. The greater the company's use of debt in its capital structure, the greater its risk.

We use financial leverage ratios to assess how much financial risk the company has taken on. There are two types of financial leverage ratios: component percentages and coverage ratios. Component percent-

EXHIBIT 4.8   Profit Margins for Pfizer, Inc., 2004

$$\text{Gross profit margin} = \frac{\text{Gross income}}{\text{Sales}} = \frac{\$44{,}975}{\$52{,}516} = 85.641\%$$

$$\text{Operating profit margin} = \frac{\text{Operating income}}{\text{Sales}} = \frac{\$17{,}024}{\$52{,}516} = 32.417\%$$

$$\text{Net profit margin} = \frac{\text{Net income}}{\text{Sales}} = \frac{\$11{,}361}{\$52{,}516} = 21.633\%$$

---

ages compare a company's debt with either its total capital (debt plus equity) or its equity capital. Coverage ratios reflect a company's ability to satisfy fixed obligations, such as interest, principal repayment, or lease payments.

The component-percentage financial leverage ratios convey how reliant a company is on debt financing by comparing the amount of debt to either the total capital of the company or to the equity capital. The *total debt-to-assets ratio* is a measure of the proportion of assets that are financed with debt (both short-term and long-term debt):

$$\text{Total debt-to-assets ratio} = \frac{\text{Total debt}}{\text{Total assets}}$$

The *long-term debt-to-assets ratio* is the proportion of the company's assets that are financed with long-term debt:

$$\text{Long-term debt-to-assets ratio} = \frac{\text{Long-term debt}}{\text{Total assets}}$$

The *debt-to-equity ratio*, also known as the *debt ratio*, indicates the relative uses of debt and equity as sources of capital to finance the company's assets, evaluated using book values of the capital sources:

$$\text{Total debt-to-equity ratio} = \frac{\text{Total debt}}{\text{Total shareholders' equity}}$$

One problem with looking at risk through a financial ratio that uses the book value of equity is that most often there is little relation between the book value and its market value. The book value of equity consists of:

■ The proceeds to the company of all the stock issued since it was first incorporated, less any treasury stock (stock repurchased by the company).
■ The accumulation of all the earnings of the company, less any dividends, since it was first incorporated.

The book value generally does not give a true picture of the investment of shareholders in the company because:

■ Earnings are recorded according to accounting principles, which may not reflect the true economics of transactions.

■ Due to inflation, the dollars from earnings and proceeds from stock issued in the past do not reflect today's values.

In contrast, the market value is the value of equity as perceived by investors. It is what investors are willing to pay, its worth. So why bother with the book value of equity? There are two reasons. First, it is easier to obtain the book value than the market value of a company's securities; second, many financial services report ratios using the book value, rather than the market value.

We may use the market value of equity in the denominator, replacing the book value of equity. To do this, we need to know the current number of shares outstanding and the current market price per share of stock and multiply to get the market value of equity.

In addition to the leverage ratios that use information about how debt is related to either assets or equity, there are a number of financial leverage ratios that capture the ability of the company to satisfy its debt obligations. There are many ratios that accomplish this, but the two most common ratios are the times interest coverage ratio and the fixed charge coverage ratio.

The *times-interest-earned ratio*, also referred to as the *interest coverage ratio*, compares the earnings available to meet the interest obligation with the interest obligation:

$$\text{Times-interest-earned ratio} = \frac{\text{Earnings before interest and taxes}}{\text{Interest}}$$

The assessment of the coverage of financial obligations may be expanded to include other obligations. For example, a fixed-charge-coverage ratio can be constructed to include any fixed charges such as lease payments and preferred dividends.[5] For example, to gauge a company's ability to cover its interest and lease payments, you could use the following ratio:

$$\text{Fixed-charge-coverage ratio} = \frac{\text{Earnings before interest and taxes} + \text{Lease payment}}{\text{Interest} + \text{Lease payment}}$$

Coverage ratios are often used in debt covenants to help protect the creditors because they require that interest be "covered," along with a

---

[5] If an obligation that is paid out of after-tax earnings is included in the denominator (such as preferred stock dividends), it is necessary to gross-up these obligations to place them on a pre-tax basis by dividing the obligation by a factor equal to one minus the tax rate.

EXHIBIT 4.9 Financial Leverage Ratios for Pfizer, Inc., 2004

$$\text{Total debt-to-assets ratio} = \frac{\text{Total debt}}{\text{Total assets}} = \frac{\$55,406}{\$123,684} = 44.796\%$$

$$\text{Long-term debt-to-assets ratio} = \frac{\text{Long-term debt}}{\text{Total assets}} = \frac{\$28,948}{\$123,684} = 23.404\%$$

$$\text{Total debt-to-equity ratio} = \frac{\text{Total debt}}{\text{Total shareholders' equity}} = \frac{\$55,406}{\$68,278} = 0.811$$

$$\text{Times-interest-coverage ratio} = \frac{\text{Earnings before interest and taxes}}{\text{Interest}}$$

$$= \frac{\$14,354}{\$347} = 41.366$$

cushion. For example, requiring an interest coverage ratio of 2 times results in a cushion of equal to the interest commitment. We provide several of the financial leverage measures for Pfizer, Inc., in Exhibit 4.9.

ANALYSIS OF RETURN-ON-INVESTMENT RATIOS

Return-on-investment ratios allow an analyst to compare benefits generated from investments. The benefit is represented in the numerator, and the resources affecting that benefit, such as the total assets of the company, are represented in the denominator.[6]

The *operating return on assets* (also referred to as the *basic earning power ratio*) is the ratio of operating earnings to assets:

$$\text{Operating return on assets} = \frac{\text{Operating income}}{\text{Total assets}}$$

It is a measure of the operating income resulting from the company's investment in total assets and is useful when comparing companies that are in the same line of business.

The *return on assets* is the ratio of net income to assets and indicates the company's net profit generated per dollar invested in total assets:

---

[6] What distinguishes return-on-investment ratios from the activity ratios (such as inventory turnover or receivable turnover) is that the numerator is the net benefit, rather than the gross benefit from an activity.

$$\text{Return on assets } = \frac{\text{Net income}}{\text{Total assets}}$$

This is a measure of what the company receives, as a whole, from the investment it's made in assets.

The *return on equity* is the ratio of net income to shareholders' equity and represents the profit generated per dollar of shareholders' investment (that is, shareholders' equity):

$$\text{Return on equity } = \frac{\text{Net income}}{\text{Shareholders' equity}}$$

The difference between the return on assets and the return on equity is the investment that is considered; the return on equity is affected by the capital structure of the company:

$$\text{Return on equity } = \frac{\text{Net income}}{\text{Shareholders' equity}}$$

$$= \frac{\text{Net income}}{\text{Total assets}} \times \frac{\text{Total assets}}{\text{Shareholders' equity}}$$

The ratio of total assets to shareholders' equity is referred to as the *equity multiplier*, which is a measure of a company's use of financial leverage: the greater the use of debt, vis-à-vis equity, the greater the equity multiplier.

We can also be more specific in terms of the type of equity. For example, we can construct a *return on common equity*, which is the ratio of net income available to common shareholders to common shareholders' equity.[7]

$$\text{Return on common equity}$$
$$= \frac{\text{Net income available to common shareholders}}{\text{Common shareholders' equity}}$$

This return is the profit generated per dollar of common shareholders' investment (that is, common shareholders' equity).

We provide the calculated values of these return metrics in Exhibit 4.10 for Pfizer, Inc. As we shall see shortly, we can relate these "bottom

---

[7] In other words, we can look at the return on common equity, removing the dividends to preferred stock from net income and considering the book value of common equity only.

EXHIBIT 4.10   Return on Investment Ratios for Pfizer, Inc., 2004

$$\text{Operating return on assets} = \frac{\text{Operating income}}{\text{Total assets}} = \frac{\$17,024}{\$123,684} = 13.764\%$$

$$\text{Return on assets} = \frac{\text{Net income}}{\text{Total assets}} = \frac{\$11,361}{\$123,684} = 9.186\%$$

$$\text{Return on equity} = \frac{\text{Net income}}{\text{Shareholders' equity}} = \frac{\$11,361}{\$68,278} = 16.639\%$$

line" measures of performance to the different financial aspects of the company's financial performance and condition.

An additional return to consider is the *return on invested capital*. Simply put, it is income from operating activities, less related taxes, divided by invested capital. *Invested capital* is the sum of all of the sources of long-term funding of the company, including equity and interest-bearing debt. However, because the numerator and denominator of this return are not reported directly on the financial statements, we must first calculate these amounts using reported accounts, making some assumptions.

The numerator is the after-tax operating income, also referred to *net operating profit after taxes* (NOPAT). One approach is to start with net income and then adjust for nonrecurring income and costs, interest expense, and taxes paid on investment and interest income. We could also start with operating income and then subtract estimated taxes on operating income. We have to make some assumptions regarding the taxes in this calculation, whether we calculate this starting with net income or operating income.[8] Generally, we use the effective tax rate (given in a footnote to the financial statements) to estimate these taxes.

Starting with operating income and using the effective rate of tax of 19%, as provided in Pfizer's Note 5 to its 2004 financial statement, we calculate operating profit after taxes of

Operating income	$17,024
Less: taxes on operating income, at 19%	3,235
Operating income after taxes	$13,789

---

[8] In the case of a company that incurs a rental expense, we generally capitalize the value of the operating leases and include this value as capital. We would also adjust net income for the after-tax effect of the implied interest on the operating lease. In past years in which goodwill was amortized, we would also add back that amortization to net income.

The invested capital for Pfizer is all long-term sources of capital:[9]

Interest bearing short-term debt	$11,266
Long-term debt	28,948
Shareholders' equity	68,278
Total capital	$108,492

The return on invested capital for Pfizer, Inc., in 2004 is therefore,

$$\text{Return on invested capital} = \frac{\text{After-tax operating income}}{\text{Invested capital}}$$

$$= \frac{\$13,789}{\$108,492} = 12.710\%$$

The return on invested capital is a measure of the company's ability to put all its financial capital to work, irregardless of how the company chooses to finance its assets; generally, the greater the return on invested capital, the better the performance of the company.

The DuPont System

The DuPont system was developed by E. I. du Pont Nemours as a means of relating the company's performance to specific aspects of the management of the company. In its simplest form, this system is a method of breaking down the return ratio into its profit margin and turnover components. Suppose the return on assets changes from 20% to 10%. We do not know whether this decreased return is due to a less efficient use of the company's assets—that is, due to lower activity—or to lower profit margins. A lower return on assets could be due to lower activity, lower margins, or both. Because we are interested in evaluating past operating performance to evaluate different aspects of the management of the company or to predict future performance, knowing the source of these returns is valuable information. The DuPont system allows us to breakdown the return ratios into components, identifying the sources of the changes in returns.

For example, we can breakdown the operating return on assets and the return on assets both into two components, margin and turnover:[10]

---

[9] Because we are interested in the total capital invested, we include short-term interest bearing debt in the amount of capital invested.

[10] An easy way to remember the DuPont breakdowns is to keep in mind that cross-cancellation of terms will produce the desired return, for example:

$$\frac{\text{Sales}}{\text{Total assets}} \times \frac{\text{Net income}}{\text{Sales}} = \frac{\text{Operating income}}{\text{Total assets}}$$

EXHIBIT 4.11   The DuPont Breakdown of the Return on Assets

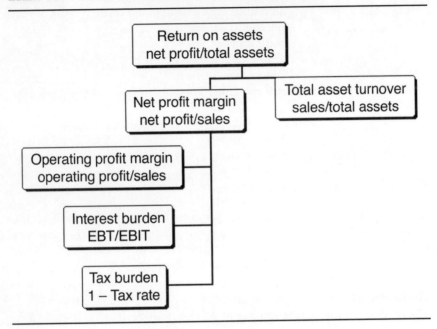

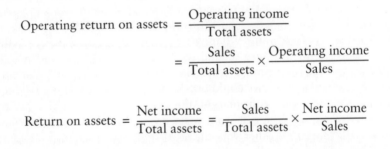

$$\text{Operating return on assets} = \frac{\text{Operating income}}{\text{Total assets}}$$

$$= \frac{\text{Sales}}{\text{Total assets}} \times \frac{\text{Operating income}}{\text{Sales}}$$

$$\text{Return on assets} = \frac{\text{Net income}}{\text{Total assets}} = \frac{\text{Sales}}{\text{Total assets}} \times \frac{\text{Net income}}{\text{Sales}}$$

By looking at the components, turnover and profit margin, and their changes from year to year, we get a better idea of what is behind changes in returns from year to year. Similarly, the return on shareholders' equity can be broken down into three components:

$$\text{Return on equity} = \frac{\text{Net income}}{\text{Total assets}}$$

$$= \frac{\text{Net income}}{\text{Sales}} \times \frac{\text{Sales}}{\text{Total assets}} \times \frac{\text{Total assets}}{\text{Shareholders' equity}}$$

The task of breaking down ratios into components can be performed on any return ratio and can reduce the ratios to their smallest components. For example, the return on equity can be broken down into five components: asset turnover, operating profit margin, fixed financial charge burden, tax burden, and financial leverage, as we demonstrate in Exhibit 4.12.

We can use the DuPont system to diagnose the source of change in returns over time. Consider Winn-Dixie prior to its bankruptcy filing in February 2005. We graph its total asset turnover, profit margin, and return on assets for the 15 years leading up to bankruptcy, as we show in Exhibit 4.13.

We can see in Panel A of Exhibit 4.13, Winn-Dixie's return on assets changed over time: significant decreases beginning after 1995, some recovery in 2001–2003, and then a decline in the fiscal year-end eight months prior to its bankruptcy filing.

What was the source of Winn-Dixie's woes? There is usually not just one source of a company's financial difficulties, but using the DuPont system allows us to get some idea of what led to Winn-Dixie's challenges.

We can see in Panel B of the exhibit that the total asset turnover did not change much from 1990 to 2002, though there was slight downward trend. If we were to compare this turnover with that of its competitors, we would see that Winn-Dixie's turnover was quite similar. However, the significant turnover in 2003 was out of line with the previous turnover, indicating something had changed.

Looking at Winn-Dixie's net profit margin, as shown in Panel C of the exhibit, we see that the changes in the net profit margin appear to have been a strong influence on Winn-Dixie's returns.

What does this mean? What we surmise from this analysis is that Winn-Dixie's difficulties are related to the management of expenses, but with issues in the deployment of its assets arose in 2003. If we wanted to get a more detailed look, we could break the net profit margin into components of the operation profit margin, the interest burden, and the tax burden to see what why the net profit margin changed over time. We would also want investigate further why the asset turnover changed dramatically in 2003, focusing especially on Winn-Dixie's inventory turnover.

Shareholder Ratios

The ratios we have explained to this point deal with the performance and financial condition of the company. These ratios provide information for managers (who are interested in evaluating the performance of the company) and for creditors (who are interested in the company's ability to pay its obligations). We now take a look at ratios that focus on the interests of the owners—shareholder ratios. These ratios translate the overall results of operations so that they can be compared in terms of a share of stock.

EXHIBIT 4.12 The Return on Equity for Pfizer, Inc. for 2004, Broken Down in Components Using the DuPont System

$$\text{Return on equity} = \text{Total asset turnover} \times \text{Net profit margin} \times \text{Equity multiplier}$$

$$\frac{\text{Net income}}{\text{Shareholders' equity}} = \frac{\text{Sales}}{\text{Total assets}} \times \frac{\text{Net income}}{\text{Sales}} \times \frac{\text{Total assets}}{\text{Shareholders' equity}}$$

$$\frac{\text{Net income}}{\text{Shareholders' equity}} = \frac{\text{Sales}}{\text{Total assets}} \times \left[\frac{\text{Operating income}}{\text{Sales}} \times \frac{\text{Income before taxes}}{\text{Operating income}} \times \left(1 - \frac{\text{Taxes}}{\text{Income before taxes}} \right) \right] \times \frac{\text{Total assets}}{\text{Shareholders' equity}}$$

$$\frac{\$11,361}{\$68,278} = \frac{\$52,516}{\$123,684} \times \left[\frac{\$17,024}{\$52,516} \times \frac{\$14,007}{\$17,024} \times \left(1 - \frac{\$2,665}{\$14,007} \right) \right] \times \frac{\$123,684}{\$68,278}$$

$$0.166 = 0.425 \times [0.324 \times 0.823 \times 0.810] \times 1.811$$

EXHIBIT 4.13 Winn-Dixie's Path to Bankruptcy
Panel A: Return on Assets

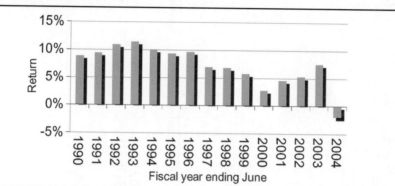

Panel B: Total Asset Turnover

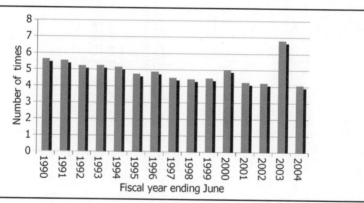

Panel C: Profit Margin

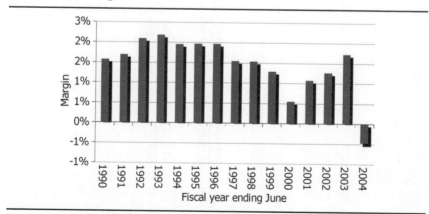

Source of data: Winn-Dixie's 10-K filings, various years.

Earnings per Share

Earnings per share (EPS) is the amount of income earned during a period per share of common stock.

$$\text{Earnings per share} = \frac{\text{Net income available to shareholders}}{\text{Number of shares outstanding}}$$

There are two numbers of earnings per share are currently disclosed in financial reports: basic and diluted. These numbers differ with respect to the definition of available net income and the number of shares outstanding.

Companies provide information on EPS in their annual and quarterly financial statement information, as well as in their periodic press releases. Generally, EPS is calculated as net income, divided by the number of shares outstanding.

Companies must report both basic earnings per share and diluted earnings per share. These EPS calculations replace the previous requirement of simple, primary, and fully diluted EPS.

Basic earnings per share is net income, minus preferred dividends, divided by the average number of shares outstanding. *Diluted earnings per share* is net income, minus preferred dividends, divided by the number of shares outstanding considering all dilutive securities (e.g., convertible debt, options).[11] Diluted EPS, therefore, gives the shareholder information about the *potential* dilution of earnings. For companies with a large number of dilutive securities (e.g., stock options, convertible preferred stock or convertible bonds), there can be a significant difference between basic and diluted EPS. You can see the effect of dilution for Pfizer—which is minimal—by comparing the basic and diluted EPS in Exhibit 4.14.

The *book value equity per share* is the amount of the book value (also known *as carrying value*) of common equity per share of common stock, calculated by dividing the book value of shareholders' equity by the number of shares of stock outstanding. As we discussed earlier, the book value of equity may differ from the market value of equity quite substantially. The market value per share, if available, is a much better indicator of the investment of shareholders in the company.

We can also compare the book value and the market value of a company, forming either the *market-to-book value ratio* or the *book-to-market value ratio*. For example,

---

[11] If dilutive securities have obligations, such as interest, that may affect the earnings available to shareholders, these obligations are added back to the numerator in the diluted EPS calculation.

EXHIBIT 4.14 Pfizer, Inc.'s, Inc., Earnings per Share, 1995–2004

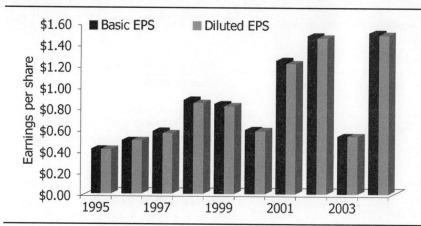

Source of data: Pfizer, Inc., 10-K filings various years.

$$\text{Market-to-book value ratio} = \frac{\text{Market value of equity}}{\text{Book value of equity}}$$

However, because the book value of equity is such a poor measure of the net assets of a company, this ratio may not be very informative. In the case of Pfizer, for example, there are many valuable assets that it owns that are not reflected on the balance sheet (i.e., drug patents) and, hence, in the book value of equity.[12]

The *price-earnings ratio* (P/E or PE ratio) is the ratio of the price per share of common stock to the earnings per share of common stock:

$$\text{Price-earnings ratio} = \frac{\text{Market price per share}}{\text{Earings per share}}$$

The earnings per share typically used in the denominator is the sum of the earnings per share for the last four quarters. In this case, the P/E ratio is often referred to as the *trailing P/E*. In contrast, the *leading P/E* or *projected P/E* ratio is calculated using earnings per share estimated for the next four quarters.

The P/E ratio is sometimes used as a proxy for investors' assessment of the company's ability to generate cash flows in the future. Histori-

---

[12] For example, Pfizer's market value of equity in July 2005 was at least three times its book value.

cally, P/E ratios for U.S. companies tend to fall in the 10–25 range, but there are periods in which P/E ratios have reached much higher. If the company has no or negative earnings, the P/E that you calculate is meaningless.

Examples of P/E ratios:

Company	P/E Ratio July 1, 2005
Abbott Laboratories	23.67
Bayer AG	22.91
Bristol-Myers Squibb	25.43
Johnson & Johnson	21.82
Merck & Co., Inc.	12.39
Novartis AG	22.49
Pfizer, Inc.	21.98

A financial analyst is often interested in how much of a company's earnings are paid out to investors. There are two common measures that address this, the dividends per share and the dividend payout ratio. *Dividends per share* (DPS) is the dollar amount of cash dividends paid during a period, per share of common stock:

$$\text{Dividends per share} = \frac{\text{Dividends paid to shareholders}}{\text{Number of shares outstanding}}$$

This represents the amount paid out in cash during a given period, but does not reflect noncash distributions such as stock dividends.

The *dividend payout ratio* is the ratio of cash dividends paid to earnings for a period:

$$\text{Dividend payout ratio} = \frac{\text{Dividends}}{\text{Earnings}}$$

The dividend payout ratio is the complement of the *plowback ratio*,

$$\text{Plowback ratio} = \frac{\text{Retained earnings}}{\text{Earnings}}$$

$$= 1 - \left[\frac{\text{Dividends}}{\text{Earnings}} \right]$$

which captures the proportion of earnings that are reinvested into the company.

We often describe a company's dividend policy in terms of either its dividend per share or its dividend payout ratio. Some companies' dividends appear to follow a pattern of constant or constantly growing dividends per share. And some companies' dividends appear to be a constant percentage of earnings. We provide the dividends per share and dividend payout for Pfizer, Inc. in Exhibit 4.15 for the period 1990 to 2005. Pfizer appears to maintain a constant growth rate in dividends (Panel A), resulting in a declining payout ratio over time (Panel B).

HOW CAN WE USE COMMON-SIZE ANALYSIS TO ANALYZE FINANCIAL STATEMENTS?

Common-size analysis is the analysis of financial statement items through comparisons among these items. In common-size analysis, we compare each item in a financial statement with a benchmark item:

- For the income statement, the benchmark is sales. For a given period, each item in the income statement is restated as a percentage of sales.
- For the balance sheet, the benchmark is total assets. For a given point in time, each item in the balance sheet is restated as a percentage of total assets.

To see how this works, consider Pfizer's financial statements for 2004. We have restated the income statements for 2003 and 2004 in Exhibit 4.16, restating each income statement item as a percentage of revenues.[13] In an analysis of this statement, we focus on the changes from year to year, looking for explanations for changes in company-specific events, economic, and market events.

The common size analysis of an income statement over several periods gives us an idea how the company's management of its expenses changes from one period to the next.

In a similar manner, we can restate each balance sheet item as a percentage of total assets and then make year-to-year comparisons. Examining changes in the asset composition tells us about how the company is altering its investments; examining changes in the liabilities and equity tells us about how the company is altering its capital structure.

---

[13] For presentation purposes, we have grouped several reported items and have rounded the percentages.

EXHIBIT 4.15   Pfizer, Inc., Dividends, 1990–2004
Panel A: Pfizer's Dividends per Share

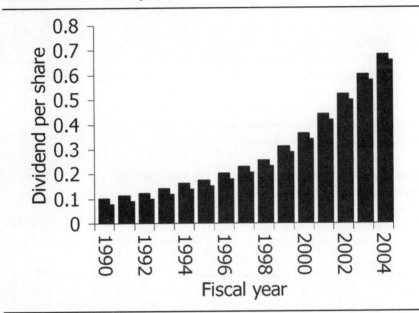

Panel B: Pfizer's Dividend Payout

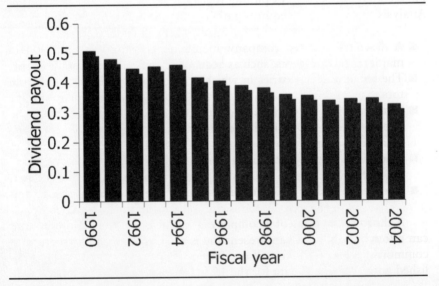

EXHIBIT 4.16   Pfizer, Inc., Common-Size Income Statement, 2003–2004

	Common-Size Statement Stated as a % of Sales	
	2004	2003
Revenues	100%	100%
Cost of sales	14%	21%
Gross profit	86%	79%
Selling, general, and administrative expenses	32%	34%
Research and development expenses	15%	17%
Amortization of intangible assets	6%	5%
Operating income	32%	23%
Interest expense and other nonoperating	5%	16%
Earnings before income taxes	27%	7%
Income tax	5%	3%
Discontinued operations, net of tax	0%	5%
Net income	22%	9%

INTEGRATED RATIO ANALYSIS

Financial analysis requires pulling together many pieces of information. Analysis of a company requires gathering information that includes:

- A description of the company, including its line(s) of business, and major corporate events, such as acquisitions and divestitures.
- The industry or industries in which it operates and its major competitors.
- Identify major factors (e.g., economic, competitive, or legal) that have affected the company in the recent past and may affect the company going forward.
- Relevant financial ratios for at least the past five years, but preferably the past 10 years.
- Common-size analysis over the past 5–10 years.

A thorough analysis of a company would require more space than we can allow here, but we can present the basic financial ratio analysis and common-size analysis. We will use Pfizer, Inc. as an example, using published annual financial data for the 15 fiscal years of 1990 through 2004.

Company Description, Industry, and Major Factors

The Pfizer, Inc. Company is a drug manufacturer that has a wide range of prescription and consumer healthcare products. There are many ways to classify this company with respect to its industry. Pfizer operates in three business segments: pharmaceuticals, consumer health, and animal health.[14]

Pfizer, Inc. is the largest drug company worldwide. Using one classification of the industry, Pfizer, Inc., has approximately 18% of the market share, with revenues in 2004 over $52 billion.[15] Its major competitors are GlaxoSmithKline PLC, Novartis AG, and Merck & Co. We show the breakdown of the market shares held by a sampling of drug companies in Exhibit 4.17.

EXHIBIT 4.17   U.S. Drug Industry, 2004

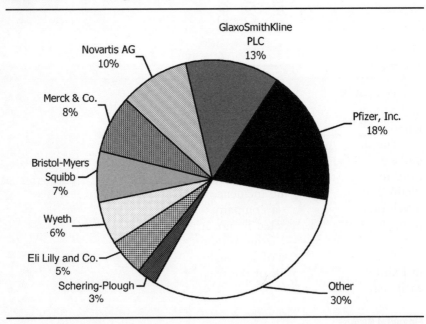

Source: Value Line Investment Survey, April 8, 2005.

---

[14] Based on its primary line of business of pharmaceutical manufacturing, its Standard Industrial Code (SIC) is 2834; its North American Industry Classification System (NAICS) code is 325412 (pharmaceutical preparation—manufacturing).

[15] This classification is based that of Value Line Investment Survey, 2005. Using classifications of other financial services, such as that by Mergent or Yahoo! Finance, we find a slightly different definition of Pfizer's Industry. For example Yahoo! Finance includes companies such as Abbott Laboratories and Bayer AG in the same industry.

EXHIBIT 4.18 Seasonality in Pfizer, Inc.'s Sales, First Quarter 2002 through Fourth Quarter 2004

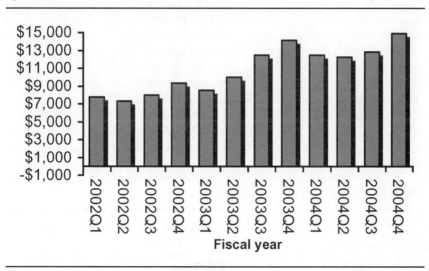

The U.S. drug industry has a few very large companies, such as Pfizer and Merck & Co., but it also has many small companies that are more narrowly focused on biotech research, such as ImClone and BioGen.

The drug industry is a noncyclical industry, which means its sales and earnings are not affected by the health of the general economy. The drug industry's growth is dependent on demographics (e.g., the aging "baby boomers") and the incidence of chronic diseases. Research and development are key to a company's growth in this industry. In addition, the industry is affected by government regulation, including drug approvals by the Federal Drug Administration.

There is some degree of seasonality in Pfizer's revenues, as we show in Exhibit 4.18. The peak of the seasonality is in the fourth quarter of each year.

Financial Ratios

Liquidity

The current and quick ratios follow similar trends during the 1990–2004 period, with a drop off in the years 1994 to 1997. A look at the management's discussion of the financial results in that period indicates that this drop-off is primarily the result of a reduction in short-term investments that was used to repay long-term debt and increase investment expenditures.

EXHIBIT 4.19   Liquidity Ratios of Pfizer, Inc., 1990–2004

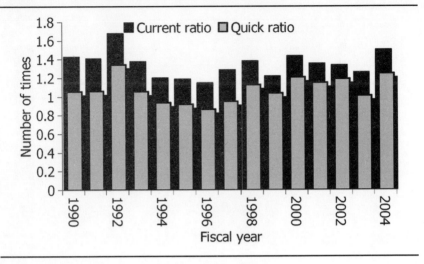

Source of data: The Pfizer, Inc. Company annual reports, various years.

You will notice a change in the physical distance of these two trend lines in this exhibit. The difference between the quick and current ratios is in the numerator, where the quick ratio excludes inventory. The tightening of these two lines indicates that inventory has declined relative to the other current assets over time. However, in the case of Pfizer, the investment in inventory is small relative to its other assets; drug companies in general do not tend to have large inventories because a large part of their cost of sales are not represented in physical inventory, but rather are the drug patents that result from the research and development activity.

Activity

We provide the turnover ratios for Pfizer for the 1990–2004 period in Exhibit 4.20. The drop off in turnover in the years 2002 to 2004 is a result of a number of factors, including the changing product mix from the acquisitions and divestitures in this period, as well as challenges with some of its major pharmaceutical products, the COX-2 inhibitor drugs.[16]

Profitability

As you can see in Exhibit 4.21, the profit margins of Pfizer, Inc. have increased over time, with the drop-off in the 2003 fiscal year, which may be attributed, in part, to changes in product mix from merger-related activities.

---

[16] For example, Pfizer merged with Warner-Lambert in 2000 and Pharmacia in 2003.

EXHIBIT 4.20   Turnover Ratios for Pfizer, Inc., 1990–2004

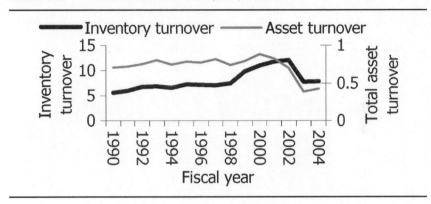

Source of data: The Pfizer, Inc. Company annual reports, various years.

EXHIBIT 4.21   Profit Margins, Pfizer, Inc., 1995–2004

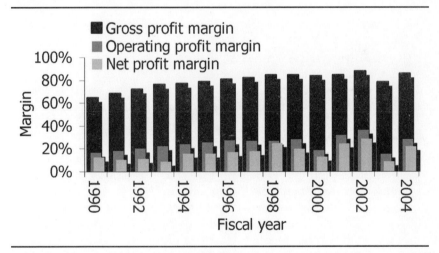

Source of data: The Pfizer, Inc. Company annual reports, various years.

The net profit margin in 2004 was affected by both the impact of the problems with its COX-2 inhibitor drugs, but also so one-time charges related to the Pharmacia merger.

Financial Leverage

Pfizer, Inc.'s use of debt has varied over the period 1990 to 2004, as we show in Exhibit 4.22. However, there has been a slight shift in to a greater reliance on short-term liabilities, as indicated by the divergence

EXHIBIT 4.22   Financial Leverage Ratios, Pfizer, Inc., 1995–2004

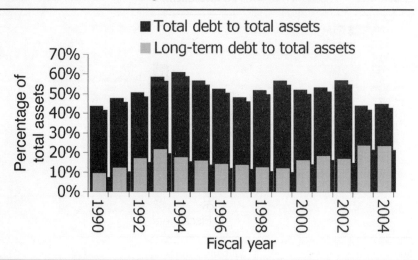

Source of data: The Pfizer, Inc. Company annual reports, various years.

of the two debt ratios. Pfizer's short-term debt consists primarily of commercial paper and unsecured notes.

Pfizer's debt is rated as high quality; Pfizer's short-term borrowing is rated P-1 and its long-term debt is rated Aaa by Moody's Investor Service.

Return and the DuPont Analysis

We plot the return on equity and return on assets for Pfizer for the years 1990 to 2004 in Exhibit 4.23. Both the return on assets and the return on equity are wide-ranging during these years.

In general, returns trended upward during most of the years up to 2002, with a drop-off in 2000. Returns declined significantly in 2003.

We provide a breakdown of the return on equity into the three components of net profit margin, asset turnover, and financial leverage, and graph these components in Exhibit 4.24. The DuPont breakdown suggests that the increased volatility of returns in the post-1999 period are attributed to changes in Pfizer's ability to manage its expenses, as represented by the net profit margin.

Other Factors

All drug companies are affected by the constant challenges from drug patent expirations and increased competition from generic drug products. One of the keys to future growth of a drug company is its spending

EXHIBIT 4.23   Pfizer, Inc., Returns on Investment, 1990–2005

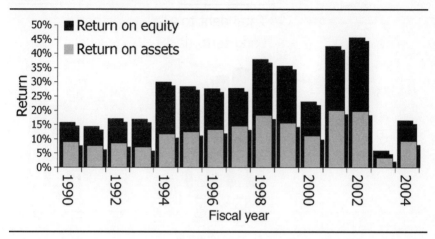

Source of data: The Pfizer, Inc. Company annual reports, various years.

EXHIBIT 4.24   DuPont Components, Pfizer, Inc., 1990–2004

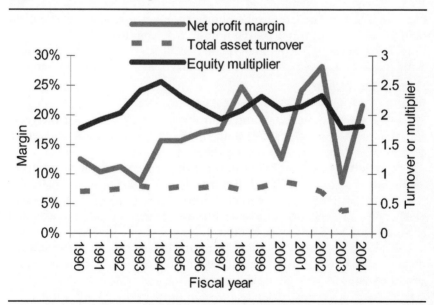

Source of data: The Pfizer, Inc. Company annual reports, various years.

EXHIBIT 4.25   Pfizer, Inc.'s Research and Development Expenses as a Percentage of Revenues, 1990–2004

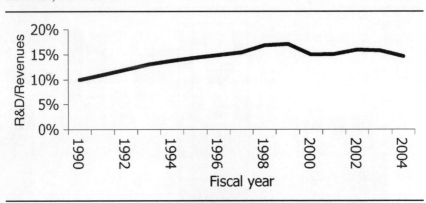

Source of data: The Pfizer, Inc. Company annual reports, various years.

on research and development. Focusing on the relation between revenues and research and development expenditures, as we show in Exhibit 4.25, we see that spending on R&D has dropped slightly since 1999. Pfizer's 2004 ratio of R&D spending to revenues of 15% is slightly less than the industry average of 17.7% and lower that its competitors of Eli Lilly and Schering-Plough.[17]

Common-Size Analysis

We can gain another perspective of the company's performance and condition through a common-size analysis of the income statement and balance sheet. We provide the common-size income statement in Exhibit 4.26 and the common size balance sheet in Exhibit 4.27.

In Exhibit 4.26, we can see the trends in the expenses and net income of the company. With the exception of 2003, we the operating costs have declined over time. The effects of the mergers, in terms of merger-related expenses, can be seen in the change in the nonoperating expenses in 2003 and 2004.

We can also see effects of the mergers in the common size balance sheets, as we show in Exhibit 4.27, Panel A. The increased proportionate investment in intangibles is a direct result to the acquisition of Pharmacia. We can see Pfizer's slight increase in its use of long-term debt in its capital structure, as shown in Panel B of this exhibit.

---

[17] Source: Standard and Poor's *Industry Survey*, "Healthcare: Pharmaceuticals."

EXHIBIT 4.26   Common-Sized Income Statements, Pfizer, Inc. Company, 1994–2004

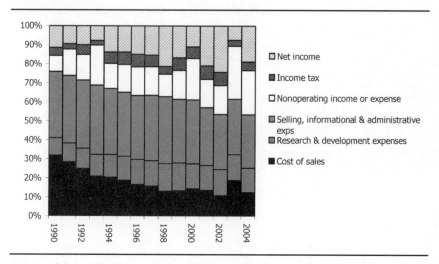

Source of data: The Pfizer, Inc. Company annual reports, various years.

WHAT ARE THE PITFALLS AND PRATFALLS OF FINANCIAL RATIO ANALYSIS?

It is an easy matter to obtain and manipulate financial data. But the important and more challenging task of making sense out all the analysis remains. There are numerous issues that arise in analyzing and comparing financial ratios across time and across companies. These issues include:

- The use of accounting data, which is generally stated using historical costs.
- Selecting the ratios to analyze and interpreting ratios appropriately for the company and the industry.
- Choosing a benchmark for comparisons, whether the industry as a whole, major competitors, or some set of aspirant or competing companies.
- The use of ratios in forecasting future performance.

There are a number of issues that arise simply from the fact that much of the financial data we use in analysis is accounting information. The problems associated with using reported accounting data include:

EXHIBIT 4.27 Common-Sized Balance Sheet, Pfizer, Inc. Company, 1994–2004
Panel A: Assets

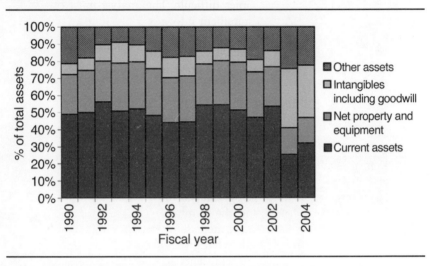

Panel B: Liabilities and Equity

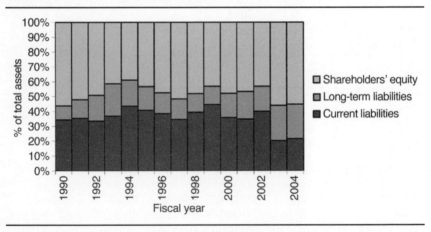

Source of data: The Pfizer, Inc. Company annual reports, various years.

■ *Use of historical costs and inflation.* Accounting data are not adjusted for inflation and represent historical cost instead of current or replacement costs for most assets. It is likely that the reported book value of assets do not reflect the market value or replacement value of a company's assets.

■ *The different methods of accounting.* Companies may select from alternative accounting procedures (e.g., LIFO versus FIFO), which makes comparisons among companies difficult. The analyst must often look beyond the basic financial statement information to remove distortions that may arise from specific accounting practices.

■ *Changes in accounting principles.* Accounting principles change over time, making it challenging to assess trends.

■ *The occurrence of extraordinary and special items.* The analyst must determine whether the effects of extraordinary and special items should be included in the analysis. In recent years, extraordinary items have become quite "ordinary," with some companies reported extraordinary items each year.

■ *The difficulty in classify "fuzzy" items.* Some accounting items are difficult to classify, especially when distinguishing between liabilities and equity accounts. Therefore, the analyst must understand not only the accounting principles behind the numbers, but also understand business practices. For example, in the case of the deferred taxes, the analyst must understand not only what gives rise to the deferred taxes, but whether this accounting item represents an ongoing difference between tax and accounting income (and is more suitably classified as equity) or whether this item represents a temporary timing difference (and is more suitably classified as a liability).

■ *Restatements.* Financial statements are restated occasionally due to errors or, unfortunately, fraud. When analyzing a company that has restated its financial statements, questions arise with regard to what data to use. As reported? As restated? Generally, when making forecasts of the company's future performance and condition, we would want to use the corrected data.[18]

Selecting and Interpreting Ratios

Interpretation of ratios one at a time is difficult since there is no "good" or "bad" value when viewed in isolation. Ratios should be selected that have meaning for that company. For example, inventory turnover for Pfizer is not very meaningful because the investment in inventory is of little consequence for a pharmaceutical company. But inventory turnover is very important for, say, a retailer such as Wal-Mart. And whereas investment in research and development is important for Pfizer, this is much less so for Wal-Mart Stores.

---

[18] Of course, if the restatement is made as a result of detected fraudulent reporting, the analyst would want to take a very close look at *why* the company's management had to restate the data—in other words, what were they hiding?

Further, some ratios do not make sense under certain circumstances. For example, if a company has negative earnings, the price-earnings ratio is meaningless. As another example, consider a company that has negative book value of equity (and, yes, this can happen). In this case, any ratio that uses book value of equity, such as the debt-equity ratio, is meaningless.

Choosing a Benchmark

To make comparisons, the analyst will likely want to compare the company with other companies. But identifying the other companies in the same or similar lines of business presents a challenge. A system that has been used for many years for classifying companies by lines of business is the Standard Industrial Classification (SIC) system, which was developed by the Office of Management and Budget. However, starting in 1997, another classification system, North American Industry Classification System (NAICS) replaces SIC codes with a system that better represents the current lines of business. Using the NAISC, we can classify a company and then compare this company with other of that class.

Classifying companies into industry groups is difficult because most companies have more than one line of business. Do we classify a company into an industry by the line of business that represents:

- The most sales revenue generated?
- The greatest investment in assets?
- The greatest share of the company's profits?

It is not clear which is the most appropriate method and a company may be classified into different industries by different financial services and analysts.

In making comparisons, there is an issue of whether the benchmark should be all other companies in the industry (say, an average), or the leading companies in the industry. Consider the case of Dow Chemical. Dow Chemical is a manufacturer of basic chemicals. The primary competitors to Dow Chemical in this industry are E. I. du Pont de Nemours and Union Carbide, though there are also a number of smaller competitors such as Georgia Gulf and Millenium Chemicals. When comparing Dow Chemical to the industry,

- Should we use just the two major competitors as the industry benchmark? If so, so we simply average DuPont's and Union Carbide's ratios or do we weight them in some manner (e.g., by market share)?
- Should we consider the smaller competitors at all?

■ Should we compare Dow Chemical with the largest or the most profitable company in the industry?

The benchmark that we choose may affect the conclusions that we draw with respect to a company's operating performance.

Using Ratios in Forecasting

We often examine trends in ratios and other financial data to predict the future, forecasting the future based on historical trends. For example, we may extrapolate a trend in sales or a trend in operating profit. And though this may result in a reasonable forecast for the immediate future, the business environment is very complex and many factors can affect the future performance or conditions of a company.

Consider forecasting Pfizer's net income for 2000 and beyond, based on net income data from 1990 to 1999. We begin by estimating the trend in the net income over this period, as we graph in Exhibit 4.28. The net income appears to follow a linear path through these years, as we show in Panel A. However, when we use this path to forecast net income for the years 2000 to 2004, we find that this trend does not fit well, as indicating in Panel B of this exhibit. That's because the forecast we make using 1990–1999 data does not consider, among other things, the company specific events such as discontinued operations and mergers that took place in the 2000–2004 period.

This illustrates why we develop forecasts using information in addition to the basic trend, such as forecasts of company-specific events, as well as economic and market conditions.

But we need to be careful in predicting the future revenues or income of a company based solely on the past. As companies mature, growth slows and this needs to be considered in making any forecasts. How much does growth slow? It depends on many factors, including industry structure (e.g., degree of competition), changing demographics, and government regulation.

SUMMARY

Financial analysis of a company requires a wealth of information. There is so much information available and so much of the analysis can be computerized, that the challenge for the analyst is to select the appropriate tools, gather the pertinent information, and interpret the information.

Financial ratio analysis requires understanding the accounting information that is used in these ratios. In addition to calculating finan-

EXHIBIT 4.28   Forecasting Net Income for Pfizer, Inc.
Panel A: Trend in Net Income, 1990–1999

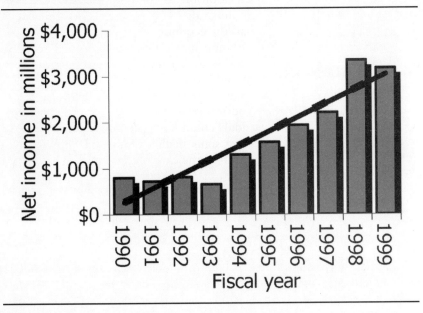

Panel B: Forecast Error in Net Income, 2000–2004

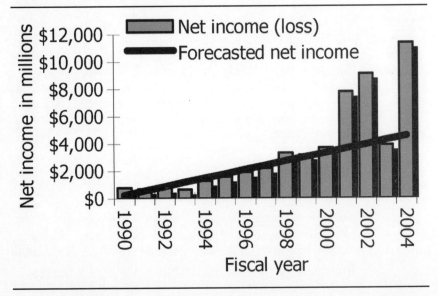

Source of data: Pfizer, Inc. 10-K filings, various years.

cial ratios, the analyst must look at company and industry specific information that helps explains the trends and changes in trends that the financial ratios may reveal. In addition to the company and industry analysis, the financial analysis must also be able to put the analysis of the financial ratios in context of the economy in general.

Analysis is becoming more important following the recent scandals as investors and financial managers are learning to become more skeptical of accounting information and look more closely at trends in data, comparisons with other companies, the relation between management compensation and earnings, and footnote disclosures. It is not necessarily the case that all of the scandals could have been detected with closer scrutiny, but there were warning signs in the trends and hints in footnotes that should have at least raised the caution flags among analysts.

CHAPTER 5

Equity Analysis

What determines the market price of a share of common stock? Like anything else, price depends on what people are willing to pay. The price of a share of stock today depends on what investors believe is today's value of all the cash flows that will accrue in the entire future from that share of stock. In other words, no one is going to pay any more today for a share of stock than they think it is worth—based on what they get out of it in terms of future cash flows. What people are willing to pay for a share of stock today determines its market value.

The theory of stock prices makes sense. If we could accurately forecast a company's cash flows in the future, we could determine the value of the company's stock today and determine whether the stock is over- or undervalued by the market. But forecasting future cash flows is difficult. As an alternative, what is typically done is to examine the historical and current relation between stock prices and some fundamental value, such as earnings or dividends, using this relation to estimate the value of a share of stock.

In this chapter, we take a closer look at the fundamental factors of earnings and dividends and their relations with share price as expressed in such commonly used ratios as the price-earnings ratio and the dividend yield.

EARNINGS

A commonly used measure of a company's performance over a period of time is its earnings, which is often stated in terms of a return—that is, earnings scaled by the amount of the investment. But earnings can really mean many different things depending on the context:

- If a financial analyst is evaluating the performance of a company's operations, the focus is on the operating earnings of the company—its earnings before interest and taxes, EBIT.
- If the analyst is evaluating the performance of a company overall, the focus is upon net income, which is essentially EBIT less interest and taxes.
- If the analyst is evaluating the performance of the company from a common shareholder's perspective, the earnings are the earnings available to common shareholders—EBIT less interest, taxes, and preferred stock dividends.
- If the analyst is forecasting future earnings and cash flows, the focus is on earnings from continuing operations. Therefore, it is useful to be very specific in the meaning of "earnings."

Can Earnings be Managed?

As we discussed in Chapter 3, there is a possibility that reported financial information may be managed by the judicious choice of accounting methods and timing. In particular, earnings can be managed using a number of devices, including the selection of inventory method (e.g., FIFO versus LIFO) and the selection of the depreciation method and depreciable lives. The possibility of earnings management exists, so the burden is on the financial analyst to understand a company's financial reporting, accounting methods, and the likelihood of manipulation.

There are many pressures that a company may face that affect the likelihood of management. These pressures include:

- Executive compensation based on earnings targets.
- Reporting ever-increasing earnings, especially when the business is subject to variations in the business cycle.
- Meeting or beating analyst forecasts.

Earnings targets comes in various forms, but typically schemes on earnings targets provide for a bonus if earnings meet or exceed a specified target such as a return on equity.

One-sided incentives such as this—rewards for beating the target return, but no penalty for not making the target—create problematic situations. Combine this with the tendency of stock prices to be affected by whether or not analysis forecasts are met or beat, and there is significant potential for problems.

If, for example, management knows that the earnings target cannot be met in a period, there may be an incentive to either (1) manage earnings, through such mechanics as accruals, changes in estimates, or changes in accounting method; or (2) take large write-offs in that period, increasing chances of making earnings targets in future periods—referred to as taking a "big bath."

Meeting analysts' forecasts presents still another pressure for the management of earnings. We know from the wealth of empirical evidence that stock prices react to earnings surprises, where surprises are defined as a difference between expected and actual earnings.[1] Because there is a market reaction to surprises—negative for earnings less than expected and positive for earnings better than expected—companies have an incentive to manage earnings to meet or exceed forecasted earnings. Frustrating the efforts to beat analysts' forecasts is the tendency of analysts to be overly optimistic about earnings.[2] In fact, the overestimation of earnings is more pronounced in cases in which companies report negative earnings.

The pressure to report constant or constantly increasing earnings may also result in earnings management, manipulation, or, in extreme cases, even fraud. The Securities and Exchange Commission (SEC) charged executives of Gateway with failing to comply with generally accepted accounting principles. In its third quarter of 2000, Gateway met analysts' expectations for earnings per share of $0.46 by overstating earnings by $0.10 per share.

Evidence suggests that there is a strong incentive to meet analysts' forecasts:

- More companies meet or beat earnings forecasts than miss these forecasts.[3]
- Stock prices are sensitive to whether earnings meet analysts' forecasts.[4]

---

[1] Rendleman, Jones, and Latane document that abnormal returns (i.e., returns in excess of that expected in absence of an earnings announcement) persist beyond the initial "surprise." See Richard J. Rendleman, Charles P. Jones, and Henry A. Latane, "Empirical Anomalies Based on Unexpected Earnings and the Importance of Risk Adjustment," *Journal of Financial Economics* 1, no. 3 (1982), pp. 269–287. The existence of abnormal returns may be the result of market inefficiency or an empirical measurement problem, as argued in Ray Ball "The Earnings-Price Anomaly," *Journal of Accounting and Economics* 15 (1992), pp. 319–345.

[2] This over-optimism is documented in Richard J. Dowen "Analyst Reaction to Negative Earnings for Large Well-Known Firms," *Journal of Portfolio Management* (Fall 1996), pp. 49–55.

[3] See Carla Hayn, "The information Content of Losses," *Journal of Accounting and Economics* 20 (1995), pp. 125–153; and Sarah McVay, Venky Nagar, and Vivki Tang, "Trading Incentives to Meet Earnings Thresholds," working paper, University of Michigan, January 2005.

[4] See E.D. Bartov, D. Givoly, and Carla Hayn, "The Rewards to Meeting or Beating Earnings Expectations," *Journal of Accounting and Economics* 33 (2002), pp. 173–204.

■ Managers are more likely to sell their shares of the company's stock after meeting or beating forecasts, than if the company fails to meet forecasts.[5]

As a result of these incentives, the financial analyst must not only look for unusual patterns in earnings, but also earnings that are perhaps *too* predictable.[6]

Even with the potential for managed earnings, is there a relation between earnings and stock value? Consider General Electric's earnings and prices over the period 1987 to 2004 shown in Exhibit 5.1. As you can see the market value of GE's common stock moves along in tandem

EXHIBIT 5.1   General Electric's Earning and Market Value of Equity, 1987–2004

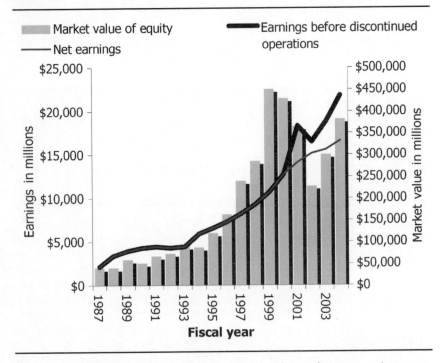

Source of data: General Electric's 10-K statements and annual reports, various years.

---

[5] McVay, Nagar, and Tang, "Trading Incentives to Meet Earnings Thresholds."

[6] The pressure to meet targets is so well known that customers and suppliers of companies under pressure can take advantage of the pressure to extract discounts or otherwise favorable terms. See Greg Ip, "Growth companies Feel Pressure to Book Sales," *Wall Street Journal* 16 September 1997, pp. C1, C13.

with GE's earnings before discontinued items. You will also notice that the relation between market value and net earnings is not as strong as that with earnings from continuing operations. This is likely because investors look beyond earnings in their valuation of future cash flows and focus on sustainable, continuing earnings.

Though the example using General Electric illustrates the relation for one company over a specific range of years, the issue is whether earnings and market value are related for most companies. The research into the relation between earnings and value concludes the following:

- Stock prices change in response to an announcement of unexpected earnings.
- Accounting earnings are correlated with stock returns, especially returns measured over a long horizon following the release of earnings.[7]

The strong relation between earnings and stock prices may be due to reported earnings being strongly correlated with true earnings (that is, earnings in absence of management). Or the earnings-stock price relation may be due to stocks' valuation being dependent on *reported* earnings.

Pro Forma Earnings

Pro forma financial information is really a misnomer—the information is neither pro forma (that is, forward looking), nor reliable financial data. What is it? Creative accounting. It started during the Internet/Tech boom in the 1990s and persists today: companies release financial information that is prepared according to their own liking, using accounting methods that they create. Why did companies start doing this? What's wrong with generally accepted accounting principles (GAAP)?

During the Internet/Tech stock boom, many startup companies quickly went public and then felt the pressures to generate profits. However, profits in that industry were hard to come by during that period of time. What some companies did is generate financial data that they included in company releases that reported earnings that were not determined by GAAP—but rather by methods of their own. In some cases, these alternative methods hid a lot of the ills of these companies.

We can see this in Exhibit 5.2 for Sabre Holdings, parent of Travelocity. Sabre Holdings began to provide "adjusted" (also referred to as "pro forma") earnings per share in the second quarter of 1999 in their

---

[7] See, for example Peter D. Easton, Trevor S. Harris, and James A. Ohlson, "Aggregate Accounting Earnings Can Explain Most of Security Returns," *Journal of Accounting and Economics* 15 (1992), pp. 119–142.

EXHIBIT 5.2   Examples of Pro Forma versus GAAP Earnings for Sabre Holdings

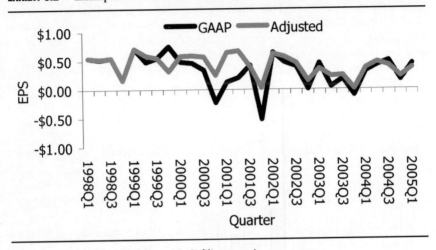

Source of data: Sabre Holdings 10-Q filings, various quarters.

press releases, initially ignoring option expense. Eventually, the adjusted EPS ignored much more, including one-time work reduction costs and the amortization of intangibles. In fact, in a couple of the quarters, the adjusted EPS was positive when the GAAP EPS was negative. It was not until the second quarter of 2002 that Sabre began presenting both GAAP and adjusted EPS in the press releases; on and after which time the GAAP and adjusted became quite similar.

The use of pro forma financial data may be misleading to investors. For example, if a press release refers to last quarter's earnings, are these pro forma or GAAP?

In response, the SEC now requires that if companies release pro forma financial data, they must also reconcile this data with GAAP.[8] Additionally, the SEC issued a cease-and-desist order proceeding against Trump Hotels & Casino Resorts, Inc., in 2002, its first enforcement action regarding pro forma statements by publicly traded companies. At issue in this case is the fact that the company discussed net income and earnings per share in the press release, but the company did not indicate whether these were prepared according to GAAP or were pro forma. And while the company discussed a one-time charge that was excluded, it was felt that investors would interpret that this one-time charge was the only difference between what was reported in the release and GAAP.

---

[8] "SEC Cautions Companies, Alerts Investors to Potential Dangers of "Pro Forma" Financials," Securities and Exchange Commission, release 2001–144, December 4, 2001.

EXHIBIT 5.3   Trading Volume and High-Low-Close Prices for Trump Hotels &
Casino Resorts, Inc., Around the Third Quarter 1999 Earnings Release

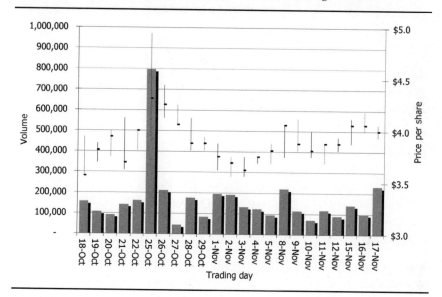

Key dates:
   October 25, 1999: Press release
   October 28, 1999: News reports revealing one-time gain as part of reported income
   November 14, 1999: 10-Q filing with the Securities and Exchange Commission
Source of data: Yahoo! Finance.

In fact, there was a one-time gain that was included in the release
income and EPS figures, but this was not disclosed as such—giving the
misleading impression that the company met analysts' forecasts.
    We can see the relation between earnings information and stock
prices in Exhibit 5.3, as we follow the price of Trump stock, using a
high-low-close diagram, and trading volume around the key dates pertaining to the earnings release. The company's press release, indicating
that the company met analysts expectations, was accompanied by an
increase in the stock's price. This stock price gain, however, dissipated
as more information was revealed.

Core Earnings

The recent experiences with financial restatements resulting from the
management of earnings and outright fraud sparked many to develop
earnings metrics that were not affected by the most obvious tools for
earnings management. Standard and Poor's (S&P) introduced a calcula-

tion in 2001 referred to as core earnings that they use to represent a company's sustainable performance.

Core earnings are defined as earnings before:[9]

- Gains from pensions
- Gains or losses from asset sales
- Merger and acquisition related expenses
- Litigation or insurance settlements
- Goodwill write-offs
- Cost of employee options[10]

In other words, earnings before the most manageable items and the most unusual and infrequent earnings.

However, we should note that core earnings are not without the potential for management, as reported in a study by Sarah McVay. Corresponding to the popularity of core earnings as a performance metric, many companies began shifting expenses to special items.[11] As she notes, such shifting does not reverse itself as do some other earnings management techniques, hence providing an inflated picture of the company's performance.[12]

Earnings per Share

Earnings per share (EPS) is earnings available for common shareholders, divided by the number of common shares outstanding:

$$\text{Earnings per share} = \frac{\text{Earnings available to owners}}{\text{Number of common shares outstanding}}$$

This ratio indicates each share's portion of how much is earned by the firm in a given accounting period.

For example, suppose a company has $5 million of earnings and 4 million shares outstanding. Its earnings per share is

---

[9] *Standard & Poor's Core Earning Technical Bulletin,* 24 October 2002.

[10] Some of the difference that we may see between core earnings and reported net income disappears when companies expense employee options. Some companies expense these options as an expense already, whereas the rest begin doing so for fiscal years beginning after December 15, 2005.

[11] Sarah E. McVay, "The Use of Special Items to Inflate Core Earnings," New York University, March 2005.

[12] She distinguishes between a shifting in expenses that results in improved operating performance from transitory shifts in operating expenses.

$$\text{Earnings per share} = \frac{\$5,000,000}{4,000,000 \text{ shares}} = \$1.25 \text{ per share}$$

This company earned \$1.25 for each common share outstanding.

The EPS does not tell us anything about the preferred shareholders. And that's acceptable because preferred shareholders, in most cases, receive a fixed dividend amount. Because the common shareholders are the residual owners of the firm—they are the last ones in line after creditors and preferred shareholders—we are interested in seeing just what is left over for them.

When we see an amount given for EPS, we have to be sure we know what it really means. But what is there to interpret? Net income available to common shares is pretty clear-cut (with some exceptions). What about the number of common shares outstanding? Can that change during the period of time under consideration? It can, affecting the calculated value of earnings per share. The number of common shares outstanding can change for two reasons:

1. *Timing.* Net income is earned over a specific period of time, yet the number of shares outstanding may change over this period.
2. *Dilutive securities.* The company may have securities outstanding that can be converted into common stock or employee stock options and warrants that may be exercisable (i.e., potentially dilutive securities), so the number of shares of common that potentially may share in this net income is greater than the number reported as outstanding.

Timing requires us to consider the net income relative to some meaningful measure of common shares outstanding during the same period. We can do this by first calculating the weighted average number of shares outstanding during the period.

Suppose the ABC company has income available for common shareholders of \$2,000,000 over 2006 and there are no potentially dilutive securities. ABC provides you with the following information:

Number of shares outstanding January 1, 2006	200,000 shares
Number of shares issued July 1, 2006	50,000 shares
Number of shares outstanding December 31, 2006	250,000 shares

The weighted average number of shares outstanding is

$$
\begin{aligned}
\text{Weighted average number of shares outstanding} &= 0.50(200,000 \text{ shares}) + 0.50(250,000 \text{ shares}) \\
&= 100,000 \text{ shares} + 125,000 \text{ shares} \\
&= 225,000 \text{ shares}
\end{aligned}
$$

What are the earnings per share for 2006?

$$\text{Earnings per share} = \frac{\$2,000,000}{225,000} = \$8.89 \text{ per share}$$

We can represent the earnings per share adjusted for the change in the shares outstanding as

$$\text{Earnings per share} = \frac{\text{Net income available for common}}{\text{Weighted average number of common shares outstanding}}$$

For a company with securities that are dilutive—meaning they could share in net income—there are two earnings per share amounts that are reported in financial statements.[13] *Basic earnings per share* are earnings (minus preferred dividends), divided by the average number of shares outstanding. *Diluted earnings per share* is earnings (minus preferred dividends), divided by the number of shares outstanding considering all dilutive securities (e.g., convertible debt, options). Companies that report earnings per share for any prior period must restate these amounts in terms of the new basic and diluted calculations.

To see how the earnings per share figures are calculated, consider Intel's 2004 earnings per share. Net income for 2004 was $7,516 million. The average number of shares for the basic earnings per share figure is 6,400 million. Therefore,

$$\text{Basic earnings per share} = \frac{\$7,516 \text{ million}}{6,400 \text{ million}} = \$1.17 \text{ per share}$$

As of 2004, Intel has the potential to issue 94 million additional shares that dilute earnings per share because of employee stock options.[14]

---

[13] Beginning with fiscal years ending after December 15, 1997, companies must report both basic and diluted earnings per share [Statement of Financial Accounting Standards No. 128, "Earnings Per Share" (Stamford: Financial Accounting Standards Board, 1997)]. This replaces the previous requirement of simple, primary, and fully diluted EPS Primary earnings per share is the earnings per share calculation that reflects the dilutive effects of securities considered likely to be transformed into common stock, such as convertible securities, options, and warrants. Fully diluted earnings per share are earnings per share that reflect the dilutive effects of all potentially dilutive securities (for example, including options that are "out-of-the-money").

[14] Date obtained from the Intel 2004 Annual Report, Note 3, p. 56.

Adding the potential shares to the weighted average outstanding shares in the denominator:

$$\text{Diluted earnings per share} = \frac{\$7,561 \text{ million}}{6,494 \text{ million}} = \$1.16 \text{ per share}$$

Accounting principles require that the diluted earnings per share may never be reported as greater than basic earnings per share.[15]

PRICE-EARNINGS RATIO

Many investors are interested in how the earnings are valued by the market. A measure of how these earnings are valued is the *price-earnings ratio* (P/E). This ratio compares the price per common share with earnings per common share:

$$\text{Price-earnings ratio} = \frac{\text{Market price per share}}{\text{Earnings per share}}$$

The result is a multiple—the value of a share of stock expressed as a multiple of earnings per share.

The inverse of this measure is referred to as the *earnings yield*, or E/P:[16]

$$\text{Earnings yield} = \frac{\text{Earnings per share}}{\text{Market price per share}}$$

Because investors are forward-looking in their valuation, earnings in this ratio represent the expected normal earnings per share for the stock. If a company has a share price of $17 and earnings per share of 80 cents, the price-earnings ratio is

$$\text{Price-earnings ratio} = \frac{\$17.00}{\$0.80} = 21.25 \text{ times}$$

---

[15] There are instances in which certain dilutive securities may be *antidilutive*; that is, the effect of the additional shares outstanding is outweighed by the adjusted to earnings in the numerator. This may occur in instances such as a convertible bond, where the effect of adding back the interest does not outweigh the dampening effect of the additional shares.

[16] Though the earnings yield provides the same information as the price-earnings ratio, it is often used to avoid the problem of dividing by zero in the cases in which earnings are zero.

EXHIBIT 5.4   Price-Earnings Ratio for the S&P Composite Index, 1881–2005

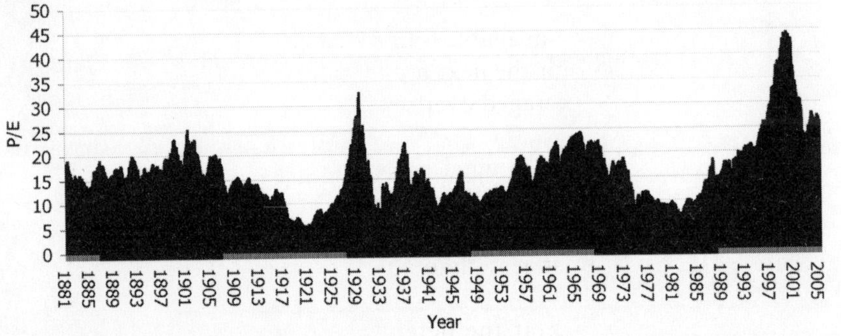

Source of data: Updated data from Robert J. Shiller's website, http://aida.econ.yale.edu/
~shiller/data.htm.

and the earnings yield is

$$\text{Earnings yield} = \frac{\$0.80}{\$17.00} = 4.71\%$$

If the market value of the stock represents today's forecast of future
earnings to common shareholders and if current earnings are an indica-
tion of future earnings, this ratio tells us that each dollar of earnings
represents $21.25 of value today.

P/E ratios vary over time for the S&P 500, typically ranging from 8 to
20 times, averaging around 14.2 times, though in recent years the P/E has
gone out of these bounds, reaching up towards record-breaking highs
toward 45 times, as we show using Robert Shiller's data in Exhibit 5.4.[17]

An interesting issue arises in deciding the appropriate inputs to this
ratio. The numerator is rather straightforward: use a recent market
price per share. The denominator presents a number of issues. Aside
from the issue of whether the denominator is the basic or diluted earnings per share, an important issue is over what period to measure earnings per share. At any point in time, the most recently ending annual
period or quarter's earnings may not usually available. Further muddying the waters is whether the P/E ratio should be measured over an historical period (backward-looking) or measured using forecasted earnings

---

[17] See also John Y. Campbell and Robert J. Shiller, "Valuation Ratios and the Long-
Run Stock Market Outlook," *Journal of Portfolio Management* (Winter 1998), p.
11.

(forward-looking). So what is the analyst to do? There are several approaches that are used:

- The sum of the latest available four reported quarters.
- Estimated earnings for the next fiscal year.
- Earning per share averaged over several historical, annual periods.

The first approach results in what is referred to as the trailing P/E ratio. The second approach is referred to as the forward P/E ratio. The latter method is suggested by Graham and Dodd and uses an EPS that is the average of EPS for "not less than five years, preferably seven or ten years."[18]

Taking a closer look at the determinant of P/E ratios, we see that this ratio is related to a number of fundamental factors:

Factor	Relationship with P/E
EPS growth	+
Stability of earnings growth	+
Earnings quality	+
Dividend payout	−
Financial leverage	−
Market capitalization	−
P/E ratio of similar stocks	+
P/E ratio of the market	+
Level of interest rates	−
Inflation	−

As pointed out by Eugene Fama and Kenneth French in their study of the relation between stock returns and fundamental factors, E/P (or its inverse P/E) includes the stock price in its construction and hence should be correlated with stock returns.[19] This has been supported in research that finds that E/P is one of the factors that explains stock returns.[20]

---

[18] Benjamin Graham and David L. Dodd, *Security Analysis*, 1st ed. (New York: McGraw-Hill) 1934, p. 452.

[19] Eugene F. Fama and Kenneth R. French. "The Cross-Section of Expected Stock Returns," *Journal of Finance* 47, no. 2 (June 1992), pp. 427–465.

[20] See, as an example, Sanjoy Basu, "The Relationship Between Earnings Yield, Market Value, and Return for NYSE Common Stocks: Further Evidence," *Journal of Financial Economics* 12, no. 1 (1983), pp. 129–156.

DIVIDENDS

Dividends are cash payments made by a corporation to its owners. Though cash dividends are paid to both preferred and common shareholders, most of the focus of the attention is on the dividends paid to the residual owners of the corporation, the common shareholders. Dividends paid to common and preferred shareholders are not legal obligations of a corporation and some corporations do not pay cash dividends.

Dividends are evaluated using three different measures:

- Dividends per share
- Dividend yield
- Dividend payout

For those companies that pay dividends, changes in dividends are noticed by investors: Increases in dividends are viewed favorably and are associated with increases in the company's stock price, whereas decreases in dividends are viewed quite unfavorable and are associated with decreases in the company's stock price.

Researchers have found a strong relation between changes in dividends and share prices, and also between dividend yields and stock prices.[21] Researchers have also found a strong relation in the aggregate between dividend payouts and earnings growth: the higher the payout—and hence the positive signal provided by the company's management—the greater the future earning growth.[22]

In this section, we look at these three measures of dividends: dividends per share, dividend yield, and dividend payout. Following our discussion of the different measures, we take a look at how dividends and stock prices are related, including a discussion of the dividend valuation model that provides the theoretical link between future dividends and current stock prices.

Dividends per Share

The value of a share of stock today is the investors' assessment of today's worth of future cash flows for each share. Because future cash flows to shareholders are dividends, we need a measure of dividends for each share of stock to estimate future cash flows per share. The *divi-*

---

[21] Jonathan Lewellen, "Predicting Returns with Financial Ratios," *Journal of Financial Economics* 74, no. 2 (November 2004) pp. 209–235.

[22] Robert D. Arnott and Clifford S. Asness, "Surprise! Higher Dividends = Higher Earnings Growth," *Financial Analysts Journal* 59, no. 1 (January/February 2003), pp. 70–87.

dends per share (DPS) is the dollar amount of dividends paid out during the period per share of common stock:

$$\text{Dividends per share} = \frac{\text{Dividends}}{\text{Number of shares outstanding}}$$

If a company has paid $600,000 in dividends during the period and 1.5 million shares outstanding, then

$$\text{Dividends per share} = \frac{\$600,000}{1,500,000} = \$0.40 \text{ per share}$$

The company paid out 40 cents in dividends per common share during this period.

There is no requirement that companies pay cash dividends. We observe, however, that many companies do pay cash dividends and, once they pay dividends only reluctantly (in cases of financial distress) lower or eliminate cash dividends. It is often the case, however, that companies that are relatively young, fast-growing companies do not pay dividends; as the companies mature they begin to pay dividends. Companies in high-growth industries tend to pay little or no dividends.

Dividend Yield

Another measure is the *dividend yield*, which is the ratio of dividends to price:

$$\text{Dividend yield} = \frac{\text{Annual cash dividends per share}}{\text{Market price per share}}$$

Historically, the dividend yield for U.S. stocks was 4.73%, but more recently the average dividend yield has dropped to around 1.6%, as you can see in Exhibit 5.5.[23]

In an exhaustive study of the relation between dividend yield and stock prices, John Campbell and Robert Shiller find that:

■ There is a weak relation between the dividend yield and subsequent 10-year dividend growth.
■ The dividend yield does not forecast future dividend growth.
■ The dividend yield predicts future price changes.

---

[23] See Campbell and Shiller, "Valuation Ratios and the Long-Run Stock Market Outlook," p. 11.

EXHIBIT 5.5   Dividend Yields

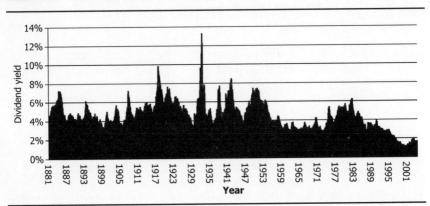

Source of data: Updated data from Robert J. Shiller's website, http://aida.econ.yale.edu/
~shiller/data.htm.

The weak relation between the current dividend yield and future
dividends may be attributed to the effects of the business cycle on dividend growth. The tendency for the dividend yield to revert to its historical mean has been observed by researchers.[24]

Dividend Payout

Another way of describing dividends paid out during a period is to state
the dividends as a portion of earnings for the period. This is referred to
as the *dividend payout ratio*:

$$\text{Dividend payout ratio} = \frac{\text{Dividends}}{\text{Earnings available to common shareholders}}$$

The complement of this ratio is the *plowback ratio*, which is the
ratio of retained earnings to earnings:

$$\text{Plowback ratio} = \frac{\text{Earnings} - \text{Dividends}}{\text{Earnings available to common shareholders}}$$

If a company pays $360,000 in dividends and has earnings of $1.2 million, the payout ratio is 30% and the plowback ratio is 70%:

---

[24] See Campbell and Shiller, "Valuation Ratios and the Long-Run Stock Market Outlook."

$$\text{Dividend payout ratio} = \frac{\$360,000}{\$1,200,000} = 0.30 \text{ or } 30\%$$

This means that the company paid out 30% of its earnings to shareholders.

The proportion of earnings paid out in dividends varies by company and industry. For example, the companies in the railroad industry typically pay out 20% of their earnings in dividends, whereas the utility companies typically pay out approximately 60% of their earnings in dividends.

If companies focus on dividends per share in establishing their dividends (e.g., a constant dividends per share), the dividend payout will fluctuate along with earnings. We generally observe that a company sets its dividend policy such that dividends per share grow at a relatively constant rate, resulting in dividend payouts that fluctuate. Consider an example of Abbott Laboratories, illustrated in Exhibit 5.6. Abbott Laboratories' dividends per share have been increasing at a relatively constant rate, as indicated by an upward-sloping curve, yet its dividend payout fluctuates within the range of 40% to 50% in the more recent years.

EXHIBIT 5.6 Abbott Laboratories' Dividends per Share and Dividend Payout, 1982–2004

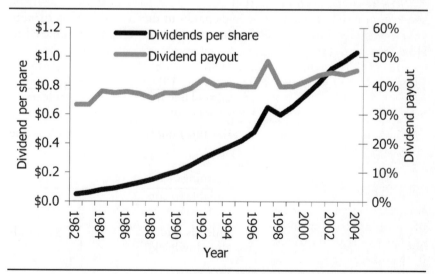

Source of dividend and earnings data: The Value Line Investment Survey, various issues.

Dividends and Stock Prices

If an investor buys a common stock, they have bought shares that represent an ownership interest in the corporation. Shares of common stock are a perpetual security—there is no maturity. The investor who owns shares of common stock has the right to receive a certain portion of any dividends—but dividends are *not* a sure thing. Whether a firm will pay dividends is up to its board of directors—the representatives of the common shareholders. Typically we see some pattern in the dividends companies pay: dividends per share are either constant or grow at a constant rate. But there is no guarantee that dividends will be paid in the future.

Preferred shareholders are in a similar situation as the common shareholders. They expect to receive cash dividends in the future, but the payment of these dividends is up to the board of directors. But there are three major differences between the dividends of preferred and common shares. First, the dividends on preferred stock usually are specified at a fixed rate or dollar amount, whereas the amount of dividends is not specified for common shares. Second, preferred shareholders are given preference: their dividends must be paid before any dividends are paid on common stock. Third, if the preferred stock has a *cumulative feature*, dividends not paid in one period accumulate and are carried over to the next period. Therefore, the dividends on preferred stock are more certain than those on common shares.

It is reasonable to figure that what an investor pays for a share of stock should reflect what he or she expects to receive from it—return on your investment. What you receive are cash dividends in the future. How can we relate that return to what a share of common stock is worth? Well, the value of a share of stock should be equal to the present value of all the future cash flows you expect to receive from that share:

$$\text{Price of share of stock} = \frac{\text{Dividends in the first period}}{(1 + \text{Discount rate})^1}$$
$$+ \frac{\text{Dividends in the second period}}{(1 + \text{Discount rate})^1} + \cdots$$

Because common stock never matures, today's value is the present value of an infinite stream of cash flows. And also, common stock dividends are not fixed, as in the case of preferred stock. Not knowing the amount of the dividends—or even if there will be future dividends—makes it difficult to determine the value of common stock.

So what are we to do? Well, we can grapple with the valuation of common stock by looking at its current dividend and making assumptions about any future dividends the company may pay.

The Dividend Valuation Model

If dividends are constant forever, the value of a share of stock is the present value of the dividends per share per period, in perpetuity. Let D represent the constant dividend per share of common stock expected next period and each period thereafter, forever, P_0 represent the price of a share of stock today, and r_e the required rate of return on common stock. The *required rate of return* is the return shareholders demand to compensate them for the time value of money tied up in their investment and the uncertainty of the future cash flows from these investments.

The current price of a share of common stock, P_0, is

$$P_0 = \frac{D}{(1 + r_e)^1} + \frac{D}{(1 + r_e)^2} + \cdots + \frac{D}{(1 + r_e)^{\yen}}$$

which we can write using summation notation,

$$P_0 = \sum_{t=1}^{\yen} \frac{D}{(1 + r_e)^t}$$

The summation of a constant amount discounted from perpetuity simplifies to

$$P_0 = \frac{D}{r_e}$$

If the current dividend is \$2 per share and the required rate of return is 10%, the value of a share of stock is

$$P_0 = \frac{\$2}{0.10} = \$20$$

Therefore, if you pay \$20 per share and dividends remain constant at \$2 per share, you will earn a 10% return per year on your investment every year. But dividends on common stock often change through time.

If dividends grow at a constant rate, the value of a share of stock is the present value of a *growing* cash flow. Let D_0 indicate *this* period's dividend. If dividends grow at a constant rate, g, forever, the present value of the common stock is the present value of all *future* dividends:

$$P_0 = \frac{D_0(1+g)^1}{(1+r_e)^1} + \frac{D_0(1+g)^2}{(1+r_e)^2} + \cdots + \frac{D_0(1+g)^{\yen}}{(1+r_e)^{\yen}}$$

Pulling today's dividend D_0, from each term,

$$P_0 = D_0\left(\frac{(1+g)^1}{(1+r_e)^1} + \frac{(1+g)^2}{(1+r_e)^2} + \cdots + \frac{(1+g)^{\yen}}{(1+r_e)^{\yen}}\right)$$

Using summation notation:

$$P_0 = D_0 \sum_{t=1}^{\yen} \frac{(1+g)^t}{(1+r_e)^t}$$

Because

$$\sum_{t=1}^{\infty} \frac{(1+g)^t}{(1+r_e)^t}$$

is approximately equal to[25]

$$\left(\frac{1+g}{r_e-g}\right)$$

$$P_0 = D_0\left(\frac{1+g}{r_e-g}\right)$$

---

[25] Our use of the term

$$\left(\frac{1+g}{r_e-g}\right)$$

to approximate for

$$\sum_{t=1}^{\infty} \frac{(1+g)^t}{(1+r_e)^t}$$

is based on integration of the latter term.

If we represent the next period's dividend, D_1, in terms of this period's dividend, D_0, compounded one period at the rate g,

$$D_1 = D_0(1 + g) \text{ or } D_0 = \left(\frac{D_1}{1+g}\right)$$

and substitute for D_0,

$$P_0 = D_0\left(\frac{1+g}{r_e-g}\right) = \left(\frac{D_1}{1+g}\right)\left(\frac{1+g}{r_e-g}\right)$$

then

$$P_0 = \left(\frac{D_1}{r_e-g}\right)$$

This equation is referred to as the *dividend valuation model* (DVM).[26]

Consider a firm expected to pay a constant dividend of $2 per share, forever. If this dividend is capitalized at 10%, the value of a share is $20:

$$P_0 = \frac{\$2}{0.10} = \$20$$

If, on the other hand, the dividends are expected to be $2 in the *next* period and grow at a rate of 6% per year, forever, the value of a share of stock is $50:

$$P_0 = \frac{\$2}{(0.10 - 0.06)} = \$50$$

---

[26] The dividend valuation model is attributed to Myron Gordon, who popularized the constant growth model. A more formal presentation of this model can be found in Myron Gordon, "Dividends, Earnings and Stock Prices," *Review of Economics and Statistics* (May 1959), pp. 99–105 and his book *The Investment Financing and Valuation of the Corporation* (Homewood, IL: Richard D. Irwin, 1962). However, the foundation of common stock valuation is laid out—for both constant and growing dividends—in Chapters 5, 6, and 7 of John Burr Williams, *The Theory of Investment Value* (Amsterdam: North-Holland Publishing Company, 1938).

Does this make sense? Yes: if dividends are expected to grow in the future, the stock is worth more than if the dividends are expected to remain the same.

If today's value of a share is $50, what are we saying about the value of the stock next year? If we move everything up one period, D_1 is no longer $2, but $2 grown one period at 6%, or $2.12. Therefore, we expect the price of the stock at the end of one year, P_1, to be $53:

$$P_1 = \frac{\$2}{(0.10 - 0.06)} = \$53$$

At the end of two years, the price will be even larger:

$$P_2 = \frac{\$2.12}{(0.10 - 0.06)} = \$56.18$$

Because we expect dividends to grow each period, we also are expecting the price of the stock to grow through time as well. In fact, the price is expected to grow at the same rate as the dividends: 6% per period.

What if the dividends are expected to decline each year? That is, what if g is negative? We can still use the dividend valuation model, but each dividend in the future is expected to be *less* than the one before it. For example, suppose a stock has a current dividend of $5 per share and the required rate of return is 10%. If dividends are expected to decline 3% each year, what is the value of a share of stock today? We know that $D_0 = \$5$, $r_e = 10\%$, and $g = -3\%$. Therefore,

$$P_0 = \frac{\$5.00(1 - 0.03)}{0.10 + 0.03} = \frac{\$4.85}{0.13} = \$37.31$$

Next period's dividend, D_1, is expected to be $4.85. We capitalize this at 13%: 10% − (−3%) or 10% + 3%. What do we expect the price of the stock to be next period?

$$P_1 = \frac{\$5.00(1 - 0.03)^2}{0.13} = \frac{\$4.70}{0.13} = \$36.19$$

The expected price goes the same way as the dividend: down 3% each year.

We illustrate the relation between the growth rate of dividends, g, and the price of the stock expected in the future in Exhibit 5.7. For a given required rate of return and dividend—in this case $r_e = 10\%$ and

EXHIBIT 5.7   Price of a Share of Stock in the Future for Different Rates of Growth in Future Dividends

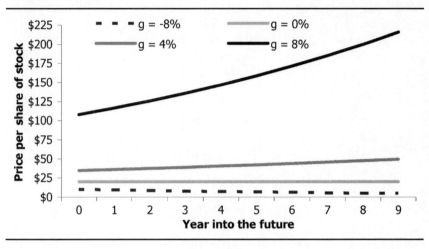

D_1 = \$2—we see that the price of a share of stock is expected to grow each period at the rate g.

Let's look at another situation, one in which growth is expected to *change* but at different growth rates as time goes on. Consider a share of common stock whose dividend is currently \$3.00 per share and is expected to grow at a rate of 8% per year for five years and afterward at a rate of 2% per year after five years. To tackle this problem, break it into two manageable parts: the first five years and after five years, or

$$P_0 = \underbrace{\frac{D_1}{(1+0.10)^1} + \frac{D_2}{(1+0.10)^2} + \frac{D_3}{(1+0.10)^3} + \frac{D_4}{(1+0.10)^4} + \frac{D_5}{(1+0.10)^5}}_{\text{Dividends growing at 8\%}}$$

$$\underbrace{+ \frac{D_6}{(1+0.10)^6} + \frac{D_7}{(1+0.10)^7} + \cdots + \frac{D_\infty}{(1+0.10)^\infty}}_{\text{Dividends growing at 2\%}}$$

The present value of the dividends in the first five years is

$$\begin{array}{rl} \text{Present value of dividends} & = \dfrac{\$3.24}{1.10} + \dfrac{\$3.50}{1.21} + \dfrac{\$3.78}{1.331} + \dfrac{\$4.08}{1.4641} + \dfrac{\$4.41}{1.6105} \\ \text{in the first five years} & \\ & = \$14.17 \end{array}$$

The present value of dividends received after the fifth year—evaluated five years from today—is the expected price of the stock in five years, P_5:

$$P_5 = \frac{D_6}{0.10 - 0.02} = \frac{D_5(1 + 0.03)}{0.10 - 0.02} = \frac{\$3.00(1 + 0.08)^5(1 + 0.02)}{0.10 - 0.02}$$

$$= \frac{\$4.41(1 + 0.02)}{0.10 - 0.02} = \frac{\$4.4982}{0.08} = \$56.23$$

The price expected at the end of five years is $56.23, which we translate into a value today by discounting it five periods at 10%:

$$\text{Present value of dividends after the first five years to infinity} = \frac{P_5}{(1 + 0.10)^5} = \frac{\$56.23}{(1 + 0.10)^5} = \$34.91$$

Putting the pieces together:

$$P_0 = \text{Present value of dividends received during first five years} + \text{Present value of all dividends received after the fifth year}$$
$$P_0 = \$14.17 + \$34.91 = \$49.08$$

The value of a share of this stock is $49.08. We can see the growth in the expected price of a share of stock in Exhibit 5.8, where the dividends grows at a rate of 8% the first five years and 2% after the fifth year.

EXHIBIT 5.8   Price and Dividends per Share for the Case of 8% Growth in Dividends for the First Five Years, 2% Thereafter

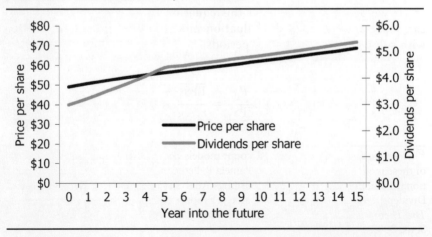

The dividend valuation model makes some sense regarding the relation between the value of a share of stock, the growth in dividends, and the discount rate:

- The greater the current dividend, the greater the value of a share of stock
- The greater the expected growth in dividends, the greater the value of a share of stock
- The more uncertainty regarding future dividends, the greater the discount rate and the lower the value of a share of stock

However, the DVM has some drawbacks. How do you deal with dividends that do not grow at a constant rate? As you can see in our example, this model does not accommodate nonconstant growth easily. What if the firm does not currently pay dividends? In that case, D_0 would be zero and the expected price would be zero—but a zero price for a share of stock does not make any sense! Therefore, the DVM may be appropriate to use to value the stock of companies with stable dividend policies, but it is not applicable for all companies.[27]

The DVM and PE

We can represent the dividend valuation model in terms of a share's P/E ratio. Let us start with the dividend valuation model with constant growth in dividends:

$$P_0 = \frac{D_1}{r_e - g}$$

If we divide both sides of this equation by earnings per share, we can represent the dividend valuation model in terms of the P/E ratio, with subscripts denoting time periods:

$$\frac{P_0}{\text{EPS}_1} = \frac{\dfrac{D_1}{\text{EPS}_1}}{r_e - g}$$

---

[27] More sophisticated dividend discount models have been developed. For a review of these models, see Chapter 11 in Pamela P. Peterson and Frank J. Fabozzi, "Traditional Fundamental Analysis III: Earnings Analysis, Cash Analysis, Dividends, and Dividend Discount Models," in Frank J. Fabozzi and Harry M. Markowitz (eds.), *The Theory and Practice of Investment Management* (Hoboken, NJ: John Wiley & Sons, 2002).

or

$$\text{Price-earnings ratio} = \frac{\text{Dividend payout ratio}}{r_e - g}$$

This tells us the P/E ratio is influenced by the dividend payout ratio, the required rate of return on equity, and the expected growth rate of dividends.

OTHER FUNDAMENTALS

Aside from the earnings for a given period, we may also be interested in knowing about how much common equity each share has. One measure of this investment is the book value of equity per share, also referred to as the *book value per share*:

$$\text{Book value of equity per share} = \frac{\text{Book value of shareholders' equity}}{\text{Number of shares outstanding}}$$

For General Electric in 2004,

$$\text{Book value of equity per share} = \frac{\$110,284 \text{ million}}{10,586 \text{ million shares}}$$

$$= \$10.418 \text{ per share}$$

In accounting terms, each common share has a shareholders' equity of $10.418.

The book value of equity may differ from the market value. The market value per share, if available, is a much better indicator of the investment of shareholders in the firm. The market value of a share of General Electric common stock was $36.05 at the end of 2004, which is substantially greater than the book value of $10.418 per share. This large difference between market and book values of equity is not unique to General Electric.

And the book value of equity could actually be negative, as we can see in Exhibit 5.9 for Rite Aid Corporation. Book value of equity (i.e., total shareholders' deficit) is negative, in large part because of the accumulated deficit. But does the negative value of equity means that Rite Aid common stock is worthless? Not at all—at the end of 2000, Rite Aid's market value of its outstanding equity is over $400 million.[28]

---

[28] There were over 135 million shares outstanding at the end of 2000, with a market value around $3 per share.

EXHIBIT 5.9   Rite Aid's Book Value of Shareholders' Equity, 1986–2004

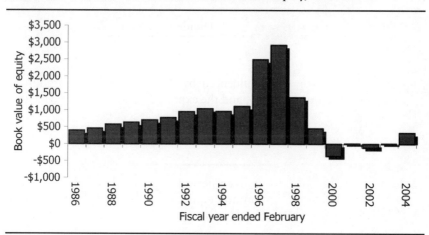

Source of data: Rite Aid's 10-K filings, various years.

BOOK-TO-MARKET RATIO

Many researchers observe that the ratio of the book value of equity to the market value of equity, BV/MV, is related to security returns: higher BV/MVs are associated with higher future returns.[29,30] The ratio is therefore:

---

[29] See, for example, Barr Rosenberg, Kenneth Reid, and Ronald Lanstein, "Persuasive Evidence of Market Inefficiency," *Journal of Portfolio Management* 11 (1985), pp. 9–17; Louis Chan, Y. Hamao, and Josef Lakonishok, "Fundamentals and Stock Returns in Japan," *Journal of Finance* 46 (1991), pp. 1739–1764; Fama and French, "The Cross-Section of Expected Stock Returns"; Eugene F. Fama and Kenneth R. French, "Size and Book-to-Market Factors in Earnings and Returns," *Journal of Finance* 50, no. 1 (March 1995), pp. 131–155; and, Robert S. Harris and Felica V. Marston, "Value versus Growth Stocks: Book-to-Market, Growth, and Beta," *Financial Analysts Journal* 50, no. 5 (September/October 1994), pp. 18–24.

[30] The relation between the market value of equity and the book value of equity is used by some in the form of MV/BV and by others in the form of the inverse, BV/MV. We use the form MV/BV to simplify the interpretation of the analysis and comparison with other performance measures: higher is better. This does not mean that higher MV/BV companies will outperform lower MV/BV companies in the future. Evidence seems to indicate that high MV/BV companies ("growth" companies) will underperform low MV/BV companies ("value" companies) in the future.

$$BV/MV = \frac{\text{Book value of shareholders' equity}}{\text{Market value of shareholders' equity}}$$

$$= \frac{\text{Book value per share}}{\text{Market value per share}}$$

In the case of the Coca-Cola Company, at the end of 2004 the BV/MV ratio was

$$BV/MV = \frac{\$6.61}{\$41.11} = 0.161$$

The relation between the book and market values of equity are sometimes reported as the inverse of the BV/MV,

$$MV/BV = \frac{\$41.11}{\$6.61} = 6.216$$

This tells us that for every $1 of book value of Coca-Cola, the market values it more than 6 times. We can see in Exhibit 5.10 for Coca-Cola that the variation in BV/MV or MV/BV ratios is due primarily to the changing market value of equity.

In studies of the relation between stock returns and fundamentals, Eugene Fama and French find that BV/MV and firm size (that is, equity

EXHIBIT 5.10   Book Value and Market Value per Share for Coca-Cola, 1990–2004

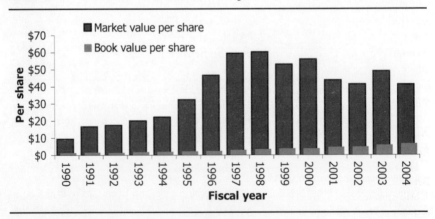

Source: Yahoo! Finance and 10-K filings of Coca-Cola.

EXHIBIT 5.11   Sorting Out the Book and Market Relationship

A . . .	also known as a . . .	is considered a	and evidence suggests that it may
high book-to-market ratio	low market-to-book ratio	value stock	outperform the market
low book-to-market ratio	high market-to-book ratio	growth stock	underperform the market

capitalization) explain cross-sectional security returns.[31] Further, they find that BV/MV explains security returns better than both beta (a measure of a stock's systematic risk) and size, where high BV/MV companies have higher returns.

Just why the book-to-market equity ratio explains security returns is not known since there is little theoretical justification for this ratio to influence returns. There are several explanations for the role of BV/MV in affecting returns. One explanation is that BV/MV is a proxy for risk: the greater the firm's BV/MV, the greater the risk of that firm's security. This explanation is consistent with efficient market theory and Fama and French's evidence if BV/MV is considered a risk factor and is therefore priced accordingly.

Another explanation for the book-to-market's relation to security returns is that it proxies for future growth: the greater the BV/MV (or, equivalently, the lower is MV/BV), the lower the firm's expected future growth prospects. This explanation is supported by other research.[32,33] Given this latter explanation, the ratio is a measure of the value-added by the firm's management: the lower the BV/MV ratio, and hence the higher the value of the MV/BV ratio, the better the firm is managing its assets to generate future value for the firm that is reflected in the current price.

It has been argued that BV/MV represents, in part, the growth options that a company has: the greater the growth options, the lower

---

[31] Fama and French, "The Cross-Section of Expected Stock Returns" and "Size and Book-to-Market Factors in Earnings and Returns."

[32] Harris and Marston, "Value versus Growth Stocks: Book-to-Market, Growth, and Beta."

[33] Still another explanation is that high BV/MV securities are underpriced; hence subsequent returns are higher for high-BV/MV stocks. However, this explanation is sufficient only if the market is inefficient. This explanation is not supported by Harris and Marston ("Value versus Growth Stocks: Book-to-Market, Growth, and Beta"), among others.

the BV/MV.[34] Related to this explanation is the hypothesis offered by Robert Haugen: the market consistently overestimates the persistence of above average future growth, which may explain why low BV/MV companies at times under–perform high BV/MV companies.[35] Or, in other words, high BV/MV companies are undervalued.

SUMMARY

Earnings are used in the valuation of stock because of the close relation that has been observed between earnings and stock prices. There are many definitions of earnings, with the appropriate definition being dependent on the particular use of earnings in the analysis.

One measure of earnings is net income, but the experience of the recent past in terms of financial reporting has taught us to be cautious of interpreting this measure. Core earnings, which adjusts for the most likely managed items in earnings, is an attempt to produce an earnings measure that is not as manageable as net income. A related measure of earnings is earnings per share (EPS). Complications arise in its calculation not only because of the definition of earnings, but in the determination of the number of shares of stock outstanding.

The relation between earnings and stock prices is often summarized using the price-to-earnings ratio (P/E), or it's inverse, the earnings yield (E/P). Calculation of the P/E or E/P is complicated by the issue of what earnings per share amount to use—historical, current, or expected.

The cash flows that are valued in a share's price are the company's future dividends. We measure dividends in a number of ways, including as dividends per share, the dividend yield, and the dividend payout

---

[34] Jonathan B. Berk, Richard C. Green, and Vasant Naik, "Optimal Investment, Growth Options, and Security Returns," *Journal of Finance* 54, no. 5 (October 1999), pp. 1553–1607. This is consistent with the evidence by Baruch Lev and Theodore Sougiannis that low book-to-market companies tend to have a greater investment in research and development in their article "Penetrating the Book-to-Market Black Box: The R&D Effect," *Journal of Business Finance & Accounting* 26, nos. 3-4 (May 1999), pp. 419–449.

[35] Robert A. Haugen, *The New Finance: The Case Against Efficient Markets* (Englewood Cliffs, NJ: Prentice-Hall). This argument is support by research by Joseph Lakonishok, Andrei Shleifer and Robert W. Vishny, "Contrarian Investment, Extrapolation, and Risk," *Journal of Finance* 49, no. 5 (December 1994), pp. 17–35, who observe that the earnings growth rates tend to converge for high BV/MV and low BV/MV securities, and that the market tends to overextrapolate earnings growth.

ratio. Dividends and stock prices are both related in theory. The dividend valuation model expresses the current stock price as a function of future dividends. This model can be applied to cases of constant dividends, dividends growing at a constant rate, and dividends growing at rates that change over time.

Other fundamental measures of a company's performance include the book value per share and the book-to market ratio. The book-to-market ratio (BV/MV) relates the accounting value of equity to the market's value of equity.

CHAPTER 6

Cash Flow Analysis

An objective of financial analysis is to assess a company's operating performance and financial condition. The information that an analyst has available includes economic, market, and financial information. Some of the most important financial data is provided by the company in its annual and quarterly financial statements. However, the choices available in the accrual accounting system make it difficult to compare companies' performance. These choices also provide the opportunity for the management of financial numbers through judicious choice of accounting methods. For example, $1 of net income for one company may not be equivalent to $1 of net income of another company.

Cash flows provide the financial analyst with a way of transforming net income based on an accrual system to a more comparable medium. Additionally, cash flows are essential ingredients in valuation: the value of a company today is the present value of its expected future cash flows. Therefore, understanding past and current cash flows may help the analyst in forecasting future cash flows and, hence determine the value of the company.

DIFFICULTIES WITH MEASURING CASH FLOW

The primary difficulty with measuring a cash flow is that it is a flow: Cash flows into the company (cash inflows) and cash flows out of the company (cash outflows). At any point in time there is a stock of cash on hand, but the stock of cash on hand varies among companies because of the size of the company, the cash demands of the business, and a company's management of working capital.

So what is cash flow? Is it the total amount of cash flowing into the company during a period? Is it the total amount of cash flowing out of

the company during a period? Is it the net of the cash inflows and outflows for a period? Well, there is no specific definition of cash flow—and
that is probably why there is so much confusion regarding the measurement of cash flow. Ideally, the analyst needs a measure of the company's
operating performance that is comparable among companies—something other than net income (e.g., net cash flow).

A simple, yet crude method of calculating cash flow requires adding
noncash expenses (e.g., depreciation) to the reported net income amount
to arrive at an approximation of cash flow, *earnings before depreciation
and amortization*, or EBDA. For example, the EBDA for J. C. Penney
Company, Inc., for 2004, is[1]

$$
\begin{aligned}
\text{EBDA} &= \text{Net income} &+& \text{ Depreciation and amortization} \\
&= \$524 \text{ million} &+& \text{ 368 million} \\
&= \$892 \text{ million}
\end{aligned}
$$

This amount is not really a cash flow, but simply earnings before depreciation and amortization. Is this estimate useful in analysis? Though not a
cash flow, EBDA does allow a quick comparison of income across firms
that may use different depreciation methods and depreciable lives.[2]

The problem with this measure is that it ignores the many other
sources and uses of cash during the period. Consider the sale of goods for
credit. This transaction generates sales for the period. Sales and the
accompanying cost of goods sold are reflected in the period's net income
and EBDA. However, until the account receivable is collected there is no
cash from this transaction. If collection does not occur until the next
period, there is a misalignment of the income and cash flow arising from
this transaction. Additionally, there are noncash items that affect net
income, but which are not cash inflows or outflows. For example, in 2004
J. C. Penney had stock based compensation of $23 million in 2004, which
was deducted to arrive at net income, but which is not a cash outflow for
the period. Therefore, the simple estimated cash flow ignores some cash
flows that, for many companies, are significant.

Another estimate of cash flow that is simple to calculate is *earnings
before interest, taxes, depreciation, and amortization* (EBITDA). We

---

[1] You can find the depreciation and amortization figure on the company's Statement
of Cash Flows.
[2] An example of the use of this estimate of cash flow, *The Value Line Investment Survey*, published by Value Line, Inc., reports a cash flow per share amount, calculated
as reported earnings, plus depreciation, minus any preferred dividends, stated per
share of common stock [*Guide to Using the Value Line Investment Survey* (New
York: Value Line, Inc.), p. 19, available at http://www.valueline.com].

calculate EBITDA by starting with operating income (that is, earning before interest and taxes or EBIT), and add back any interest expense. For J. C. Penney, EBITDA in 2004, in millions, is

Income from continuing operations before income taxes	$1,020
Add: interest expense	233
Add: depreciation and amortization	368
EBITDA	$1,621

EBITDA is useful not only for its simplicity, but because it allows us to compare companies based on operations, without considering how companies choose to finance their assets. In analyzing companies in industries that require heavy capital investments, such as telecommunications, EBITDA may give a better measure of performance than, say, net income because the large depreciation expenses do not affect EBITDA.

However, EBITDA suffers from the accrual-accounting bias in EBITDA, which may result in the omission of significant cash flows. Additionally, EBITDA is before interest and taxes, which may also be substantial cash outflows for some companies.[3,4]

These two rough estimates of cash flows—EBDA and EBITDA—are used in practice not only for their simplicity, but because they experienced widespread use prior to the disclosure of more detailed information in the statement of cash flows. Currently, the measures of cash flow are wide ranging, including these simplistic cash flows measures, measures developed from the statement of cash flows, and measures that seek to capture the theoretical concept of "free cash flow."

CASH FLOWS AND THE STATEMENT OF CASH FLOWS

Prior to the adoption of the statement of cash flows, the information regarding cash flows was quite limited. The first statement that addressed

---

[3] For a more detailed discussion of the EBITDA measure and its limitations, see Kent Eastman, "EBITDA: An Overrated Tool for Cash Flow Analysis," *Commercial Lending Review* 12, no. 2 (Spring 1997), p. 64; and Pamela M. Stumpp, "Critical Failings of EBITDA as a Cash Flow Measure," Chapter 6 in Frank J. Fabozzi (ed.), *Bond Credit Analysis: Framework and Case Studies* (Hoboken, NJ: John Wiley & Sons, 2001).

[4] EBITDA, in fact, became popular in company discussion of earnings by Internet companies in the late 1990s and early 2000s because EBITDA does not reflect the substantial interest expense and amortization that they experienced, thus providing a rosier financial picture than net income or cash flow from operations. There is no standard for calculating EBITDA, so investors should be cautious in interpreting companies' reports of EBITDA, as they would with any pro forma earnings value.

the issue of cash flows was the AICPA Statement of Financial Position, which was required beginning in 1971.[5] This statement was quite limited, requiring an analysis of the sources and uses of funds using one of a variety of formats. In its earlier years of adoption, most companies provided this information using what is referred to as the working capital concept—a presentation of working capital provided and applied during the period. Over time, many companies began presenting this information using the cash concept, which is a more detailed presentation of the cash flows provided by operations, investing, and financing activities.[6]

Consistent with the cash concept format of the funds flow statement, the statement of cash flows is now a required financial statement.[7] As discussed in Chapter 2, this statement requires the company to classify cash flows into three categories based on the activity: operating, investing, and financing. Cash flows are summarized by activity and within activity by type (e.g., asset dispositions are reported separately from asset acquisitions).

The reporting company may report the cash flows from operating activities on the statement cash flows using either the *direct method*—reporting all cash inflows and outflows—or the *indirect method*—starting with net income and making adjustments for depreciation and other non-cash expenses and for changes in working capital accounts. The direct method provides more information about the sources of a company's cash flows. Though the direct method is recommended it is also the most burdensome for the reporting company to prepare.[8] As a result, most companies report cash flows from operations using the indirect method.[9]

---

[5] *APB Opinion No. 19*, "Reporting Changes in Financial Position" (New York: AICPA, 1971). Prior to this APB, *APB Opinion No. 3* "The Statement of Source and Application of Funds" (New York: AICPA, 1963) encouraged, but did not require, companies to report a information regarding the changes in cash over a period (referred to as the *flow of funds*).

[6] This change in format generally followed the recommendations of the Financial Executives Institute and the Financial Accounting Standards Board recommendations [*FASB Discussion Memorandum*, "Conceptual Framework for Accounting and Reporting" (Stamford, CT: Financial Accounting Standards Board, 1974)].

[7] Statement of Financial Accounting Standards No. 95, "Statement of Cash Flows," (Stamford, CT: Financial Accounting Standards Board, 1987).

[8] As argued by O. Whitfield Broome, the direct method provides more useful information for the financial analyst. In addition to the reconciliation of net income and cash flow from

[9] Interestingly, a survey of CEOs, CFOs, and managers revealed that there are (1) some industries that tend to use one method versus the other; and (2) the indirect method may be preferred by users because of it is easier to understand. See Tantatape Brahmasrene, C. David Strupick, and Donna Whitten, "Examining Preferences in Cash Flow Statement Format," *The CPA Journal* (October 2004).

The indirect method produces a cash flow from operations that is similar to the estimated cash flow measure discussed previously, yet it encompasses the changes in working capital accounts that the simple measure does not. For example, J. C. Penney's cash flow from operating activities (taken from their 2004 statement of cash flows) is $1,127 million, which differs substantially from the cash flows we estimated earlier.

The classification of cash flows into the three types of activities provides useful information that can be used by the analyst to see, for example, whether the company is generating sufficient cash flows from operations to sustain its current rate of growth. However, the classification of particular items is not necessarily as useful as it could be. Consider some of the classifications:[10]

- Cash flows related to interest expense are classified in operations, though they are clearly financing cash flows.
- Income taxes are classified as operating cash flows, though taxes are affected by financing (e.g., deduction for interest expense paid on debt) and investment activities (e.g., the reduction of taxes from tax credits on investment activities).
- Interest income and dividends received are classified as operating cash flows, though these flows are a result of investment activities.

Whether these items have a significant affect on the analysis depends on the particular company's situation. J. C. Penney, for example, has very little interest and dividend income, and its interest expense of $280 million is not large relative to its earnings before interest and taxes of $1,300 million. Adjusting J. C. Penney's cash flows for the interest expense only (and related taxes) changes the complexion of its cash flows slightly to reflect greater cash flow generation from operations and less cash flow reliance on financing activities:[11]

	As reported (in millions)	As adjusted (in millions)
Cash flow from operations	$1,127	$1,309
Cash flow from (for) investing activities	4,288	4,288
Cash flow from (for) financing activities	(2,607)	(2,789)

---

[10] The International Financial Reporting Standards allow more flexibility with respect to the classification of these items, yet the U.S. generally accepted accounting principles do not yet permit such flexibility.

[11] The data source for the table is the J. C. Penney 2004 Annual Report. Note that the adjustment is for $280 million of interest and other financing costs, less its tax shield (the amount that the tax bill is reduced by the interest deduction) of $98 (estimated from the average tax rate of 35% of $280): adjustment = $280 (1 − 0.35) = $182.

For other companies, however, this adjustment may provide a different perspective on a company's cash flows. Consider Amazon.com's 2004 cash flows:[12]

	As reported (in millions)	As adjusted (in millions)
Cash flow from operations	$566.6	$645.6
Cash flow from (for) investing activities	(317.6)	(289.4)
Cash flow from (for) financing activities	(97.3)	(204.6)

The reclassification of interest income and interest expense offers a different picture of the cash outflows related to Amazon.com's investing and financing: less investment activity and less reliance on financing.

Looking at the relation among the three cash flows in the statement gives the analyst a sense of the activities of the company. A young, fast growing company may have negative cash flows from operations, yet positive cash flows from financing activities (i.e., operations may be financed to a large part with external financing). As a company grows, it may rely to a lesser extent on external financing.

The typical, mature company generates cash from operations and reinvests part or all of it back into the company. Therefore, cash flow related to operations in a healthy company is positive (i.e., a source of cash) and cash flow related to investing activities is negative (i.e., a use of cash). As a company matures, it may seek less financing externally and may even use cash to reduce its reliance on external financing (e.g., repay debts). We can classify companies on the basis of the pattern of their sources of cash flows, as shown in Exhibit 6.1. Though additional information is required to assess a company's financial performance and condition, examination of the sources of cash flows, especially over time, gives us a general idea of the company's operations.

Though we can classify a company based on the sources and uses of cash flows, more data are needed to put this information in perspective. What is the trend in the sources and uses of cash flows? What market, industry or company-specific events affect the company's cash flows? How does the company being analyzed compare with other companies in the same industry in terms of the sources and uses of funds?

Let us take a closer look at the incremental information provided by cash flows. Consider Wal-Mart Stores, Inc., which had growing sales

---

[12] The data source for the table is the Amazon.com, Inc., 2004 Annual Report. Note that Amazon.com, Inc., did not pay taxes in 2004 due to the substantial tax loss carryover applied in this year, so no adjustment was made to interest income and expense for taxes.

EXHIBIT 6.1 Patterns of Sources of Cash Flows

	Financing Growth Externally and Internally	Financing Growth Internally	Mature	Temporary Financial Downturn	Financial Distress	Downsizing
Cash flow: Operations	−	+	+	−	−	+
Cash flow: Investing activities	−	−	−	+	−	+
Cash flow: Financing activities	+	−	+ or −	+	−	−

EXHIBIT 6.2 Wal-Mart Stores Net Income and Revenues, 1990–2004

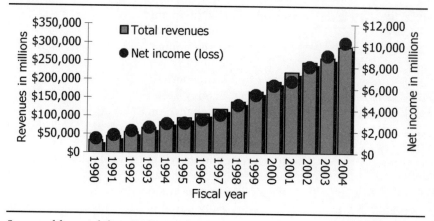

Source of financial data: Wal-Mart Stores, Inc., 10-K filings, various years.

and net income over the past 10 years, as summarized in Exhibit 6.2. We see that net income grew each year, with the exception of 1995, and that sales grew each year.

We get additional information about Wal-Mart by looking at the cash flow and their sources, as graphed in Exhibit 6.3. We see that the growth in Wal-Mart was supported by both internally generated funds and, to a lesser extent, through external financing. Wal-Mart's pattern of cash flows suggests that Wal-Mart is a mature company that has become less reliant on external financing in recent years, funding most of its growth in recent years with internally generated funds.

EXHIBIT 6.3   Wal-Mart Stores, Inc., Sources of Cash Flow, 1990–2004

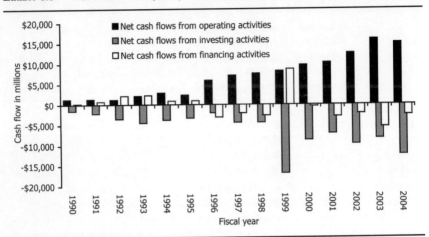

Source: Wal-Mart Stores, Inc., Annual Report, various years.

EXHIBIT 6.4   Amazon.com, Inc., Cash Flows, 1994–2004

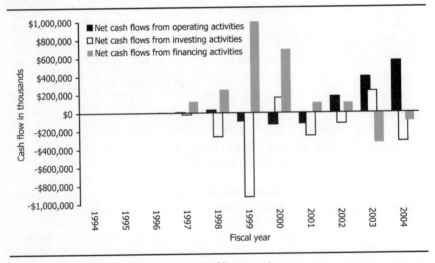

Source of data: Amazon.com, Inc., 10-K filings, various years.

We can see the typical pattern of a fast-growing company in the reported cash flow of Amazon.com, Inc., which we show in Exhibit 6.4. Here we see the company's cash flows from its origin in 1994 through high growth/heavy investment phase of 1994 to 2000 and into the period in which it is able to sustain itself primarily through cash flows from operations.

FREE CASH FLOW

Cash flows without any adjustment may be misleading because they do not reflect the cash outflows that are necessary for the future existence of a firm. An alternative measure, *free cash flow*, was developed by Michael Jensen in his theoretical analysis of agency costs and corporate take-overs.[13] In theory, free cash flow (FCF) is the cash flow left over after the company funds all positive net present value projects. Positive net present value projects are those projects (i.e., capital investments) for which the present value of expected future cash flows exceeds the present value of project outlays, all discounted at the cost of capital.[14] In other words, free cash flow is the cash flow of the firm, less capital expenditures necessary to stay in business (i.e., replacing facilities as necessary) and grow at the expected rate (which requires increases in working capital).

The perspective that we have taken in this definition of free cash flow is that of the shareholders: What is left for shareholders after the company makes necessary capital expenditures. That is why this definition of free cash flow is often referred to as *free cash flow to equity* or FCFE. We could take a broader perspective and consider the *free cash flow to the firm* (FCFF), which is FCFE with after-tax interest added.[15] FCFF therefore provides a measure of how much cash flow is available to all suppliers of capital—lenders and creditors. For J.C. Penney, the 2004 free cash flow for the firm is

	(in millions)
Cash flow from operations	$1,127
Deduct: Capital expenditures	412
Free cash flow to equity (FCFE)	$715
Add: After-tax interest [$280 (1 − 0.35)]	182
Free cash flow to the firm (FCFF)	$897

The theory of free cash flow was developed by Jensen to explain behaviors of companies that could not be explained by existing economic theories. Jensen observed that companies that generate free cash flow should

---

[13] Michael Jensen, "Agency Costs of Free Cash Flow, Corporate Finance, and Take-overs," *American Economic Review* 76, no. 2 (May 1986), pp. 323–329.

[14] The cost of capital is the cost to the company of funds from creditors and shareholders. The cost of capital is basically a hurdle: if a project returns more than its cost of capital, it is a profitable project.

[15] We add after-tax interest because this produces a cash flow figure that indicates how much cash flow was available before paying suppliers of capital. This is similar to what we accomplished in reclassifying interest expense from an operating cash flow to a financing cash flow.

disgorge that cash rather than invest the funds in less profitable invest-ment, wasting funds. There are many ways in which companies may dis-gorge this excess cash flow, including the payment of cash dividends, the repurchase stock, and debt issuance in exchange for stock. The debt-for stock exchange, for example, increases the company's leverage and future debt obligations, obligating the future use of excess cash flow. If a company does not disgorge this free cash flow, there is the possibility that another company—a company whose cash flows are less than its profitable invest-ment opportunities or a company that is willing to purchase and lever-up the company—will attempt to acquire the free-cash-flow-laden company.

As a case in point, Jensen observed that the oil industry illustrates the case of wasting resources: The free cash flows generated in the 1980s were spent on low-return exploration and development and on poor diversification attempts through acquisitions. He argues that these companies would have been better off paying these excess cash flows to shareholders through share repurchases or exchanges with debt.

By itself, the fact that a company generates free cash flow is neither good nor bad. What the company *does* with this free cash flow is what is important. And this is where it is important to measure the free cash flow as that cash flow in excess of profitable investment opportunities. Consider the simple numerical exercise with the Winner Company and the Loser Company:

	Winner Company	Loser Company
Cash flow before capital expenditures	$1,000	$1,000
Capital expenditures, positive net present value projects	750	250
Capital expenditures, negative net present value projects	0	500
Cash flow	$250	$250
Free cash flow	$250	$750

These two companies have identical cash flows and the same total capital expenditures. However, the Winner Company spends only on profitable projects (in terms of positive net present value projects), whereas the Loser Company spends on both profitable projects and wasteful projects. The Winner Company has a lower free cash flow than the Loser Company, indicating that they are using the generated cash flows in a more profitable manner. The lesson is that the existence of a high level of free cash flow is not necessarily good—it may simply sug-gest that the company is either a very good takeover target or the com-pany has the potential for investing in unprofitable investments.

Positive free cash flow may be good news or bad news; likewise, negative free cash flow may be good or bad news:

	Good News	Bad News
Positive free cash flow	The company is generating substantial operating cash flows, beyond those necessary for profitable projects.	The company is generating more cash flows than it needs for profitable projects and may waste these cash flows on unprofitable projects.
Negative free cash flow	The company has more profitable projects than it has operating cash flows and must rely on external financing to fund these projects.	The company is unable to generate sufficient operating cash flows to satisfy its investment needs for future growth.

Therefore, once the analyst calculates free cash flow, other information (e.g., trends in profitability) must be considered to evaluate the operating performance and financial condition of the firm.

Calculating Free Cash Flow

There is some confusion when the theoretical concept of free cash flow is applied to actual companies. The primary difficulty is that the amount of capital expenditures necessary to maintain the business at its current rate of growth is generally not known; companies do not report this item and may not even be able to determine how much of a period's capital expenditures are attributed to maintenance and how much is attributed to expansion.

Some analysts estimate free cash flow by assuming that all capital expenditures are necessary for the maintenance of the current growth of the company. Though there is little justification in using all expenditures, this is a practical solution to an impractical calculation. This assumption allows us to estimate free cash flows using published financial statements.

There is no one correct method of calculating free cash flow and different analysts may arrive at different estimates of free cash flow for a company. The problem is that it is impossible to measure free cash flow as dictated by the theory, so many methods have arisen to calculate this cash flow. A simple method is to start with the cash flow from operations and then deduct capital expenditures. For J. C. Penney in 2004:

Cash flow from operations	$1,127
Deduct capital expenditures	412
Free cash flow	$715

J. C. Penney provides a free cash flow from continuing operations in its Executive Report in the 10-K filing. The free cash flow that they provides differs slightly from the above in two ways: the deduction of dividends and the inclusion of the proceeds from the sale of assets:[16]

Cash flow from operations	$1,127
Deduct capital expenditures	412
Deduct dividends	150
Add proceeds from the sale of assets	34
Free cash flow from continuing operations	$599

This calculation presumes that:

1. The measure of capital expenditures to meet replacement and growth opportunities is the net of capital expenditures and proceeds from the sale of assets.
2. Dividends are not a discretionary expenditure.

This is an example of some of the variations that you will see in the free cash flow calculations. Because there is no one, right way to calculate free cash flow, for a given company you may see different values.

Using a the simple definition of free cash flow and applying to Winn-Dixie Stores, as shown in Exhibit 6.5, we see that in the year prior to its bankruptcy filing, Winn-Dixie's did not have free cash flow and

EXHIBIT 6.5   Winn-Dixie's Free Cash Flow, 1990–2004

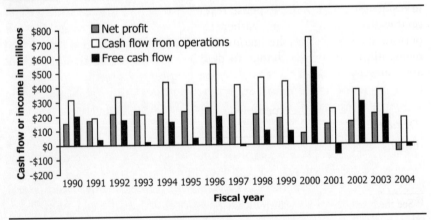

Source of data: Winn-Dixie's 10-K filings, various years.

---

[16] J. C. Penney 2004 10-K, p. 6.

that Winn-Dixie's ability to generate cash flows in excess of its capital expenditures is sporadic during the 15 years leading up to bankruptcy.

NET FREE CASH FLOW

There are many variations in the calculation of cash flows that are used in analyses of companies financial condition and operating performance. As an example of these variations, consider the alternative to free cash flow developed by Fitch Investors Service.[17] This cash flow measure, referred to as *net free cash flow* (NFCF), is free cash flow less interest and other financing costs, and taxes. In this approach, free cash flow is defined as earnings before depreciation, interest, and taxes, less capital expenditures. Capital expenditures encompass all capital spending, whether for maintenance or expansion and no changes in working capital are considered.

The basic difference between NFCF and free cash flow above is that the financing expenses—interest and, in some cases dividends—are deducted. If preferred dividends are perceived as nondiscretionary—that is, investors come to expect the dividends—dividends can be included with the interest commitment to arrive at net free cash flow. Otherwise, dividends are deducted *from* net free cash flow to produce cash flow. Another difference is that NFCF does not consider changes in working capital in the analysis.

Further, cash taxes are deducted to arrive at net free cash flow. Cash taxes are the income tax expense restated to reflect the actual cash flow related to this obligation, rather than the accrued expense for the period. Cash taxes are the income tax expense (from the income statement) adjusted for the change in deferred income taxes (from the balance sheets).[18]

	Income tax expense
Deduct	Increase in deferred income tax
Equals	Cash taxes

---

[17] See the research reports at http://www.fitchibca.com for descriptions of this method.

[18] Cash taxes require taking the tax expense and either increasing this to reflect any decrease in deferred taxes (that is, the payment this period of tax expense recorded in a prior period) or decreasing this amount to reflect any increase in deferred taxes (that is, the deferment of some of the tax expense).

	EBIT
Add	Depreciation and amortization
Equals	Earnings before interest, taxes, depreciation, and amortization
Deduct	Capital expenditures
Equals	Free cash flow
Deduct	Interest
Deduct	Cash taxes
Equals	Net free cash flow
Deduct	Cash common dividends
Equals	Net cash flow

For J. C. Penney in 2004, the net cash flow is $528 million:

	(in millions)
Earnings before interest, taxes, depreciation, and amortization	$1,621
Subtract: Capital expenditures	412
Free cash flow	$1,209
Deduct: Interest expense	280
Deduct: Cash taxes [$353 − ($1,318 − 1,217)]	252
Net free cash flow	$677
Deduct: Cash common dividends	149
Net cash flow	$528

Net cash flow gives the analyst an idea of the unconstrained cash flow of the company. This cash flow measure may be useful from a creditor's perspective in terms of evaluating the company's ability to fund additional debt. From a shareholder's perspective, net cash flow (i.e., net free cash flow net of dividends) may be an appropriate measure because this represents the cash flow that is reinvested in the company.

THE USEFULNESS OF CASH FLOWS IN FINANCIAL ANALYSIS

The usefulness of cash flows for financial analysis depends on whether cash flows provide unique information or provide information in a manner that is more accessible or convenient for the analyst. The cash flow information provided in the statement of cash flows, for example, is not necessarily unique because most, if not all, of the information is available through analysis of the balance sheet and income statement. What the statement does provide is a classification scheme that presents information in a manner that is easier to use and, perhaps, more illustrative of the company's financial position.

An analysis of cash flows and the sources of cash flows can reveal information to the analyst, including:

- *The sources of financing the company's capital spending.* Does the company generate internally (i.e., from operations) a portion or all of the funds needed for its investment activities? If a company cannot generate cash flow from operations, this may indicate problems up ahead. Reliance on external financing (e.g., equity or debt issuance) may indicate a company's inability of to sustain itself over time.
- *The company's dependence on borrowing.* Does the company rely heavily on borrowing that may result in difficulty in satisfying future debt service?
- *The quality of earnings.* Large and growing differences between income and cash flows suggests a low quality of earnings.

Ratio Analysis

One use of cash flow information is in ratio analysis, much like we did in Chapter 4 primarily with the balance sheet and income statement information. In that chapter we used a cash flow-based ratio—the cash flow interest coverage ratio—as a measure of financial risk. There are a number of other cash flow-based ratios that the analyst may find useful in evaluating the operating performance and financial condition of a company.

A useful ratio to help further assess a company's cash flow is the *cash flow to capital expenditures ratio*, or *capital expenditures coverage ratio*:[19]

$$\text{Cash flow-to-capital expenditures} = \frac{\text{Cash flow}}{\text{Capital expenditures}}$$

This ratio gives the analyst information about the financial flexibility of the company and is particularly useful for capital-intensive firms and utilities.[20] The larger the ratio, the greater the company's financial flexibility. Consider IBM's cash flow to capital expenditures ratio over the period 1990 to 2004 shown in Exhibit 6.6.[21] Using this ratio, we see that IBM's financial flexibility has improved since 1997.

---

[19] The cash flow measure in the numerator should be one that has not already removed capital expenditures; for example, including free cash flow in the numerator would be inappropriate.

[20] Martin Fridson, *Financial Statement Analysis: A Practitioner's Guide* (New York: John Wiley & Sons, 1995), p. 173.

[21] Because of the varied nature of IBM's fixed assets, we use the net of the cash flows expenditures for plant and equipment, software, and acquisitions in this capital expenditure calculation.

EXHIBIT 6.6   IBM Cash Flow to Capital Expenditures Ratio, 1990–2004

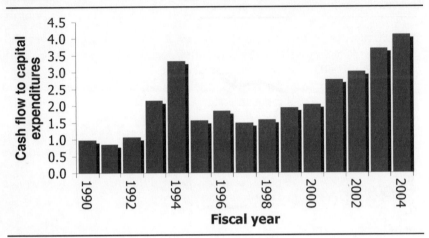

Source of data: IBM 10-K filings, various years.

The analyst, however, must carefully examine the reasons why this ratio may be changing over time and why it might be out of line with comparable firms in the industry. For example, a declining ratio can be interpreted in two ways. First, the firm may eventually have difficulty adding to capacity via capital expenditures without the need to borrow funds. The second interpretation is that the firm may have gone through a period of major capital expansion and, therefore, it will take time for revenues to be generated that will increase the cash flow from operations to bring the ratio to some normal long-run level.

Another useful cash flow ratio is the *cash flow to debt ratio*:

$$\text{Cash flow-to-debt} = \frac{\text{Cash flow}}{\text{Debt}}$$

where debt can be represented as total debt, long-term debt, or a debt measure that captures a specific range of maturity (e.g., debt maturing in five years). This ratio gives a measure of a company's ability to meet maturing debt obligations. A more specific formulation of this ratio is Fitch's *CFAR ratio*, which compares a company's three-year average net free cash flow to its maturing debt over the next five years.[22] By comparing the company's average NFCF to the expected obligations in the near term (i.e., five year), this ratio provides information on the company's credit quality.

---

[22] Daniel J. McConville, "Cash Flow Ratios Gains Respect as Useful Tool for Credit Rating," *Corporate Cashflow Magazine*, January 1996, p. 18.

EXHIBIT 6.7   Cash Flow-to-Debt Using Alternative Estimates of Cash Flow for Weirton Steel, 1990–2004

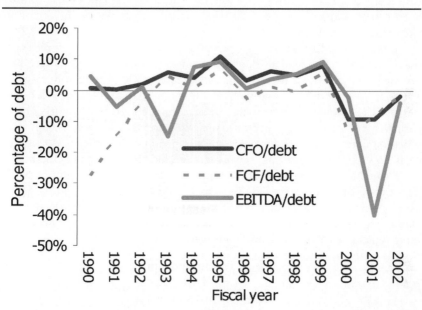

Source: Weirton Steel 10-K filings, various years.

We will see divergences between the cash flow to debt ratio when different definitions of cash flow are used. Consider the cash flow-to-debt ratio calculated using three different measures of cash flow—EBITDA, free cash flow, and cash flow from operations (from the statement of cash flows)—each compared with long-term debt, as shown in Exhibit 6.7 for Weirton Steel, which went public in 1989. You can see the effect of capital expenditures in the 1990–1992 period, which causes the difference between the free cash flow measure and the other two measures of cash flow; both EBITDA and cash flow from operations ignore capital expenditures, which were substantial outflows for this company is the earlier period. In the years after 1999, however, all three indicators agree and suggest there is a problem. The FCF/debt and CFO/debt ratios are similar because capital expenditures in these years were minimal. The severe drop in EBITDA/debt reflects the fact that the cost of sales was substantially greater than net sales in those years (2001 and 2002). Cash flow from operations and, therefore, free cash flow did not drop as dramatically in those years because the company benefited from tax loss carryovers, which provided benefit to net income and these cash flows. EBITDA provided a strong signal that there were problems.

Patterns of Cash Flows

The analysis of cash flows provides information that can be used along with other financial data to help the analyst assess the financial condition of a company.

Cash flow information may help the analyst identify companies that may encounter financial difficulties. Consider the study by Largay and Stickney that analyzed the financial statements of W. T. Grant during the 1966–1974 period preceding its bankruptcy in 1975 and ultimate liquidation.[23] They noted that financial indicators such as profitability ratios, turnover ratios, and liquidity ratios showed some down trends, but provided no definite clues to the company's impending bankruptcy. A study of cash flows from operations, however, revealed that company operations were causing an increasing drain on cash, rather than providing cash.[24] This necessitated an increased use of external financing, the required interest payments on which exacerbated the cash flow drain. Cash flow analysis clearly was a valuable tool in this case because W. T. Grant had been running a negative cash flow from operations for years. Yet none of the traditional ratios discussed above take into account the cash flow from operations. Use of the cash flow-to-capital expenditures ratio and the cash flow-to-debt ratio would have highlighted the company's difficulties.

Dugan and Samson examined the use of operating cash flow as an early warning signal of a company's potential financial problems.[25] The subject of the study was Allied Products Corporation because for a decade this company exhibited a significant divergence between cash flow from operations and net income. For parts of the period, net income was positive while cash flow from operations was a large negative value. In contrast to W. T. Grant that went into bankruptcy, the auditor's report in the 1991 Annual Report of Allied Products Corporation did issue a going concern warning. Moreover, the stock traded in the range of $2 to $3 per share. There was then a turnaround of the company by 1995. In its 1995 annual report, net income increased dramatically from prior periods (to $34 million) and there was a positive cash flow from operations ($29 million). The stock traded in the $25 range by spring

---

[23] J. A. Largay III and C. P. Stickney, "Cash Flows, Ratio Analysis and the W. T. Grant Company Bankruptcy," *Financial Analysts Journal* (July–August 1980), pp. 51–54. An analysis of EBITDA, for example, would not have revealed the problems W. T. Grant was experiencing.

[24] For the period investigated, a statement of changes of financial position (on a working capital basis) was required to be reported prior to 1988.

[25] Michael T. Dugan and William D. Samson, "Operating Cash Flow: Early Indicators of Financial Difficulty and Recovery," *Journal of Financial Statement Analysis* (Summer 1996), pp. 41–50.

1996.[26] As with the W. T. Grant study, Dugan and Samson found that the economic realities of a firm are better reflected in its cash flow from operations.

The importance of cash flow analysis in bankruptcy prediction is supported by the study by Benjamin Foster and Terry Ward, who compared trends in the statement of cash flows components—cash flow from operations, cash flow for investment, and cash flow for financing—between healthy companies and companies that subsequently sought bankruptcy.[27] They observe that healthy companies tend to have relative stable relations among the cash flows for the three sources, correcting any given year's deviation from their norm within one year. They also observe that unhealthy companies exhibit declining cash flows from operations and financing and declining cash flows for investment one and two years prior to the bankruptcy. Further, unhealthy companies tend to expend more cash flows to financing sources than they bring in during the year prior to bankruptcy. These studies illustrate the importance of examining cash flow information in assessing the financial condition of a company.

We can see this pattern for Weirton Steel, which went public in 1989 and filed for bankruptcy in 2003. The cash flows follow the pattern outlined by Foster and Ward as shown in Exhibit 6.8.

EXHIBIT 6.8   Cash Flows for Weirton Steel, 1990–2002

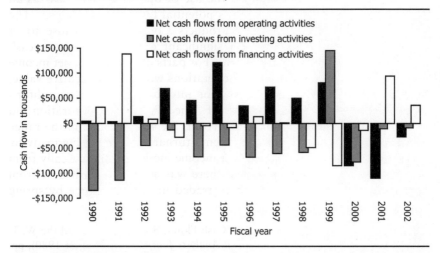

Source: Weirton Steel 10-K filings, various years.

---

[26] As noted for the W. T. Grant study by Largay and Stickney, cash flow from operations had to be constructed from the statement of changes in financial positions that companies were required to report prior to 1988.

[27] Benjamin P. Foster and Terry J. Ward, "Using Cash Flow Trends to Identify Risks of Bankruptcy," *The CPA Journal* 67, no. 9 (September 1997), p. 60.

Company Performance

Cash flow and free cash flow are often used as metrics to gauge whether the financial performance of a company is sustainable. A company that is able to consistently generate cash flow in excess of capital expenditures is considered to have the flexibility to expand as new investment opportunities arise and/or to pay additional dividends to shareholders.

Consider the CFO *Cash Free Flow Scorecard*, which is a ranking of companies on the basis of their free cash flow.[28] In this case, free cash flow is calculated by deducting both capital expenditures and preferred dividends from cash flow from operations, producing a free cash flow measure specifically from the common shareholders' perspective. Companies that are ranked high in terms of free cash flow are considered to be financially able to continue to pay dividends and/or make investments necessary to continue growing.

We see from the example with J. C. Penney that the cash flow that we estimate depends on the specific definition that we are using. Consider the different cash flows that we can calculate for J. C. Penney based on the estimates that we discuss in this chapter:

	Cash Flows (in millions)
Earnings before depreciation and amortization	$892
Earnings before interest, taxes, depreciation, and amortization	$1,621
Cash flow from operations, as reported	$1,127
Cash flow from operations, as adjusted	$1,309
Free cash flow to equity	$715
Free cash flow to the firm	$897
Free cash flow (as reported by the company)	$599
Net free cash flow	$677
Net cash flow	$528
Free cash flow, per CFO *Cash Flow Scoreboard* calculation	$1,060

Which do you use? It depends on the focus of your analysis:

■ If you are evaluating the company's ability to generate cash flow from its operations, you would want to focus on the cash flow from operations, adjusting it appropriately.

---

[28] Ronald Fink, "Serving up Dividends: The 2004 Free Cash Flow Scorecard," *CFO.com*, 1 January 2005.

■ If you are assessing the company's ability to generate cash flows and sustain its growth in the future, you would want to focus on the free cash flow estimates.

■ If you are evaluating the ability of the company to generate cash flows to its owners, you would want to focus on the free cash flow to equity or net free cash flow.

■ If you are evaluating the financial flexibility of the company, you would want to focus on the unconstrained cash flow measures of net free cash flow or net cash flow.

Another use of cash flow in performance is in executive compensation. Part of the compensation of the CEO of General Electric is in the form of performance shares that are granted based on the growth of cash flow from operations.[29] And General Electric is not the only company tying compensation to a measure of cash flow; other examples include Comcast Corporation, Dow Chemical Company, Kraft Foods, Inc., Motorola, Inc., Walt Disney Company, and The Washington Post Company.

SUMMARY

The term "cash flow" has many meaning and the analyst's challenge is to determine the cash flow definition and calculation that is appropriate. The simplest calculation of cash flow is the sum of net income and non-cash expenses. This measure, however, does not consider other sources and uses of cash during the period. The statement of cash flows provides a useful breakdown of the sources of cash flows: operating activities, investing activities, and financing activities. Though attention is generally focused on the cash flows from operations, the analyst must also examine what the company does with the cash flows (i.e., investing or paying off financing obligations) and the sources of invested funds (i.e., operations versus externally financing). Minor adjustments can be made to the items classified in the statement of cash flows to improve the classification.

The analyst can examine different patterns of cash flow to get a general idea of the activities of the company. For example, a company whose only source of cash flow is from investing activities, suggesting the sale of property or equipment, may be experiencing financial distress.

Free cash flow is a company's cash flow that remains after making capital investments that maintain the company's current rate of growth. It is not possible to calculate free cash flow precisely, resulting in many

---

[29] Marie Leone, "Compensation and Cash Flow," *CFO.com*, 21 January 2004.

different variations in calculations of this measure. A company that generates free cash flow is not necessarily performing well or poorly. However, the existence of free cash flow must be taken in context with other financial data and information on the company. Variations in the calculation of free cash flow include free cash flow for the firm and net free cash flow. These are measures of the funds available to service additional obligations to suppliers of capital.

Applying Financial Analysis

Measuring Company Performance

As we saw in previous chapters, financial statement information and ratio analysis of these statements can give us an idea of a company's performance. However, financial statement information may be problematic. Accounting principles are continually updated to provide for the best representation of a company's operating performance and financial position; yet because we apply a set of general accounting principles to companies in a variety of businesses and because that financial information can be managed through a judicious use of accounting principles, the financial analyst must be careful in the evaluation of the financial statement information in financial analysis and valuation. Further, just looking at the values and income from the reported financial statements does not provide all the information we need to make projections about the future performance of a company.

So why not just look at stock prices as a measure of performance? If we dispose of financial statement information and focus solely on stock prices we have simply substituted one set of concerns for another. Evaluating a company's performance is much more challenging than looking at stock prices. If stock prices rise in a given period, does that mean the company is doing well? Not necessarily—the stock price may not be as high as it should be, given economic and market conditions. If a company's stock price declines during a given period, does that mean that the company is doing poorly? Not necessarily—the stock's price may be higher than expected given current economic and market conditions.

Arising from the need for better methods of evaluating performance, several consulting companies advocate performance evaluation
methods that are applied to evaluate a company's performance as a
whole and to evaluate specific managers' performances. These methods
are, in some cases, supplanting traditional methods of measuring performance, such as the return on assets. As a class, these measures are often
referred to as *value-based metrics* or *economic value-added measures*,
though there is a cacophony of acronyms to accompany these measures,
including *economic value added* (EVA®), *market value added* (MVA),
cash flow return on investment (CFROI), *shareholder value added*
(SVA), *cash value added* (CVA), and *refined economic value added*
(REVA).

A company's management creates value when decisions are made
that provide benefits that exceed the costs. These benefits may be
received in the near or distant future, and the costs include both the
direct cost of the investment, as well as the less obvious cost, the cost of
capital. The *cost of capital* is the explicit and implicit cost associated
with using investors' funds. It is the attention to the cost of capital that
sets the value-based metrics apart from traditional measures of performance.

Value creation is a basic theme of capital budgeting: A company
should only invest in projects that enhance the value of the company. So
where do these value-enhancing projects come from? In a competitive
market for investment opportunities where many companies compete
for available investment opportunities, there should be no value-
enhancing projects. In other words, the cost of a project should be bid
upward through competition so there is no net benefit from investing in
the project. This explanation is rather gloomy and ignores the true
source of value-enhancing projects: a company's comparative or competitive advantage. It is only through some advantage vis-a-vis one's
competitors that allows companies to invest in projects that enhance
value.[1] In cases where there are no impediments to investment (that is,
there is a competitive market for investments), it is only through having
some type of advantage that a company can invest in something and get
more back in return. Stepping back from looking at individual projects
to looking at an entire company, we can apply the same basic principles.
If the company's investments provide future benefits greater than its
costs, the investments enhance the value of the company. If the com-

---

[1] A *comparative advantage* is the advantage one company has over others in terms
of the cost of producing or distributing goods or services. A *competitive advantage*
is the advantage one company has over another because of the structure of the markets (input and output markets) in which they both operate.

pany's investments provide future benefits that are less than the investments costs, this is detrimental to the value of the company.[2,3]

From the perspective of analysts, the focus of performance evaluation is on the company as a whole, not on individual investment decisions within the company. The key to evaluating a company's performance is therefore whether the company's investment decisions, as a whole, are producing value for the shareholders. But there is no obvious technique to accomplish this because (1) we do not have the ability to perfectly forecast future cash flows from these investments; (2) we do not have accurate measures of the risks of each investment; and (3) we do not know the precise cost of capital. Therefore, we are left with using proxies (however imperfect) to assess a company's performance.

In the next section we first look at the sources of value added, using Michael Porter's "five forces" that help us focus on the company's competitive advantage. We then look at methods of measuring the value added of companies.[4]

PORTER'S FIVE FORCES

Michael Porter analyzed competitive structure of industries and identified five competitive forces.[5] These forces capture an industry's competitive rivalry:

---

[2] The idea of producing current value from future investment opportunities is reflected in the concept of franchise value, which is discussed by Kogelman and Liebowitz in their decomposition of the price-earnings (P/E) ratio into a franchise P/E and a base P/E. (See S. Kogelman and M. L. Liebowitz, "The Franchise Factor Valuation Approach: Capturing the Company's Investment Opportunities," in *Corporate Financial Decision Making and Equity Analysis* (Charlottesville, PA: ICFA Continuing Education, Association for Investment Management and Research, 1995), pp. 5–10.) In their analysis, future investment opportunities in excess of market returns are reflected in above-market P/E ratios.

[3] This is what Warren Buffett is talking about when he refers to a "sustainable competitive advantage" or "enduring competitive advantage" in his letters to shareholders of Bershire Hathaway. See, for example, Letters to Shareholders in 1999, 2000, and 2004, available at www.berkshirehathaway.com.

[4] For a further discussion of the value-based approach to portfolio management, see: James A. Abate, James L. Grant, and Bennett G. Stewart III, "The EVA Style of Investing," *Journal of Portfolio Management* (Summer 2004), pp. 61–72; James L. Grant and James A. Abate, *Focus on Value: A Corporate and Investor Guide to Wealth Creation* (New York: John Wiley & Sons, 2001), and; Frank J. Fabozzi and James L. Grant (eds.), *Value-Based Metrics: Foundations and Practice* (New York: John Wiley & Sons, 2000).

[5] Michael Porter, *Competitive Strategy: Techniques for Analyzing Industries and Competitors* (New York: Simon & Schuster, 1998).

- Bargaining power of suppliers
- Threat of new entrants
- Threat of substitute products
- Bargaining power of buyers
- Degree of rivalry

The bargaining power of suppliers is a force related to the providers of inputs—both goods and services. Suppliers' bargaining power is greater when the market in which they operate is dominated by a few large companies, there are no substitutes for the input, the cost of switching inputs is high, the buyers are fragmented with little buying power, or the suppliers may integrate forward to capture higher prices and margins. The bargaining power of customers is high when they purchase large quantities of goods or services, the buyers are concentrated, the suppliers have high fixed costs, there are ready substitutes or the buyer could produce the good or service itself.

The threat of new entrants is high when there are few barriers to entry. A barrier to entry is an impediment such as economies of scale, high initial, startup costs, cost advantages due to experience of existing

EXHIBIT 7.1   Porter's Five Forces

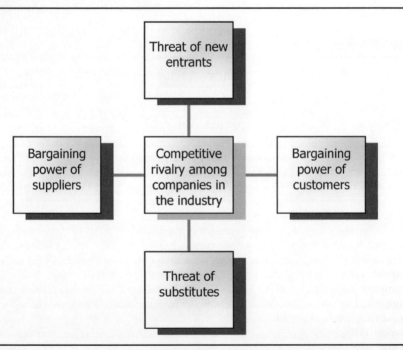

participants, loyalty among customers, protections such as patents, licenses, or copyrights, or regulatory or government action that limits entrants into the industry.

The threat of substitutes is high when there is little brand loyalty among customers, there are no close customer relations, there are low costs to switching goods or services, and there are substitutes that are lower priced.

The competitive rivalry among existing members of the industry is affected by the number and relative size of the companies in the industry, the strategies of the companies, the differentiation among products, and the growth of the sales in the industry.

Porter's forces are, basically, an elaboration of the theories of economics that tell us how a company creates economic profit. Though Porter's forces may be criticized for being over-simplistic in a dynamic economy, they provide a starting point for analysis of a company's ability to add value. Porter argues that an individual company may create a competitive advantage through relative cost, differentiation, and relative prices. A financial analyst, in evaluating a company's current and future performance, can use these forces and strategies to identify a company's competitive advantage. For it is through a competitive advantage that a company creates value.

MEASURES OF VALUE ADDED

The most prominent of recently developed techniques to evaluate a company's performance is the value-added measures of economic profit and market value added (MVA).[6,7] These measures have links to our fundamental valuation techniques. Value-added measures are based on

---

[6] A particular calculation of economic profit, promoted by the consultant firm of Stern Stewart, is economic value added (EVA®). A detailed description of the value-added methods can be found in G. Bennett Stewart III, *The Quest for Value* (New York: Harper Collins Publishers, 1991). We refer to economic value added by its original name of *economic profit*.

[7] Another prominent valuation approach is the discounted cash flow approach, advocated by McKinsey and Co. This approach involves forecasting future periods' free cash flows, forecasting a company's continuing value at the end of the forecast period, and discounting the future free cash flows and the continuing value at the company's weighted average cost of capital. Because this approach involves valuation based on forecasts, it is not a suitable device for evaluating performance, though it is useful in setting performance targets [T. Copeland, T. Koller, and J. Murrin, *Valuation: Measuring and Managing the Value of Companies*, second edition, New York: John Wiley & Sons, 1994, p. 116)].

the same valuation principles as the net present value capital budgeting technique. But remember: value is not created out of thin air, but rather from a company's competitive advantage.

A net present value for a specific investment project is the estimate of change in the value of equity if the company invests in the project. The value-added measures also produce an estimate of the change in the value of the company, but relate to the company as a whole, rather than a specific project. Further, whereas net present value is forward looking, assisting management in making decisions dealing with the use of capital in the future, measuring a period's performance using value-added measures focuses on the decisions that have been made during a period and the cost of capital that supported those investment decisions to help us gauge how well the company has performed.

There are a number of value-added measures that an analyst can calculate. The most commonly used measures are economic profit and market value added. Key elements of estimating economic profit are:

- The calculation of the company's operating profit from financial statement data, making adjustments to accounting profit to better reflect a company's results for a period
- The calculation of the company's cost of capital
- The comparison of operating profit with the cost of capital

The difference between the operating profit and the cost of capital is the estimate of the company's economic profit, or economic value added.

A related measure, market value added, focuses on the market value of capital, as compared to the cost of capital. The key elements of market value added are:

- The calculation of the market value of capital
- The calculation of the capital invested
- The comparison of the market value of capital with the capital invested

The difference between the market value of capital and the amount of capital invested is the market value added. The primary distinctions between economic value added and market value added are that the latter incorporates market data in the calculation and it uses the market value of capital, which is forward looking.

What makes a good performance measure? Ideally, a measure of a company's performance should have several characteristics:

1. The measure should not be sensitive to the choice of accounting methods.
2. The measure should evaluate the company's current decisions in light of the expected future results.
3. The measure should consider the risk associated with the decisions made by the company.
4. The measure should neither penalize nor reward the company for factors outside of their control, such as market movements and unanticipated changes in the economy.

We look at these criteria when discussing the particulars of the different performance measures.

TRADITIONAL PERFORMANCE MEASURES

The most widely cited performance measures are return on investment ratios, including the return on assets and the return on equity. Generally, we associate higher return ratios with better performance. Return ratios are typically used in two ways. First, we often compare return ratios over time for a given company, where it is the trend, rather than the actual return for a particular period, which indicates performance. Second, we often compare return ratios across companies or with a benchmark, such as an industry average return or the return for the industry leaders.

An advantage of using return ratios in evaluating companies' performances is the ease of calculation. All information necessary for the calculation is readily available, either from financial statements or from market data. And, since the return is expressed as a percentage of the investment, its interpretation is straightforward.

An attractive feature of return ratios is the ability to break down the return ratio to examine the source of changes in returns. As we saw in Chapter 4, we can use the DuPont system to analyze return ratios, breaking the return ratios into their activity, profit, and other components. This allows us to further evaluate the source of the return changes from year-to-year and to evaluate differences across companies.

Return on investment measures may not be the best measures of performance for a number of reasons. First, we form return on investment ratios using financial statement data in the numerator and/or the denominator and therefore these ratios are sensitive to the choice of accounting methods. And this sensitivity to accounting methods makes it difficult to compare return ratios across companies and across time, requiring an adjustment of the accounting data to place return ratios on the same accounting basis.

Second, in creating these ratios, we are using financial data that is an accumulation of monetary values from different time periods. For example, the gross plant account includes the cost of assets purchased at different points in time. If there is significant inflation in some of the historical periods, this results in an "apples and oranges" addition problem for most accounts that affect total assets and equity, distorting the calculated returns on investment.

Third, return on investment ratios are backward looking, not forward looking. Though the immediate effects of current investments influence the return ratios, the expected future benefits from current period decisions are generally not incorporated in the return ratios.

A fourth reason for the deficiency of return-on-investment ratios is that they fail to consider risk. These ratios simply use historical financial statement data that in no way reflect the uncertainty the company faces.

Finally, the return-on-investment ratios do not adjust for controllable versus noncontrollable factors. Ideally, we would want to isolate the performance of the company from factors that are outside the control of management. Return on investment ratios simply reflect the bottom line and do not consider any other factors.

A CLOSER LOOK AT VALUE ADDED MEASURES

It is difficult to measure whether a company's management has increased or decreased a company's value during a period since a company's value may be affected by many factors. Currently advocated performance measurement techniques, such as Stern Stewart's EVA® and MVA, are based on valuation principles. However, there is an important distinction between valuation and performance measurement: valuation relies on forecasts, whereas performance measurement must rely on actual results.

Economic Profit

Many U.S. corporations embraced a method of evaluating and rewarding management performance that is based on economic profit, rather than for its accounting profit. What is economic profit? *Economic profit* is the difference between revenues and costs, where the costs include not only expenses, but also the cost of capital. Though the application of economic profit is relatively new in the measurement of performance, the concept of economic profit is not new—it was first noted by Alfred Marshall in the 19th century.[8] What this recent emphasis on economic profit has done is focus attention away from accounting profit and towards economic profit.

The *cost of capital* is the rate of return that is required by the suppliers of capital to the company. For a business that finances its operations or investments using both debt and equity, the cost of capital includes not only the explicit interest on the debt, but also the implicit minimum return that owners require. This minimum return to owners is necessary so that owners keep their investment capital in the company.

So, where does economic profit come from? From the company's competitive or comparative advantage. The challenge that the analyst faces is examining the company in light of Porter's "five forces" and identifying what advantages, if any, a company has. For it is only through these advantages that a company can generate a sustainable economic profit and, hence, create value. In other words, a company creates value when it generates profit over and above that expected for the level of risk it assumes—therefore, "clearing" the hurdle that is its cost of capital.

Economic Profit versus Accounting Profit

There are two important distinctions between accounting profit and economic profit. The first distinction deals with the cost of capital. Accounting profit is the difference between revenues and costs, based on the representation of these items according to accounting principles. Economic profit is also the difference between revenues and costs, but, unlike the determination of accounting profit, we include the cost of capital in the costs.

The second distinction between accounting and economic profit deals with the principles of recognition of revenues and costs. We determine accounting profits based on the accrual method, whereas we calculate economic profits using cash-basis accounting. However, because the only data reported in financial statements is in terms of accrual accounting, analysts calculating economic profits must first start with accounting profits and then make adjustments to place the data on a cash basis. This adjustment is imperfect, but does help us better gauge performance than relying solely on accounting profits.

Further we make adjustments to accounting profits to compensate for distortions that may arise from the choice of particular accounting

---

[8] Alfred Marshall, *Principles of Economics*, vol. 1 (New York: Macmillan & Co., 1890), p. 142.

methods. For example, companies with operating leases account for these leases as rental expense, with no liability on the balance sheet; however, analysts often capitalize these leases to make their presentation similar to that of capital leases. Unlike accounting profit, economic profit (if measured accurately) cannot be managed through the choice of accounting methods.

In addition to the use of economic profit measures for compensating managers, financial analysts are incorporating the basic principles of economic profit in their assessment of corporate success. Performance measures based on economic profit are known by several different names, including market value added (MVA), economic value added (EVA®), and excess shareholder value.[9]

Economic Profit and Net Present Value

We estimate economic profit in a manner analogous to the net present value method of evaluating investments. Though attractive in principle, there are many pitfalls associated with its application of the net present value capital budgeting technique to actual companies. These pitfalls include (1) the use of accounting data to determine economic profit and (2) the estimation of the cost of capital.[10]

Just as the net present value of a project produces results that are sensitive to the cost of capital, so does the economic profit approach. Any slight change in the cost of capital estimate may change the estimated value added from positive to negative or vice versa. In other words, whether we view of a company's performance as value-destroying to value-enhancing is sensitive to the estimates used in the calculation.

The net present value method, as applied in the context of evaluating performance of companies and management, was brought to prominence by Bennett Stewart III, in his 1991 book *A Quest for Value* and through the consulting work by Stern Stewart.

Calculating Economic Profit

Economic profit, referred to as economic value added, is the difference between operating profits and the cost of capital, where the cost of capital is expressed in dollar terms. The application to an entire company involves, essentially, calculating the net present value of all investment projects, both those involving existing assets (that is, past investment decisions) and those projected.

---

[9] EVA is a registered trademark of Stern Stewart.
[10] The cost of capital is an opportunity cost of funds, measured as the weighted average of the marginal costs of debt and equity capital.

Economic profit can be written as[11]

$$\text{Economic profit} = \begin{pmatrix} \text{Net operating profit} \\ \text{after taxes} \end{pmatrix} - \begin{pmatrix} \text{Cost of} \\ \text{capital} \times \text{Capital} \end{pmatrix}$$

or, equivalently, using the spread between the rate of return and the percentage cost of capital,

$$\text{Economic profit} = \begin{pmatrix} \text{Return on} \\ \text{capital} \end{pmatrix} - \begin{pmatrix} \text{Cost of} \\ \text{capital} \end{pmatrix} \times \text{Capital}$$

where the return on capital is the ratio of net operating profit after taxes to capital.

Application of this formula produces an estimate of the economic profit for a single period. In evaluating a company's performance for a given period, economic profit reflects whether value is added (a positive economic profit) or reduced (a negative economic profit). Each element of this formula is discussed in detail below.

Net Operating Profit after Taxes   There are two important elements in the calculation of *net operating profit after taxes* (NOPAT): operating profit after depreciation and cash operating taxes. NOPAT is income from operations, but only after we remove the taxes on a cash basis that are related to operating income. Cash-operating taxes are taxes on operating income, placed on a cash basis.

Operating income *after* depreciation is used rather than the traditional operating income before depreciation because depreciation is considered an economic expense: Depreciation is a measure of how much of an asset is used up in the period, which gives us an idea of how much must be expended to maintain operations at the existing level.

In addition to using cash-operating taxes instead of the tax expense on the income statement, there are several adjustments intended to alter accounting profit to better reflect economic profit. However, because these adjustments involve adjusting accounting profit to arrive at economic profit, these adjustments must be tailored to the company's specific accounting practices and situation.

Whether you start with operating profit after depreciation (the "bottom-up" approach),

---

[11] Bennett, *The Quest for Value*, p. 136.

NOPAT = Operating profit after depreciation and amortization

$$+ \left(\begin{array}{c} \text{Implied interest expense on operating leases} \\ \text{Increase in LIFO reserve} \\ \text{Increase in bad debt reserve} \\ \text{Increase in net capitalized research and developent} \end{array} \right)$$

– Cash-operating taxes

or begin with sales (the "top-down" approach),

NOPAT = Sales

$$+ \left(\begin{array}{c} \text{Increase in LIFO reserve} \\ \text{Implied interest expense on operating leases} \\ \text{Other income} \end{array} \right)$$

$$- \left(\begin{array}{c} \text{Cost of goods sold} \\ \text{Selling, general, and administrative expenses} \\ \text{Depreciation} \end{array} \right)$$

– Cash-operating taxes

we arrive at net operating profit after taxes.

Let us calculate 2004 NOPAT for McDonald's Corporation to see how these adjustments are made to actual company data. Using the basic income statement data as presented as an example in Exhibit 7.2, balance sheet data in Exhibit 7.3, financial statement note information (not shown in the exhibit), and using the bottom-up approach, we begin with operating profit after depreciation and amortization (i.e., operating income) of $3,540.5 million.

Most of the information necessary to make the adjustments is available directly from the financial statements or the notes to financial statements. The only adjustment applicable to McDonald's is for implied interest on operating leases, which is implied from future rental commitments, as detailed in *McDonald's Corporation 2004 Annual Report*, "Leasing arrangements" note.[12] McDonald's implied interest expense on operating leases must be calculated using this footnote information. The interest expense is estimated as the interest cost on the change in the average value of leases during the year. This requires estimating the present value of leases at the beginning and end of the year.

---

[12] Information on change in bad debt reserve is not available in McDonald's financial statement, likely because these items are immaterial. Therefore, these adjustments are not made. This illustrates a potential problem in calculating economic profit: The information needed may not be available in published financial reports.

EXHIBIT 7.2 McDonald's Balance Sheet

	2004 (in millions)	2003 (in millions)
ASSETS		
Cash and cash equivalents	$1,379.8	492.8
Accounts and notes receivable	745.5	734.5
Inventories	147.5	129.4
Prepaid expenses and other current assets	585.0	528.7
Total current assets	$2,857.8	$1,885.4
Notes receivable due after one year		
Investments in and advances to affiliates	$1,109.9	$1,089.6
Goodwill	1,828.3	1,665.1
Miscellaneous	1,338.4	1,273.2
Total other assets	$2,137.9	$1,931.4
Gross plant, property and equipment	$30,507.8	$28,740.2
Less: Accumulated depreciation and amortization	9,804.7	8,815.5
Net plant, property and equipment	$20,703.1	$19,924.7
Total assets	$27,837.5	$25,838.0
LIABILITIES		
Accounts payable	$714.3	$577.4
Taxes payable	331.3	334.2
Other taxes	245.1	222.0
Accrued interest	179.4	193.1
Accrued restructuring and restaurant closing costs	71.5	115.7
Accrued payroll and other liabilities	1,116.7	918.1
Long-term debt due in one year	862.2	388.0
Total current liabilities	$3,520.5	$2,748.5
Long-term debt	$8,357.3	$9,342.5
Other liabilities	976.7	699.8
Deferred taxes	781.5	1,065.3
SHAREHOLDERS' EQUITY		
Common stock	16.6	16.6
Additional paid-in capital	2,186.0	1,837.5
Guarantee of ESOP Notes	−82.8	−90.5
Retained earnings	21,755.8	20,172.3
Accumulated other comprehensive income	−96.0	−635.5
Less: Common stock in treasury	9,578.1	9,318.5
Total shareholders' equity	$14,201.5	$11,981.9
TOTAL LIABILITIES AND EQUITY	$27,837.5	$25,838.0

Source: McDonalds' Corporation, 2004 Annual Report.

EXHIBIT 7.3   McDonald's Income Statement

	2004 (in millions)	2003 (in millions)
REVENUES		
Sales by Company operated restaurants	$14,223.8	$12,795.4
Revenues from franchised and affiliated restaurants	4,840.9	4,345.1
Total revenues	$19,064.7	$17,140.5
OPERATING COSTS AND EXPENSES		
Company operated restaurants	$12,099.8	$11,006.0
Franchised restaurants—occupancy expenses	1,003.2	937.7
Selling and general administrative expense	1,980.0	1,833.0
Other operating (income) expense—net	441.2	531.6
Total operating costs and expenses	$15,524.2	$14,308.3
Operating income	$3,540.5	$2,832.2
Interest expense	358.4	388.0
Nonoperating income and expense	−20.3	97.8
Income before provision for income taxes	$3,202.4	$2,346.4
Provision for income taxes	923.9	838.2
Net income before cumulative effect of accounting changes	$2,278.5	$1,508.2
Cumulative effect of accounting change, net of tax benefits	0	−36.8
Net income	$2,278.5	$1,471.4

Source: McDonald's Corporation, 2004 Annual Report.

The present value of operating leases is determined by discounting minimum rental commitments on operating leases for the next five years. These minimum rental commitments are disclosed in a footnote to the financial statements. In the case of McDonald's, the expected future commitments beyond 2004 are as follows:

	Operating lease rental commitment	
Year following	2004 (in millions)	2003 (in millions)
First year	$1,061.7	$998.0
Second year	$999.7	$939.5
Third year	$929.1	$876.6
Fourth year	$865.0	$814.7
Fifth year	$806.6	$757.7
Beyond the fifth year	$6,780.5	$6,531.5

Using a discount rate of 5% (the approximate yield on McDonald's debt in 2004), the present value of the first five years of commitments is $4,064 million. Because many companies disclose only rental commitments for the next five years, the value of the commitments beyond the fifth year are often ignored in the determination of capital. In the case of McDonald's, this may amount to a large difference in estimated debt capital.[13] Repeating the same analysis for 2003, the present value of the operating leases is $3,824 million. The average lease value for 2004 is, therefore, ($4,064 + 3,824)/2 = $3,944 million. Using an interest rate of 5%, the interest on the leases is estimated to be $3,944 × 0.05 = $197.2 million. This implied interest is backed out of operating profit because it represents a financing cost that was deducted to arrive at reported operating profit.

Starting with the operating profit after depreciation and amortization from the 2004 income statement, adjusted operating profit before taxes for McDonald's is calculated as:

	Amount (in millions)
Operating profit after depreciation and amortization	$3,540.5
Add: Implied interest on operating leases	197.2
Adjusted operating profit before taxes	$3,737.7

Cash-Operating Taxes

Cash-operating taxes are estimated by starting with the income tax expense and adjusting this expense for: (1) changes in deferred taxes; (2) the tax benefit from the interest deduction (for both explicit and implicit interest) to remove the tax effect of financing with debt; and (3) taxes from other nonoperating income or expense and special items.[14] The change in deferred taxes is removed from the income tax expense because:

- An increase in deferred taxes means that a portion of the income tax expense that is deferred is not a cash outlay for the period

---

[13] If McDonald's rental commitments beyond the fifth year are, say $800 million per year, the difference in estimated debt capital (using a 5% discount rate) is over $12,000 million: discount the $800 per year as a perpetuity to the end of the fifth year ($800/0.05 = $16,000), and then discount this amount back five years (present value = $12,536 million).

[14] The adjustment for the taxes on other nonoperating income is suggested by Thomas Copeland, Tim Koller, and Jack Murrin, *Valuation: Measuring and Managing the Value of Companies*, 2nd ed. (New York: John Wiley & Sons, 2000), though the amount is typically small.

■ A decrease in deferred taxes means that the income taxes expense understates the true cash expense.

The tax benefit from interest is added back to taxes so that the cash taxes reflect the taxes from operations. This gross-up of taxes isolates the taxes from any financing effects. This tax benefit is the reduction of taxes from the deductibility of interest expense:

$$\text{Tax benefit from interest} = \text{Interest expense} \times \text{Marginal tax rate}$$

The taxes from other nonoperating income and special items (e.g., sales of investment interest) are also removed so that the cash taxes reflect solely those taxes related to operations.

Let us look at an example using the McDonald's 2004 financial data. First, we calculate cash taxes, using a marginal tax rate of 35%:

	Amount in Millions	Source of Information
Income tax expense	$923.9	Income statement
Add: Decrease in deferred taxes	283.8	Difference between deferred taxes on balance sheets for 2004 and 2003: [$781.5 − 1,065.3 = $283.8]
Add: Tax benefit from interest expense	158.4	Interest expense from income statement, times the marginal tax rate [$358.4 × 0.35 = $158.36]
Add: Tax benefit from interest on leases	69.0	Implied interest from footnote information, times marginal tax rate [$197.2.4 × 0.35 = $69.0]
Subtract: Tax benefit on non-operating expense	−7.1	Nonoperating expense from income statement, times marginal tax rate [$20.3 × 0.35 = $7.1]
Cash-operating taxes	$1,428.0	

Subtracting cash-operating taxes from the adjusted operating profit produces net operating profit after taxes:

	Amount in millions
Adjusted operating profit before taxes	$3,737.7
Less: Cash operating taxes	−1,428.0
Net operating profit after taxes (NOPAT)	$2,309.7

This approach to calculating NOPAT is a bottom-up approach since it starts with operating profit after depreciation and amortization and builds to NOPAT. Another approach is a "top-down" approach, where we start with sales and adjust to arrive at NOPAT. In the case of McDonald's for 2004:

	Amount in Millions	Source of Information
Revenues	$19,064.7	Income statement
Less: Operating costs and expenses	−15,524.2	Income statement (costs and expenses of company operated restaurants and franchised restaurants)
Add: Implied interest on operating leases	197.2	Calculated from "Leasing arrangements" note
Adjusted operating profit before taxes	$3,737.7	
Less: Cash operating taxes	−1,428.0	(see previous calculation)
Net operating profit after taxes (NOPAT)	$2,309.7	

Whether we use the top-down approach or the bottom-up approach, we can arrive at the NOPAT of $2,082.7 million.

Capital

Capital is defined in this context as the sum of net working capital, net property and equipment, goodwill, and other assets. Another way of looking at capital is that it is the sum of the long-term sources of financing, both debt and equity, that are invested in the company. Therefore, this sum is often referred to as *invested capital*.

Several adjustments to reported accounts are made to correct for possible distortions arising from accounting methods. For example, we adjust inventory for any last in, first out (LIFO) reserve, we include the present value of operating leases as part of invested capital, and we add back any accumulated goodwill amortization to capital.

We must peruse the footnotes for the financial statements to arrive at these adjustments. The calculation of capital should, ideally, be tailored to reflect each company's financial accounting. You will also notice that the adjustments we made to arrive at NOPAT have companion adjustments to arrive at capital. And, as with the NOPAT calculations, we can arrive at capital by starting at either of two points: total assets (the asset approach) or book value of equity (sources-of-financing approach).

Using the asset approach, we begin with net operating assets and then make adjustments to reflect total invested capital:

$$\text{Capital} = \text{Net operating assets}$$
$$+ \begin{pmatrix} \text{LIFO reserve} \\ \text{Net plant and equipment} \\ \text{Other assets} \\ \text{Goodwill} \\ \text{Accumulated goodwill amortization} \\ \text{Present value of operating leases} \\ \text{Bad debt reserve} \\ \text{Capitalized research and development} \\ \text{Cumulative write-offs of special items} \end{pmatrix}$$

For example, it can be argued that goodwill generated from paying more when acquiring a company than its assets' book value is an investment. Using this reasoning, we add both goodwill and prior periods' amortization of goodwill to capital to reflect the company's asset investment.[15]

Using another approach, the source-of-financing approach, we begin with the book value of common equity and add debt, equity equivalents and debt equivalents:

$$\text{Capital} = \text{Book value of common equity}$$
$$+ \begin{pmatrix} \text{Preferred stock} \\ \text{Minority interest} \\ \text{Deferred income tax reserve} \\ \text{LIFO reserve} \\ \text{Accumulated goodwill amortization} \end{pmatrix}$$
$$+ \begin{pmatrix} \text{Interest-bearing short-term debt} \\ \text{Long-term debt} \\ \text{Capitalized lease obligations} \\ \text{Present value of operating leases} \end{pmatrix}$$

Continuing our example using McDonald's, we estimate capital using the asset approach. We begin with net operating assets and adjust for plant and equipment, other assets, and the value of the operating leases. *Operating current assets* include cash, marketable securities, receivables, inventories, and other current assets. For McDonald's in 2004, these amount to $2,857.8.[16] *Net operating assets* are operating current assets, less operating current liabilities, such as accounts payable.

---

[15] Though goodwill amortization is no longer permitted, many companies have amortized goodwill in the past such that the value reflected on the balance sheet is net of amortized goodwill from years in which goodwill was amortized.

We calculate McDonald's capital using the asset approach as $29,422.6 million:[17]

	Amount in Millions	Source of Information
Begin with net operating assets	$378.9	Current assets, less accounts payable, taxes payable, and accrued expenses, all from the balance sheet
Add: Net plant, property, and equipment	20,703.1	Balance sheet
Add: Other assets	2,448.3	Balance sheet
Add: Intangibles	1,828.3	Balance sheet (assumption: all intangibles represent goodwill)
Add: Present value of operating leases	4,064.0	Implied from data in note
Capital	$29,422.6	

Alternatively, we may use the source-of-financing approach, starting with the book value of equity and arriving at the same amount of capital:

	Amount in Millions	Source of Information
Begin with Book value of equity	$14,201.5	Balance sheet
Add: Deferred income taxes	781.5	Balance sheet
Total equity and equity equivalents	$14,983.0	
Add: Book value of long-term debt	$8,357.3	Current and long-term portions of debt from balance sheet
Add: Accrued interest	179.4	Balance sheet
Add: Interest-bearing short-term debt	862.2	Notes payable from balance sheet
Add: Present value of operating leases	4,064.0	Calculated from note data
Add: Other liabilities	976.7	Balance sheet
Total debt and debt equivalents	$14,439.6	
Capital	$29,422.6	

---

[16] Information on bad debt reserve, capitalized research and development, and cumulative write-offs was not available in the financial statements. The extent to which these omissions affect the resultant economic value-added measure is unknown, but these items are also omitted in published examples of economic value added due to unavailability of the data. See, for example, the explanations accompanying the Wal-Mart example in Stewart, *The Quest for Value*, p. 99.

[17] Net operating assets are operating current assets less accounts payable [$714.3], taxes payable [$576.4], and accrued expenses other than accrued interest [$1,188.2], $2,857.8 − 2,478.9 = $378.9.

Some consultants make a further distinction between invested capital (as described previously) and operating capital.[18] *Operating capital* is invested capital less goodwill. In other words, operating capital is the amount of the investment employed in operations. Goodwill is removed as capital because it tends to be distorted by premiums paid in acquiring other companies.[19] Goodwill for McDonald's in 2004 is $1,828.3 million and accumulated goodwill amortization is not determinable from published financial statements. Removing goodwill from invested capital produces operating capital of $27,594.3 million.

Return on Capital

We calculate the *return on capital* by dividing operating income after taxes by capital. This measure is a return on investment measure, using NOPAT instead of accounting profit:

$$\text{Return on capital} = \frac{\text{Net operating profit after taxes}}{\text{Capital}}$$

The return on capital for McDonald's is the ratio of the NOPAT to invested capital, or

$$\text{McDonald's return on capital} = \frac{\$2,309.7 \text{ million}}{\$29,422.6 \text{ million}} = 7.85\%$$

The return on operating capital for McDonald's is somewhat higher:

$$\text{McDonald's return on operating capital} = \frac{\$2,309.7 \text{ million}}{\$27,594.3 \text{ million}} = 8.37\%$$

Which return measure is best to use in evaluating McDonald's? It depends on whether you are focusing on (1) McDonald's ability to profitably and efficiently use investors' funds (including funds used to acquire other companies at a premium), which requires use of the former measure; or (2) McDonald's ability to profitably and efficiently

---

[18] Copeland, Koller, and Murrin, *Valuation: Measuring and Managing the Value of Companies*, 2nd ed.

[19] Another possible adjustment is for excess cash and marketable securities. Excess cash and marketable securities are those in excess of the typical need for cash and marketable securities. Copeland, Koller, and Murrin estimate that the need for cash and marketable securities is between 0.5% and 2% of sales, varying by industry.

use its operating assets (allowing better comparability across companies in the same industry), which requires the use of the latter measure.

Cost of Capital

The cost of capital is the cost of raising additional funds from debt and equity sources. For each source, there is a cost. Once the cost of each source of capital is determined, the cost of capital for the company is calculated as a weighted average of each cost, where the weight represents the proportionate use of each source.

The cost of debt is the after-tax cost of debt, r_d^*, adjusted for the benefit from the tax-deductibility of interest:

$$r_d^* = r_d(1 - \text{Marginal corporate tax rate})$$

where the before-tax rate, r_d, is the prevailing yield on long-term bonds of companies with similar credit risk. For example, at the end of 2004, bonds of similar risk to McDonald's yielded approximately 5%. Using the marginal tax rate of 35%, the after-tax cost of debt for McDonald's is

$$r_d^* = 0.05(1 - 0.35) = 3.25\%$$

There are different methods used to estimate the *cost of equity capital*, which is the return that shareholders require on their investment. Using the widely accepted approach that is based on the capital asset pricing model, the cost of equity capital is the sum of the risk-free rate of interest and the premium for bearing market risk:

$$r_e = r_f + \beta(r_m - r_f)$$

where r_f is the risk-free rate of interest, r_m is the expected return on the market, and β is the stock's beta.[20] This calculation is not as straightforward as it looks. One issue is the appropriate proxy for the risk-free rate. The risk-free rate of interest should, theoretically, be the return on a zero-beta portfolio with a duration similar to the holding period of the investor. Because this estimation task is extremely difficult, an alternative is to proxy the risk-free rate using rates on securities with no default risk; that is, U. S. government debt. If a government obligation with a short duration is used, such as a Treasury bill, there is a mismatch of the duration between the Treasury bill and the

---

[20] *Beta* is the estimated slope coefficient that relates the returns on the stock to the returns on the market computed using regression analysis.

risk-free portfolio. A more suitable proxy is the 10-year government bond, because this matches the duration of the market portfolio.[21]

Another issue is the premium for market risk, $(r_m - r_f)$. Stewart advocated a 6% market risk premium, based on the historical spread between the return on the market and the return on long-term government bonds. Thomas Copeland, Tim Koller, and Jack Murrin, on the other hand, advocate a slightly different approach, using the difference between the geometric mean return on the market and that of the long-term government bonds, both calculated over a long time frame. They estimate that the risk premium may range between 3% and 8%, and that the estimate is sensitive to the period over which the estimate is made. Aswath Damodaran uses a value in between these two, 5.5%, in his estimations.[22] For the purposes of demonstrating the calculation, we use a 5.5% market risk premium.

The market risk premium is tailored to the company's specific risk premium by multiplying the market risk premium by the company's common stock beta, β. The beta is a measure of the sensitivity of the returns on the company's stock to changes in the returns on the market. Estimates of beta and are readily available from financial services such as MSCI Barra, Standard and Poor's Compustat, Yahoo! Finance, or Value Line. We'll use a beta of 0.95 for McDonald's for the purposes of this example.[23] Using the 10-year Treasury bond rate of 4.23%, a market risk premium of 5.5%, and a beta of 0.9, McDonald's cost of equity is

$$r_e = 0.0423 + 0.95\,(0.055) = 0.095 = 9.5\%$$

In sum, the cost of capital of McDonald's is comprised of the cost of debt of 3.25% and the cost of equity of 9.5%. We weight the costs of debt and equity using the proportion each represents in the capital structure to arrive at a cost of capital for the company.

The first step is to determine the book values of debt and equity. One method is to use the debt and equity book values that we determined in the calculation of capital. Another method is to estimate the

---

[21] See Copeland, Koller, and Murrin for a discussion of the comparability of durations. Stewart specifies that this rate should be the rate on a long-term government bond. Copeland, Koller, and Murrin are more specific, advocating the rate on a 10-year U.S. Treasury bond. Using the latter approach, the risk-free rate for 2004 is 4.23%.

[22] Available at the web site of Aswath Damodaran, http://pages.stern.nyu.edu/~adamodar/. You can find an explanation of the methods typically used in estimating this premium in Aswath Damodaran "Estimating Equity Risk Premiums," available at his web site.

[23] The beta 0.95, taken from *Value Line Investment Survey*, agrees with the beta reported by Yahoo! Finance.

market value of the capital components. This requires estimating the market value of both debt and equity.

McDonald's capital structure at the end of 2003 (and the beginning of 2004) consists of:[24]

Capital	Book Value in Millions	Book Value Proportions	Market Value in Millions	Market Value Proportions
Debt capital	$14,447.4	52.5%	$14,447.4	31.5%
Equity capital	13,047.2	47.5%	31,333.0	68.4%
Total	$27,494.6	100.0%	$45,780.4	100.0%

McDonald's capital structure at the end of 2004 consists of:

Capital	Book Value in Millions	Book Value Proportions	Market Value in Millions	Market Value Proportions
Debt capital	$14,439.6	49.1%	$14,439.6	26.2%
Equity capital	14,983.0	50.9%	40,635.3	73.8%
Total	$29,422.6	100.0%	$55,074.9	100.0%

Additions and subtractions to debt and equity capital are made throughout the year. Because of this and the lack of specific data on changes in capital, we can approximate the capital proportions by averaging the beginning and ending capital proportions for the year. Using book values, this gives us approximately 51% debt and 49% equity. The weighted average cost of capital using the book weights and a 9.5% cost of equity, is

$$\text{Cost of capital} = [0.51\,(0.0325)] + [0.49\,(0.095)] = 0.063 \text{ or } 6.3\%$$

Using market value weights, the cost of capital is greater because approximately 71.1% of its capital is equity:

$$\text{Cost of capital} = [0.289(0.0325)] + [0.711(0.095)] = 0.077 \text{ or } 7.7\%$$

Which do we use: 6.3% or 7.7%? In most applications, we choose the method that best reflects the marginal cost of funds. If the company

---

[24] In addition to estimating the company's most recent market value capital components, it is useful to look at the capital structure of other companies in the industry and to consider the trends in the company's capital structure over time, because the capital structure of a company at a point in time may not reflect the company's target capital structure.

raises an additional dollar of capital, in what proportion does it raise these funds? We usually think of this in terms of the market value proportions, and would, therefore, use the 7.7% cost of capital. But in this particular application, we are applying this cost of capital against the invested capital, which is most often stated in terms of book values. Mixing a market value determined cost of capital with book value of invested capital results in distortions.[25] Therefore, we use the book value weighted cost of capital in determining economic profit (that is, the 6.3%).

Economic Profit and Performance

Economic profit is the profit generated during the period in excess of what is required by investors for the level of risk associated with the company's investments. Economic profit is analogous to the net present value of capital budgeting, and represents the value added by the company's management during the period.

Suppose we assume that McDonald's cost of capital is 6.3%. Using the two, equivalent economic profit calculations, we see that McDonald's management generated an economic profit in 2004:

$$\begin{aligned}
\text{McDonald's economic profit} &= \text{Net operating profit after taxes} - \left(\frac{\text{Cost of}}{\text{capital}} \times \text{Capital}\right) \\
&= \$2,309.7 \text{ million} - (0.063 \times \$29,422.6 \text{ million}) \\
&= \$2,309.7 \text{ million} - \$1,853.6 \text{ million} \\
&= \$456.1 \text{ million}
\end{aligned}$$

or

$$\begin{aligned}
\text{McDonald's economic profit} &= \left(\frac{\text{Rate of}}{\text{return}} - \frac{\text{Cost of}}{\text{capital}}\right) \times \text{Capital} \\
&= (0.785 - 0.063) \times \$29,422.6 \text{ million} \\
&= \$456.1 \text{ million}
\end{aligned}$$

McDonald's earned an economic profit of $456.1 million in 2004. In other words, McDonald's management added value during 2004.

Though it seems that McDonald's added value during the period, as represented by the estimate of economic profit, the estimate of economic profit is sensitive to the estimate of the cost of capital. Because the cost of capital is something that is difficult to measure, we should look at the

---

[25] The extent of the distortion depends on the relation between the market value of capital and the book value of capital.

sensitivity of the estimated economic profit to the cost of capital. Consider the sensitivity of our estimate of McDonald's cost of capital to plus and minus 100 basis points:

$$\frac{\text{McDonald's economic profit}}{\text{if the cost of capital is } 7.3\%} = \$2,309.7 - \$2,147.8 = \$161.9 \text{ million}$$

$$\frac{\text{McDonald's economic profit}}{\text{if the cost of capital is } 5.3\%} = \$2,309.7 - \$1,559.4 = \$750.3 \text{ million}$$

Consequently, drawing a conclusion regarding the degree of profitability depends, in large part, on the estimated cost of capital. In our example of McDonald's, we see that the company created value in 2004, even in the case of a cost of capital of 7.3%.

Market Value Added

A measure closely related to economic profit is market valued added. Market value added is the difference between the company's market value and its capital. Essentially, market value added is a measure of what the company's management has been able to do with a given level of resources (the invested capital):

$$\text{Market value added} = \text{Market value of the firm} - \text{Capital}$$

Like economic profit, market value added is in terms of dollars and the goal of the company is to increase added value. However, being top of the list of companies ranked on the basis of market value added does not mean that the company has outperformed other companies. It merely means that the company has the greatest difference between is book and market values of capital—accumulated over time. Rather, performance is evaluated by looking at the *change* in market value added over a period. The change in the market value added is a measure of how effectively the company's management employs capital to enhance the value of capital to *all* suppliers of capital, not just common shareholders.[26] The change in market value added is the change in the market value of capital (debt and equity), less the change in the book value of capital.

Looking once again at McDonald's, we see the following for 2004 and 2003:

---

[26] A related issue is whether the company's management should be striving to maximize the value of the company or to maximize the value of common equity. The market-value-added measure focuses on the former, whereas more common measures, such as stock returns, focus on the latter. In general, maximizing the value of the company will result in the maximization of shareholders' wealth.

Capital	2004 (in millions)	2003 (in millions)	Change (in millions)
Market value of equity, plus market value of debt	$55,074.9	$45,780.4	$9,294.5
Less: Invested capital	29,422.6	27,494.6	1,928.0
Market value added	$25,652.3	$18,285.8	$7,366.5

This analysis tells us that McDonald's management has increased the market value added in 2004, adding $7,366.5 million more in market value in excess of invested capital.

It is often the case in application that the book value of debt and the book value of preferred stock are used in estimating both the market value of capital and the book value of capital.[27] Therefore, the change in market value added from one year to the next amounts to the change in the market value of common equity, plus the change in the book value of debt and preferred stock. Because of this measurement of market value added, the change in market value added is determined, in large part, by the change in the market value of the common stock. Therefore, the change in market value is affected by the change in the value of the market in general.

RECONCILING ECONOMIC VALUE ADDED WITH MARKET VALUE ADDED

There are two different value-added measures: economic value added (economic profit) and market value added. Economic value added is based on the adjusted operating earnings (after taxes), invested capital, and the company's weighted average cost of capital. Market value added is based on a comparison of invested capital with the market value of capital. These two measures are both designed to help evaluate the performance of a company.

There is a logical link, however, between market value added and economic profit. The market value added should be equal to the present value of future periods' economic profit, discounted at the cost of capital. If we assume that the company will generate future-period economic profit equivalent to this period's economic profit, in perpetuity, the relation between market value and economic profit is a simple one:

---

[27] See, for example, Stewart, *The Quest for Value*, pp. 153–154.

$$\text{Market value added} = \frac{\text{Economic profit}}{\text{Cost of capital}}$$

Yet, the perpetuity assumption is not valid for most companies because of a very basic notion: economic profits are generated only when a company has some comparative or competitive advantage. Most companies cannot maintain these advantages for long periods of time; for example, government regulations may change, patents are not perpetual, and demographics change, all of which can erode a company's advantage and, as a result, its economic profit. Therefore, the assumption of a perpetual stream of the current period's economic profit is not reasonable in most cases.

Another reason why this relation does not hold in application is that the methods of determining economic profit and market value added are quite different. Economic value added is a single-period measure, estimated using accounting data and an estimated cost of capital. Market value added employs market values, which are more forward-looking estimates of performance.

Still another reason why this relation does not hold true is that the estimates of economic profit are just that—estimates. Economic profit is estimated by starting with accounting data and making adjustments to better reflect economic reality. However careful an analyst is in adjusting the accounting data, the estimated economic profit cannot precisely reflect true economic profit.

Economic profit and market value added may result in conflicting evaluations of performance. For example, in the 2002 ranking by Stern Stewart, Intel Corporation is ranked 10th among the Russell 3000 companies in terms of its market value added (of $77.4 billion), implying that Intel is one of the best companies in terms of providing value to its shareholders. But Intel has a negative economic profit (of $3.7 billion), which implies the company's management lost value in its most recent fiscal year. This apparent contradiction between economic profit and market value added may be due to the fact that economic profit, while theoretically forward-looking, is based on historical, single-period accounting data, whereas market value added is based on forward-looking stock prices.[28,29]

---

[28] As we have shown previously, slight differences in the estimated cost of capital can result in quite different conclusions regarding economic profit and performance.

[29] As you can see, this equation is nonsensical in the case in which there is an economic loss and a positive market value added.

Challenges in Applying Value-Added Measures

Even advocates of economic profit do not prescribe a particular formula for calculating economic profit. Economic profit has ambiguous elements, most notably the adjustments to operating income and the cost of capital.[30] Conceivably, two analysts could calculate economic profit, yet draw different conclusions regarding companies' relative performance.

The calculation of operating income (NOPAT) requires that each company be treated as an individual case. The adjustments to arrive at operating profits after taxes are different for each company and there may be over 150 adjustments applied. This makes it difficult to apply from the perspective of the financial analyst who must rely on financial statements and other publicly available information to determine economic profit. Though a formula could be developed to deal with the most common adjustments, there are always exceptions to the general rules that must be dealt with.

There are also many ambiguities regarding the measurement of the cost of capital. One problem is determining the best model for the estimate of the cost of equity. Should the analyst use the capital asset pricing model or the dividend valuation model?[31] Suppose the analyst uses the capital asset pricing model, which requires specifying a market risk premium (that is, the additional required return for bearing market risk). Should the market risk premium be 5%? 6%? In some cases the choice matters, making the difference between a value-adding company and a value-destroying company. Another problem with the estimation of the cost of capital is the choice of weights to apply to the difference costs of capital. Though market weights are theoretically appealing, many apply weights based on book values.

BUT ARE VALUE-ADDED MEASURES BETTER?

Whether the value-added measures aid the financial analyst in assessing the operating performance and financial condition of a company is

---

[30] This is not the fault of economic profit *per se*, but rather the starting point of the calculations: reported financial statements prepared according to generally accepted accounting principles.

[31] Most applications of economic profit use a CAPM-based cost of equity. The CAPM has been challenged as inadequately capturing the risk and return relationship. See, for example, Eugene F. Fama and Kenneth. R. French, "The Cross-Section of Expected Stock Returns," *Journal of Finance* (June 1992), pp. 427–465.

really an empirical issue.[32] What we know from an analysis of the economic profit (also known as *economic value added*) is that it has a solid foundation in economic and financial theory. Using economic profit instead of accounting earnings is attractive because it avoids the problems associated with accounting earnings.

Are companies that generate more economic profit than others better companies? Not necessarily. First, we estimate economic profit as a single-period measure, using the current period's financial information. Just like a return on investment ratio, focusing on economic profit is short-sighted. It may be the case that the company is sacrificing future profitability to generate current period economic profit.

Second, we calculate economic profit using the company's cost of capital as the "hurdle." But if the company has taken on activities that are riskier than the company's typical activities, the calculation of the cost of capital and economic profit may not reflect this increased risk-taking, resulting in an over-statement of current profitability.

Third, the estimates of NOPAT and the cost of capital are just that—estimates. Even slight variations in the assumptions and estimates can result in dramatic changes in measured profitability.

Fourth, we state economic profit in dollar terms, but this is misleading when comparing companies of different sizes. According to the Stern Stewart's 2002 Russell-3000 rankings, Microsoft generated $2,201 million of economic value added, whereas Proctor & Gamble Company generated $2,315.[33] So which one performed better? Comparing economic value added, Procter & Gamble appears to be approximately the same as Microsoft, but once you look at the amount of invested capital (that is, what they invested to generate that economic profit), you get a different picture: Procter & Gamble's invested capital is almost twice that of Microsoft's.

We show the economic profit, market value added, and capital over time for the Coca-Cola Company.[34] We use this data to compare eco-

---

[32] Evidence suggests that economic profit is not a better predictor of future stock value than the traditional measures. The primary challenge in using economic profit as a performance measure is the estimating economic profit. See, for example, Jeffrey M. Bacidore, John A. Boquist, Todd T. Milbourn, and Anjan V. Thakor "The Search for the Best Financial Performance Measure," *Financial Analysts Journal* 53 (May–June), pp. 11–20; and by Pamela P. Peterson and David R. Peterson, *Company Performance and Measures of Value Added* (Charlottesville, VA: The Research Foundation of the Institute of Chartered Financial Analysts, 1996).

[33] Richard Teitelbaum, "America's Greatest Wealth Creators," *Fortune*, 10 November 1997, pp. 265–276.

[34] The Coca-Cola Company did not continue reporting economic profit beyond 2002.

nomic profit and net income in Panel A of Exhibit 7.4. Here we see that economic profit and net income track closely. Continuing the example of Coca-Cola, we provide the book value and market value of capital for the same period, in Panel B of Exhibit 7.4. We have assumed that the book value of debt is equal to the market value of debt; this assumption does not affect the general conclusion that the market value of capital is driven, in large part, by general market movements.[35]

EXHIBIT 7.4   The Coca-Cola Company's Economic Profit and Capital, 1984–2002
Panel A: Economic Profit and Net Income

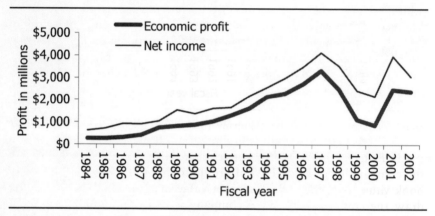

Panel B: Book Value and Market Value of Capital

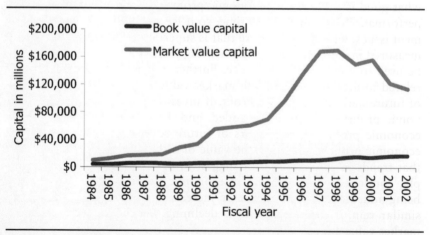

---

[35] In book value terms, debt is approximately one-third of Coca-Cola's capital.

EXHIBIT 7.4 (Continued)
Panel C: Return on Capital

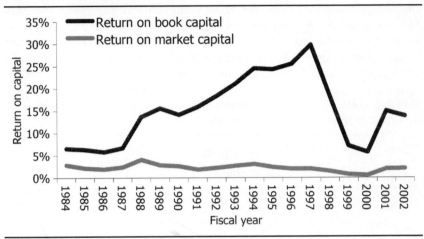

Source of data: The Coca-Cola Company 10-K filings, various years.

In Panel C of Exhibit 7.4, we see that the conclusions with regard to the company's return on capital are quite different whether we use the book value of capital or the market value of capital. In either case, we draw the conclusion that the company is consistent in creating value each year.

So if there are problems associated with measuring economic profit, what good is it? In theory economic profit is a measure of a company's performance over a period of time; so if we can overcome the measurement issues, we have a measure that is superior to accounting income. If measured in a consistent manner across companies or across time, it can be used to compare performance. Further, economic profit in theory is related to market value added: market value added is the present value of future periods' economic profit. If investors' valuation of future economic profit is market value added, and if current and recent periods' economic profits are predictors of future economic profit, we can use economic profit in assessing the value of a share of stock. This suggests that trends in economic profit suggest future value changes. For example, continued improvements in economic profit suggest that value is being added and we should see an increase in market value added. In a similar vein, if economic profit is declining, we should see a decline in market value added.

Suppose that we focus on market value added. Is this a better measure of the performance of a company than, say, return on assets? Going back to the definition of market value added, we see that a company increases its market value when the change in the market value of its capital (that is, the market value of its debt and equity) exceeds the change in its invested capital (that is, book value of its debt and equity). Because most of the measures of market value added use the market value of equity and assume that the market value of debt is equal to the book value of debt, the change in the market value added is really attributed to the change in the stock's price. Therefore, it should be no surprise that the change in the market value added is highly correlated with a company's stock's return and sensitive to general movements in the stock market.

SUMMARY

The value-added measures of economic profit and market value added are really nothing new—it is their application in performance measurement within firms and in financial analysis that is new. Economic profit (also called economic value added) is the operating profit of a company less its cost of capital. The calculation of operating profit for this purpose requires adjustments to remove distortions resulting from the application selected accounting principles. There can be more than 150 adjustments and these adjustments must be tailored for the individual company.

Traditional performance measures, such as the return on assets, are not forward looking, do not capture risk, and do not control for factors outside of the control of the company. Additionally, unless care is taken in the construction of these measures, these measures may be affected by the choice of accounting methods.

The calculation of economic profit requires financial statement data, notes to financial statements, and, in most cases, information beyond published financial information. This makes the calculation of economic profit challenging to the financial analyst. Calculating economic profit also requires determining the amount of company's invested capital. Adjustments to arrive at operating income for the economic profit calculation have companion adjustments to arrive at invested capital. The cost of capital is generally determined by using a weighted average of the costs of capital. However, there are many assumptions and complexities in the calculation of the cost of capital and any estimate is subject to possible measurement error because a company's cost of capital cannot be observed.

Market value added is the difference between the market value of a company's capital and the amount of invested capital (i.e., book values of capital). Performance measurement requires determining the change in market value added because the total market value added is measured over the company's entire history.

If used with the understanding of what the value added measures can and cannot do, the financial analyst may benefit from including these measures along with the traditional measures.

CHAPTER 8

Credit Analysis

Credit analysis involves the analysis of a multitude of quantitative and qualitative factors over the past, present, and future. The past and present are introductions to what the future may hold. Corporate bond credit analysis involves an analysis of an issuer that is not done in isolation but in conjunction with a review of the issuer's place within the industry and an overall analysis of where the industry fits within the national economy and, with increasing frequency, the global economy.

In the previous chapter, we discussed equity analysis. Corporate bond credit research and equity research areas historically have been viewed as separate. With the development and application of option theory, these two areas of financial research are now considered to be complementary. Now credit risk models that are grounded in option theory are commercially available to investors.

Our purpose in this chapter is to discuss the general principles of corporate credit analysis. We begin with a discussion of the types of credit risk an investor faces when investing in a bond. We then explain the factors to consider in credit analysis: character, capacity, collateral, and covenants.

TYPES OF CREDIT RISK

An investor who lends funds to a corporation by purchasing its debt obligation is exposed to credit risk. But what is credit risk? Credit risk encompasses three types of risk:

- Default risk
- Credit spread risk
- Credit downgrade risk

Default risk is the likelihood that the issuer of debt is not able to meet the promised obligations to pay interest and repay the obligation. *Credit spread risk* is the uncertainty that the difference between the yield on a debt instrument and the yield for a benchmark will change. *Credit downgrade risk* is the risk of an increase in default risk. We refer to this risk as *downgrade risk* because we often observe that the company's credit rating is downgraded as default risk increases.

Default Risk

If a corporate bond issuer fails to make timely payment of interest and principal due to the bondholders or if it violates any provisions set forth in the bond indenture, the issuer is said to default. In that case, the issuer is required to payoff the bond issue immediately. If this cannot be done, the bankruptcy laws take over. The petition for bankruptcy can be filed either by the company itself, in which case it is called a voluntary bankruptcy, or be filed by its creditors, in which case it is called an involuntary bankruptcy

The laws governing bankruptcy are set forth in the U.S. Bankruptcy Code. Under these rules, a business may file for reorganization under Chapter 11 or liquidation under Chapter 7 of the Code. The liquidation of a corporation means that all the assets will be distributed to the holders of claims of the corporation and no corporate entity survives. In reorganization, a new corporate entity results. Some holders of the claim of the bankrupt corporation receive cash in exchange for their claims, others may receive new securities in the corporation that results from the reorganization, and others may receive a combination of both cash and new securities in the resulting corporation.

Many companies that file for Chapter 11 reorganization ultimately are liquidated. For example, Eastern Airlines filed for bankruptcy in March of 1989 and then liquidated under Chapter 7 in January of 1991.[1] When a company is liquidated, creditors receive distributions based on the *absolute priority rule* to the extent assets are available. The absolute priority rule is the principle that senior creditors are paid in full before junior creditors are paid anything. For secured and unsecured creditors, the absolute priority rule guarantees their seniority to equity holders.

Credit default risk is the risk that the corporate borrower will fail to satisfy the terms of the obligation with respect to the timely payment of interest and repayment of the amount borrowed resulting in a loss inter-

---

[1] At the time Eastern filed for Chapter 11 bankruptcy, its net worth was more than $1 billion, which would have been sufficient to pay the creditors in full. However, by the time Eastern Airlines was liquidated, the company had incurred $1.7 in losses and legal fees, leaving unsecured creditors unsatisfied.

est and principal. Analysis of the credit default risk of an issuer or issuer is a time-consuming process. While many large institutional investors have a staff of credit analysts to analyze the credit default risk, most investors rely on form credit ratings assigned to issues by specialist companies referred to as rating agencies. As of this writing, the three major rating agencies are Moody's Investors Service, Standard & Poor's Corporation, and Fitch Ratings.

A credit rating is an indicator of the potential default risk associated with a particular debt obligation. It represents in a simplistic way the rater's assessment of an issuer's ability to meet the payment of principal and interest in accordance with the terms of the debt contract. Credit rating symbols or characters are uncomplicated representations of more complex ideas. In effect, they are summary opinions.

A credit rating is a formal opinion given by a rating agency of the credit default risk faced by investing in a particular issue of debt securities. Rating agencies provide credit ratings for long-term and short-term debt obligations. For the long-term debt obligations (debt with an original maturity of more than one year), a credit rating is a forward-looking assessment of the probability of default and the relative magnitude of the loss should a default occur. For short-term debt obligations (debt with an original maturity of 12 months or less), a credit rating is a forward-looking assessment of the probability of default. While rating agencies analyze a company when making their determination of what credit rating to assign, the credit rating is specific to the issue not the issuer.

The rating systems of the rating agencies use similar symbols. Ratings systems are uncomplicated representations of more complex ideas. There are different rating systems for a given rating agency for short-term and long-term debt. In the rating systems of all three rating agencies, the term "high grade" means low credit risk, or conversely, high probability of future payments. The highest-grade bonds are designated by Moody's by the letters Aaa, and by the others as AAA. The next highest grade is Aa (Moody's), and by the others as AA; for the third grade all rating agencies use A. The next three grades are Baa (Moody's) or BBB, Ba (Moody's) or BB, and B, respectively. There are also C grades. S&P and Fitch use plus or minus signs to provide a narrower credit quality breakdown within each class. Moody's uses 1, 2, or 3 for the same purpose. Bonds rated triple A (AAA or Aaa) are said to be "prime"; double A (AA or Aa) are of high quality; single A issues are called "upper medium grade"; and triple B are "medium grade." Lower-rated bonds are said to have "speculative" elements or be" distinctly speculative." Bond issues that are assigned a rating in the top four categories are referred to as investment-grade bonds. Bond issues that carry a rating below the top four categories are referred to as noninvestment grade bonds or more popularly as high-yield bonds or junk bonds. Thus, the bond market can be divided into two sectors: the investment grade sector and the noninvestment grade sector. Distressed debt is a subcategory of noninvestment grade bonds. These bonds may be in bankruptcy proceedings, may be in default of coupon payments, or may be in some other form of distress.

Credit Spread Risk

The price performance of a corporate debt obligation and its return over some investment horizon depends on how the credit spread changes. If the credit spread increases, the market price of the debt obligation declines. The risk that an issuer's debt obligation will decline due to an increase in the credit spread is called credit spread risk.

Credit spread risk exists for an individual issue, debt obligations in a particular industry or economic sector, and for all debt issues in the economy. For example, during economic recessions investors are concerned that issuers will face a decline in cash flows that will be used to service debt obligations. As a result, the credit spread increases for all corporate issuers and the prices of all corporate debt obligations in the market decline.

While there are portfolio managers who seek to allocate funds among different sectors of the bond market to capitalize on anticipated changes in credit spreads, an analyst investigating the credit quality of an individual issue is concerned with the prospects of the credit spread increasing for that particular issue. But how does the analyst assess whether he or she believes the market will change the credit spread attributed to the issue?

To understand this form of credit risk, we need to review some basic yield relationships for debt obligations.

First, the price of a bond changes in the opposite direction to the change in the yield required by the market. Thus, if yields in the bond market increase, the price of a bond declines, and vice versa. Second, the yield on a corporate debt instrument is made up of two components:

1. The yield on a similar maturity U.S. Treasury issue
2. A premium to compensate for the risks associated with the corporate debt instrument that does not exist in a Treasury issue

The risk premium is referred to as a *spread*. In the United States, we often use the yield on U.S. Treasury issues as the benchmark yield because these issues have no credit default risk, are highly liquid, and Treasury issues are not callable. The part of the risk premium or spread attributable to credit default risk is called the *credit spread*. In a well functioning bond market, we observe that the higher the credit rating, the smaller the credit spread (see Exhibit 8.1).[2]

The price performance of a corporate bond and its return over some investment horizon depends on how the credit spread changes over time. If the credit spread increases, the market price of the bond declines. The risk that an issuer's bond will decline due to an increase in the credit spread is what we refer to as *credit spread risk*. Changes in credit spreads affect the value of the portfolio and can lead to losses for bond traders or underperformance relative to a benchmark for portfolio managers. Credit spread risk exists for an individual bond issue, bonds in a particular industry or economic sector, and for all bonds issues in the economy.

To gauge the exposure of portfolio or an individual bond to credit spread risk requires the use of measures developed in the bond market. More specifically, credit spread risk is approximated by *spread duration*. To understand this measure, we must first understand what is meant by the duration of a bond or a bond portfolio. *Duration* is a measure of the approximate change in the value of a bond or a bond portfolio when interest rates change. A useful way of thinking of duration is that it is the approximate percentage change in the value of a bond for a 100 basis point change in "interest rates." The interest rate that is assumed to change is the Treasury rate. So, if the duration of a bond is 5, this means that for a 100 basis point increase in interest rates, the bond's price will decline by approximately 5%.

As we mentioned earlier, the yield on a corporate bonds is the sum of the Treasury yield and the credit spread. A measure of how a corporate bond's price is likely to change if the credit spread sought by the market changes is what we refer to as the *spread duration*. For example, a spread duration of 1.7 for a corporate bond means that for a 100 basis point increase in the credit spread (holding the Treasury yield constant), the bond's price will change by approximately 1.7%.

Credit Downgrade Risk

Once a credit rating is assigned to a corporate bond, a rating agency monitors the credit quality of the issuer and can reassign a different credit rating. An improvement in the credit quality of an issue or issuer is rewarded with a better credit rating, referred to as an *upgrade*; deterioration in the

---

[2] In a study of the determinants of credit spreads, Pierre Collin-Dufresne, Robert S. Goldstein, and J. Spencer Martin examine a number of possible factors that may explain credit spreads. They conclude that changes in credit spreads are driven primarily by supply and demand, rather than factors that affect the issuer's credit risk and liquidity ("The Determinants of Credit Spread Changes," *Journal of Finance* 56, no. 6 (December 2001), pp. 2177–2207).

EXHIBIT 8.1   Yields and Credit Spreads for Aaa and Baa Rated Bonds, 1985–2005

Panel A: Yields

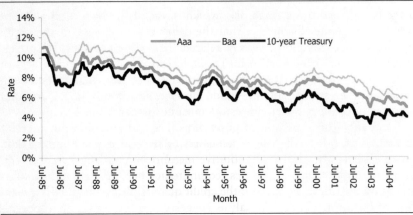

Panel B: Spreads

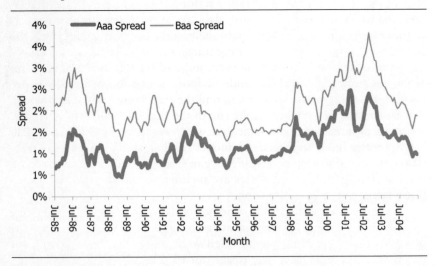

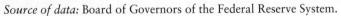

Source of data: Board of Governors of the Federal Reserve System.

credit quality of an issue or issuer is penalized by the assignment of an inferior credit rating, referred to as a *downgrade*. An unanticipated downgrading of an issue or issuer increases the credit spread sought by the market, resulting in a decline in the price of the issue or the issuer's debt obligation. This risk is credit downgrade risk, which is often also referred to as *migration risk* because it is the risk that the debt's risk will migrate to another risk class. It is obviously closely related to credit spread risk because a downgrade is one reason why the credit spread will increase.

Consequently, a credit rating is not a measure of the other aspects of credit risk (that is, credit ratings do not measure credit spread risk and credit downgrade risk). Yet, investors must be aware of how rating agencies gauge credit default risk for purposes of assigning ratings in order to understand credit downgrade risk. When assessing the credit quality of an issuer, an analyst often evaluates quantitative measures such as financial ratios in terms of what the rating agencies require to achieve a certain rating. When an analyst expresses a view that the credit quality has deteriorated, typically the analyst means that the analysis suggests that the issue may be downgraded because the quantitative measures identified in the analysis are inferior to the benchmarks for the issue to maintain its current credit rating.

To help gauge credit downgrade risk for corporate bonds in general, the rating agencies periodically publish data about how issues that they rated change over time. This data is published in the form of a table which is called a rating migration table, rating transition table, or transition matrix. Each cell in the table shows the percentage of bonds rated by the rating agency at the beginning of the study period that had their rating change to another rating. For example, we can find the percentage of bonds rated AA that had a rating of single A at the end of the period. These tables are published for different lengths of time over which rating changes are analyzed.

Attempts have been made to model credit migration using the transition matrix. For example, in JPMorgan's modeling of migration, credit spreads and default probabilities are included in addition to the transition matrix to explain migration.[3]

Is there actually migration among bonds to different rating classes? Christopher Gootkind reports that from 1973 to 2000, the percentage of bonds that were high-quality rated went from 58% to 25%, and the percentage of bonds rated Baa rose from 10% to 32%.[4] He also demon-

---

[3] Bill Demchak, "Modelling Credit Migration," in Angelo Arvantis and Jon Gregory (eds.), *Credit: The Complete Guide to Pricing, Hedging and Risk Management* (London: Risk Books, 2001), pp. 276–388.

[4] Christopher L. Gootkind, "Improving Credit Risk Analysis," in *Fixed-Income Management: Credit, Covenants, and Core-Plus* (Charlottesville, VA: Association for Investment Management and Research, 2003), pp. 11–18.

strates that there is increased credit volatility, with upgrades and down-grades following a more dramatic cyclical pattern.

FACTORS TO CONSIDER IN CORPORATE CREDIT ANALYSIS

In conducting this credit examination, the analyst considers the four Cs of credit:

- Character
- Capacity
- Collateral
- Covenants

The first of the Cs stands for *character* of management, the founda-tion of sound credit. This includes the ethical reputation as well as the business qualifications and operating record of the board of directors, management, and executives responsible for the use of the borrowed funds and repayment of those funds. The next C is *capacity* or the abil-ity of an issuer to repay its obligations.

The third C, *collateral*, is looked at not only in the traditional sense of assets pledged to secure the debt, but also to the quality and value of those nonpledged assets controlled by the issuer. In both senses the col-lateral is capable of supplying additional aid, comfort, and support to the debt and the debtholder. Assets form the basis for the generation of cash flow which services the debt in good times as well as bad. The final C is for *covenants*, the terms and conditions of the lending agreement. Covenants are restrictions on how management operates the company and conducts its financial affairs. Covenants may restrict management's discretion. A default or violation of any covenant may provide a mean-ingful early warning alarm enabling investors to take positive and cor-rective action before the situation deteriorates further. Covenants have value as they play an important part in minimizing risk to creditors. They help prevent the unconscionable transfer of wealth from debt holders to equity holders.

Analysis of an Issuer's Character

In 1912, the Pujo Committee, a subcommittee of the House Banking and Currency Committee, investigated the "Money Trust monopoly." The following is an exchange between the committee's counsel, Samuel Untermeyer, and the well-known financier John Pierpont Morgan:

Untermeyer:	Is not commercial credit based primarily upon money or property?
Morgan:	No, sir, the first thing is character.
Untermeyer:	Before money or property?
Morgan:	Before money or anything else. Money cannot buy it . . . because a man I do not trust could not get money from me on all the bonds in Christendom.

The issue of character is important, as evidenced by the financial scandals of the past few years. Investors who ignore character do so at their own peril. The analysis of characters involves reviewing the history of the business, as well as an analysis of the experience and quality of management. In discussing the factors it considers in assigning a credit rating, Moody's Investors Service notes the following regarding the quality of management:

> Although difficult to quantify, management quality is one of the most important factors supporting an issuer's credit strength. When the unexpected occurs, it is a management's ability to react appropriately that will sustain the company's performance.[5]

In assessing management quality, the rating analysts at Moody's, for example, try to understand the business strategies and policies formulated by management. Following are factors that are considered: (1) strategic direction, (2) financial philosophy, (3) conservatism, (4) track record, (5) succession planning, and (6) control systems.[6]

Analysis of the Capacity to Pay

In assessing the ability of an issuer to pay, an analyst evaluates the company's financial condition and operating performance, as we discussed in earlier chapters. The goal in evaluating a company's capacity to pay is to assess whether the company's future cash flows are sufficient to satisfy the obligations to pay interest and repay the debt as promised. However, we should note that there are generally many factors contributing to a company's lack of capacity to pay and there is no well-specified theory of why companies fail. Therefore, assessing a company's capacity to pay is not straightforward.

---

[5] "Industrial Company Rating Methodology," *Moody's Investors Service: Global Credit Research* (July 1998).
[6] "Industrial Company Rating Methodology," p. 7.

Factors to Consider

In a study of credit quality of U.S. corporate debt, Marshall Blume, Felix Lim, and Craig MacKinlay examine the financial characteristics of bonds that are rated in the four investment grade categories (AAA, AA, A, and BBB).[7] The financial characteristics they examine are the interest coverage ratio, the operating margin, the long-term debt-to-assets ratio, and total debt-to-assets ratio. They found that these financial characteristics distinguish the bonds in the different rating categories. Higher quality bonds are distinguished by their lower financial risk and higher profitability. Blume, Lim, and MacKinlay also observe that higher-quality bonds are issued by larger firms (as measured by market capitalization), which suggests some consideration for factors beyond financial ratios (e.g., established product lines).

In addition to management quality, the factors examined by analysts at Moody's include:

1. Industry trends
2. Regulatory environment
3. Basic operating and competitive position
4. Financial position and sources of liquidity
5. Company structure (including structural subordination and priority of claim)
6. Parent company support agreements
7. Special event risk[8]

Industry trends are critical to the analysis. It is only within the context of an industry is a company analysis valid. For example, if the annual growth rate of a company is 20%, on a standalone basis, that may appear attractive. However, if the industry is growing at 40% per annual, the company is competitively weak.

In considering industry trends, analysts should look at the following eight factors:[9]

■ Economic cyclicality
■ Growth prospects

---

[7] Marshall E. Blume, Felix Lim, and Craig Mackinlay, "The Declining Credit Quality of U.S. Corporate Debt: Myth or Reality," *Journal of Finance* (August 1998), pp. 1389–1413.

[8] "Industrial Company Rating Methodology," p. 3.

[9] Frank J. Fabozzi, "Credit Analysis for Corporate Bonds," Chapter 32 in Frank J. Fabozzi (ed.), *The Handbook of Fixed Income Securities* (New York: McGraw-Hill, 2005), p. 735.

- Research and development expenses
- Competition
- Sources of supply
- Degree of regulation
- Labor
- Accounting

The analyst must be sure to look at the vulnerability of the company to economic cycles, the barriers to entry, and the exposure of the company to technological changes. For firms in regulated industries, proposed changes in regulations must be analyzed to assess their impact on future cash flows. At the company level, diversification of the product line and the cost structure are examined in assessing the basic operating position of the firm.

In addition to the measures described in previous chapters for assessing a company's financial position over the past three to five years, an analyst must look at the capacity of a firm to obtain additional financing and backup credit facilities. *Backup credit facilities* are additional sources of financing that may be called upon if needed. There are various forms of backup facilities. The strongest forms of backup credit facilities are those that are contractually binding and do not include provisions that permit the lender to refuse to provide funds. An example of such a provision is one that allows the bank to refuse funding if the bank feels that the borrower's financial condition or operating position has deteriorated significantly.[10] Noncontractual facilities such as lines of credit that make it easy for a bank to refuse funding should be of concern to the analyst. The analyst must also examine the quality of the bank providing the backup facility.

Analysts should also assess whether the company can use securitization as a funding source for generating liquidity. *Asset securitization* involves using a pool of loans or receivables as collateral for a security. The decision of whether to securitize assets to borrow or use traditional borrowing sources is done on the basis of cost. However, if traditional sources dry up when a company faces a liquidity crisis, securitization may provide the needed liquidity. An analyst should investigate the extent to which management has considered securitization as a funding source.

Other sources of liquidity for a company may be third-party guarantees, the most common being a contractual agreement with its parent company. When such a financial guarantee exists, the analyst must undertake a credit analysis of the parent company.

---

[10] Such a provision is called a material adverse change clause.

Bankruptcy Prediction Models

Analysts and researchers use various statistical techniques to assess the potential likelihood of bankruptcy. These techniques include multiple discriminant analysis, linear probability models, and hazard models. The models that use these techniques all use financial ratios in some manner to predict whether the company is likely to fail.[11]

For example, we can use multiple discriminant analysis (MDA) to identify those financial characteristics that distinguish companies on the basis of capacity to pay. In analyzing credit default risk, the primary advantage of using MDA is that allows an analyst to simultaneously consider a large number of characteristics and does not restrict the analysis to a sequential evaluation of each individual attribute. In his 1967 dissertation, Edward I. Altman established the baseline of bankruptcy prediction, using MDA to discriminate between bankrupt and nonbankrupt companies. The financial variables that have been found by Edward Altman to be important for predicting corporate bankruptcy using MDA are:[12]

X1: Working capital to total assets

X2: Earnings retention, measured as the ratio of retained earnings to total assets

X3: Operating return on assets, which is the ratio of earnings before interest and taxes (EBIT) to total assets

X4: Market value of equity/Total capitalization

X5: Total asset turnover, which is net revenues divided by total assets.

In his original work, published in 1968, Altman estimates the following model:

---

[11] There are also more sophisticated credit risk models that have been developed in recent years. These models fall into two general categories. Structural models and reduced form models. *Structural models* are based on option theory viewing the bondholders as having granted the stockholders a call option on the company's assets and that the decline in the value of the assets below some default threshold will trigger a default. These models do not use financial ratios other than the leverage of a firm. Reduced form models treat bankruptcy as a surprise and do not use financial ratios. For a discussion of these models, see Chapter 9 and 10 in Mark J. P. Anson, Frank J. Fabozzi, Moorad Choudhry, and Ren-Raw Chen, *Credit Derivatives: Instruments, Pricing, and Applications* (Hoboken, NJ: John Wiley & Sons, 2004).

[12] See Chapters 8 and 9 in Edward I. Altman, *Corporate Financial Distress and Bankruptcy: A Complete to Predicting and Avoiding Distress and Profiting from Bankruptcy* (New York: John Wiley & Sons, 1993); and Edward I. Altman, Robert G. Haldeman, and Paul Narayann, "Zeta Analysis: A New Model to Identify Bankruptcy Risk of Corporations," *Journal of Banking and Finance* (June 1977), pp. 29–54.

$$Z = 1.2\ X1 + 1.4\ X2 + 3.3\ X3 + 0.6\ X4 + 0.999\ X5$$

The output of the MDA is a score (hence MDA is called a *credit-scoring model*) that is used to classify firms with respect to whether or not there is potentially a serious credit problem that would lead to bankruptcy. If the calculated value of z (referred to as the "z-score") is above 2.675, this indicates a low risk of bankruptcy; if the z-score is below 1.81, this indicates a high risk of bankruptcy and if the z-score fall between 1.81 and 2.675, it is unclear.[13]

A modification of this model to accommodate nonmanufacturers is to drop the turnover ratio and use reestimated coefficients:[14]

$$Z^* = 6.56\ X1 + 3.26\ X2 + 6.72\ X3 + 1.05\ X4$$

Let us apply the basic model and the variation for nonmanufacturers to actual companies. When we applied the models to Wal-Mart Stores, we found z and z^* scores of 5.185 and 5.194, respectively. This indicates that the company has a low risk of bankruptcy. We can see the pattern of z and z^*-scores in panel A of Exhibit 8.2. Wal-Mart Stores has scores that are well above the 2.675 cutoff.

EXHIBIT 8.2   Z-Scores and Z*-Scores for Selected Companies, 1998–2004
Panel A: Wal-Mart Stores

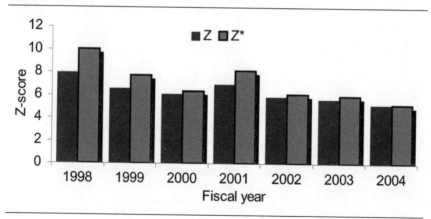

---

[13] This is the range that Altman refers to as the "zone of ignorance."

[14] This is a model shown in Edward I. Altman, "Predicting Financial Distress of Companies: Revisiting the Z-Score and ZETA® Models," working paper, New York University, July 2000.

EXHIBIT 8.2 (Continued)
Panel B: Winn-Dixie

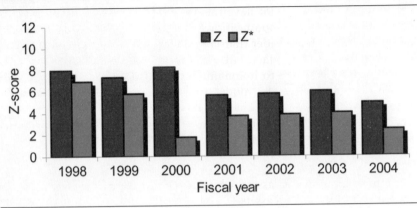

Panel C: Delta Air Lines

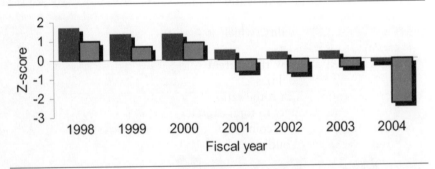

Source of data: Financial data from 10-K filings by the respective companies, various years and stock price data from Yahoo! Finance.

Winn-Dixie Stores, as we show in panel B, has declining z-scores, with z^*-scores in the range that indicates a high risk of bankruptcy in both 2000 and 2004. Winn-Dixie filed for bankruptcy seven months after its June 2004 fiscal-year end.

In panel C, we show the scores for Delta Air Lines. In all years shown and for both z-score metrics, Delta Air Lines falls into the high risk of bankruptcy category.[15]

---

[15] Delta Air Lines' received "bail-out" money under the Air Transportation Safety and System Stabilization Act passed in September 2001, but Delta was already struggling prior to 2001. Delta Air Lines filed for bankruptcy in September 2005.

In 1977, Edward Altman, Robert Haldeman, and P. Narayanan updated the basic model, creating the ZETA® model.[16] This is a proprietary model, so we do not have the ability to report the details here or apply it. The primary modifications that the researchers made were to adapt the model to consider that large firms—that once were considered too large to fail—do, in fact, fail. Another modification was to make the model more applicable to nonmanufacturing sectors. A further modification was to update the model to consider changes in accounting. Many of these accounting changes relate to the movement of off-balance sheet debt to the balance sheet, which then changes the estimated role of each variable in the model.

The ZETA® model consists of seven variables:

- Operating return on assets, which is the ratio of earnings before interest and taxes to total assets
- Variability of operating earnings, measured as the standard error of estimate of EBIT/Total assets (normalized) for 10 years
- Debt service, which is the ratio of earning before interest and taxes to interest charges
- Cumulative profitability, which is measured as the ratio of retained earnings to total assets
- Liquidity, captured by the current ratio, which is the ratio of current assets to current liabilities
- Capitalization, which is the ratio of the five-year average market value of shareholders' equity to total capital
- Size, measured as the company's total tangible assets, normalized to reduce the effect of outliers

Altman, Haldeman, and Narayanan find that the most important variable in this model in terms of discriminating between healthy and nonhealthy companies is the cumulative profitability. The next most important variable is the variability of operating earnings.

Carol Osler and Gijoon Hong report z-scores for a large sample of companies in the U.S. for the Altman model and variations to this model, such as the hazard model of Tyler Shumway.[17,18] They observe

[16] E. Altman, R. Haldeman, and P. Narayanan, "ZETA Analysis: A New Model to Identify Bankruptcy Risk of Corporations," *Journal of Banking and Finance* 1 (June 1977), pp. 29–35.

[17] Carol Osler and Gijoon Hon, "Rapidly Rising Corporate Debt: Are Firms Now Vulnerable to an Economic Slowdown?" *Federal Reserve Bank of New York: Current Issues in Economics and Finance* 6, no. 7 (June 2000).

[18] Tyler Shumway, "Forecasting Bankruptcy More Accurately: A Simple Hazard Model," *Journal of Business* 74, no. 1 (January 2001), pp. 101–124.

that the z-scores rose, on average, over the 1995–1999 period due to the run-up in prices in the market that was fueled by Internet companies. Market value of equity is the numerator of the $X4$ variable in the original Altman model and, hence inflated stock prices affect the z-score.

Whereas credit scoring models have been found to be helpful to analysts and bond portfolio managers, they do have limitations as a replacement for human judgment in credit analysis. Marty Fridson, for example, provides the following sage advice about using MDA models:

> . . . quantitative models tend to classify as troubled credits not only most of the companies that eventually default, but also many that do not default. Often, firms that fall into financial peril bring in new management and are revitalized without ever failing in their debt service. If faced with a huge capital loss on the bonds of a financially distressed company, an institutional investor might with to assess the probability of a turnaround—an inherently difficult-to-quantify prospect—instead of selling purely on the basis of a default model.[19]

Fridson also notes that one must recognize that "companies can default for reasons that a model based on reported financial cannot pick up."

In addition to MDA, there are several other statistical techniques that can be used in predicting bankruptcy. Several of these fall into the class of multiple regression models: linear probability model, probit regression model, and logit regression model. In all of these models applied to predicting default, the dependent variable is "default" or "nondefault."[20] A linear probability model is the simplest type however a major drawback of the model is that the predicted value may be negative. Probit regression model is a nonlinear regression model where predicted values (the probabilities) fall between 0 and 1 because what is being predicted is based on the standard normal cumulative probability distribution. As with the probit regression model, the logit regression model is a nonlinear regression model and the predicted value is also based on a cumulative probability distribution. However, rather than being a standard normal cumulative probability distribution, it is stan-

---

[19] Martin S. Fridson, *Financial Statement Analysis: A Practitioner's Guide, Second Edition* (New York: John Wiley & Sons, 1995), p.195.
[20] The primary difference among these models is the underlying assumption regarding the distribution of the probability of bankruptcy as it lies between 0% and 100%.

dard cumulative probability distribution of a distribution called the logistic distribution.

Another, related technique that can be used is a *hazard model*. A hazard model is similar to the regression models, but each company's life span as a healthy company enters into the estimation. An example of this is the model by Tyler Shumway. Using Altman's 5-variable z-score model but estimating the model using hazard function, he finds that operating return on assets and capitalization are the most discriminating of the variables.

Analysis of the Collateral[21]

A corporate debt obligation may be secured or unsecured. As explained earlier, in the case of the liquidation of the company, the proceeds from a bankruptcy are distributed to creditors based on the *absolute priority rule*. This rule states that senior creditors are paid before junior creditors, and that all creditors are paid before owners receive anything. However, in the case of reorganization, the absolute priority rule rarely holds.[22] That is, unsecured creditors may receive distributions for the entire amount of their claim and common stockholders may receive something, while secured creditors may receive only a portion of their claim. The reason is that reorganization requires approval of all the parties. Consequently, secured creditors are willing to negotiate with both unsecured creditors and stockholders in order to obtain approval of the plan of reorganization.

The question is then, what does a secured position mean in the case of reorganization if the absolute priority rule is not followed in reorganization? The claim position of a secured creditor is important in terms of the negotiation process. However, because absolute priority is not followed and the final distribution in reorganization depends on the bargaining ability of the parties, some analysts place less emphasis on collateral compared to the other factors discussed earlier and covenants discussed later.

The types of collateral used for a corporate bond issue are broadly classified as mortgage debt and other secured debt. *Mortgage debt* is

---

[21] For a more detailed discussion, see Richard S. Wilson and Frank J. Fabozzi, *Corporate Bonds: Structures and Analysis* (New York: John Wiley, 1996).

[22] Many researchers have found that there are violations of the absolute priority rule in over 75% reorganizations. See, for example, Julian R. Franks and Walter N. Torous "An Empirical Investigation of U.S. Firms in Reorganization," *Journal of Finance* 44, no. 3 (July 1989), pp. 747–769; and Brian L. Betker, "Management's Incentives, Equity's Bargaining Power, and Deviations from Absolute Priority in Chapter 11 Bankruptcies," *Journal of Business* 68, no. 2 (April 1995), pp. 161–183..

debt secured by real property such as plant and equipment is called mortgage debt. The largest issuers of mortgage debt are electric utility companies. There are instances when a company might have two or more layers of mortgage debt outstanding with different priorities.[23]

Debt may be secured by many different assets. Collateral trust bonds and notes are secured by pledges of financial assets such as cash, receivables, other notes, debentures or bonds, and not by real property. Generally, the market value of the collateral must be at least some minimum percentage of the bonds or notes outstanding.

Railroads and airlines have financed much of their rolling stock and aircraft with secured debt. These securities go by various names such as *equipment trust certificates* (ETCs) in the case of railroads, and *secured equipment certificates*, *guaranteed loan certificates*, and *loan certificates* in the case of airlines. If a railroad, for example, buys a piece of equipment, the title to that equipment is transferred to a trustee, who, in turn, leases the equipment to the railroad and sells the trust certificates to investors.

Analysis of Covenants[24]

Covenants deal with limitations and restrictions on the borrower's activities. Some covenants are common to all indentures, such as

- To pay interest, principal, and premium, if any, on a timely basis.
- To maintain an office or agency where the securities may be transferred or exchanged and where notices may be served upon the company with respect to the securities and the indenture.
- To pay all taxes and other claims when due unless contested in good faith.
- To maintain all properties used and useful in the borrower's business in good condition and working order.
- To maintain adequate insurance on its properties.
- To submit periodic certificates to the trustee stating whether the debtor is in compliance with the loan agreement.
- To maintain its corporate existence.

The covenants listed above are often called *affirmative covenants* because they call upon the debtor to make promises to do certain things.

---

[23] This situation usually occurs because the companies cannot issue additional first mortgage debt (or the equivalent) under the existing indentures.

[24] The discussion in this section draws from Wilson and Fabozzi, *Corporate Bonds: Structures and Analysis.*

In contrast to affirmative covenants, *negative covenants* are those which require the borrower not to take certain actions. There is an infinite variety of restrictions that can be placed on borrowers, depending on the type of debt issue, the economics of the industry and the nature of the business, and the lenders' desires. Some of the more common restrictive covenants include various limitations on the company's ability to incur debt, since unrestricted borrowing can lead a company and its bondholder to ruin. Thus, debt restrictions may include limits on the absolute dollar amount of debt that may be outstanding or may require a ratio test—for example, debt may be limited to no more than 60% of total capitalization or that it cannot exceed a certain percentage of net tangible assets.

There may be an interest or fixed charge coverage test of which there are two types. One, a *maintenance test*, requires the borrower's ratio of earnings available for interest or fixed charges to be at least a certain minimum figure on each required reporting date (such as quarterly or annually) for a certain preceding period. The other type, a *debt incurrence test*, only comes into play when the company wishes to do additional borrowing. In order to take on additional debt, the required interest or fixed charge coverage figure adjusted for the new debt must be at a certain minimum level for the required period prior to the financing. Debt incurrence tests are generally considered less stringent than maintenance provisions. There could also be cash flow tests or requirements and working capital maintenance provisions.

Some indentures may prohibit subsidiaries from borrowing from all other companies except the parent. Indentures often classify subsidiaries as restricted or unrestricted. Restricted subsidiaries are those considered to be consolidated for financial test purposes; unrestricted subsidiaries (often foreign and certain special-purpose companies) are those excluded from the covenants governing the parent. Often, subsidiaries are classified as unrestricted in order to allow them to finance themselves through outside sources of funds.

Limitations on dividend payments and stock repurchases may be included in indentures. Often, cash dividend payments will be limited to a certain percentage of net income earned after a specific date plus a fixed amount. Sometimes the dividend formula might allow the inclusion of the net proceeds from the sale of common stock sold after the specified date. In other cases, the dividend restriction might be so worded as to prohibit the declaration and payment of cash dividends if tangible net worth (or other measures, such as consolidated quick assets) declines below a certain amount. There are usually no restrictions on the payment of stock dividends. In addition to dividend restrictions, there are often restrictions on a company's repurchase of its common stock if such purchase might cause a violation or deficiency in the dividend determination formulae. Some holding company indentures might limit the right of the company to pay dividends in the common stock of its subsidiaries.

Another part of the covenant article may place restrictions on the disposition and the sale and leaseback of certain property. In some cases, the proceeds of asset sales totaling more than a certain amount must be used to repay debt. This is seldom found in indentures for unsecured debt but at times some investors may have wished they had such a protective clause. At other times, a provision of this type might allow a company to retire high coupon debt in a lower interest rate environment, thus causing bondholders a loss of value. It might be better to have such a provision where the company would have the right to reinvest the proceeds of asset sales in new plant and equipment rather than retiring debt, or to at least give the investor the option of tendering his bonds.

SUMMARY

Credit analysis of a corporation involves the analysis of a multitude of quantitative and qualitative factors over the past, present, and future based on the issuer's, and, if applicable, the guarantor's, operations and need for funds. In conducting a credit examination, an analyst must consider the four C's of credit—character, capacity, collateral, and covenants.

Character analysis involves the analysis of the quality of management, including trying to understand the business strategies and policies formulated by management.

Assessing the capacity of an issuer to pay involves an analysis of the financial statements, including the analysis of industry trends (i.e., vulnerability of the company to economic cycles, the barriers to entry, and the exposure of the company to technological changes), the regulatory environment, basic operating and competitive position, financial position and sources of liquidity, company structure, parent company support agreements (if any), and special event risk.

Statistical models have been used that based on financial data seek to predict corporate bankruptcy (multiple discriminant analysis) or the probability of bankruptcy (linear probability model, probit regression model, and logit regression model).

Analysis of collateral involves an analysis of the claim position of the bondholder. In the liquidation of a corporation, proceeds are distributed to creditors based on the principle of absolute priority while in a reorganization absolute priority rarely holds because reorganization requires approval of all the parties. The claim position of a secured creditor is important in terms of strength in the negotiation process in reorganization.

Covenants deal with limitations and restrictions on the borrower's activities. Affirmative covenants call upon the debtor to make promises to do certain things (e.g., make timely payment of interest and repayment of principal). Negative covenants are those which require the borrower not to take certain actions.

CHAPTER 9

Analysis of Risk Using Fundamentals

Throughout this book, we have described various measures computed from financial statements and ratios that have combined financial statement data and market data. We discussed how these measures can be used to evaluate the economic prospects of a company. In Chapter 5, we began the process of showing how a company's stock can be valued using a discounted value approach, and we presented several dividend discount models that are used by practitioners. In this chapter, we look at another dimension of valuation, risk. While there are different models that explain risk, our focus in this chapter is on so-called *fundamental factor models*. Such models use the various measures discussed in this book as inputs to the model.

Our objective is not to discuss how factor models are built. It is simply to demonstrate how the measures discussed are used in a model to estimate the expected return and risk of stocks. We also explain how a fundamental factor model can be used in managing portfolios.

MEASURING RISK

It is well known that there is a positive relationship between risk and expected return. That is, the greater the risk, the higher the expected return that investors want. This is a basic principle of financial theory. The tough part is figuring out the appropriate way to define risk and to how to quantify that risk. The term "risk" is used very casually in the financial press and in day-to-day conversations about investments. Financial theory provides a more specific definition of risk. There are several models in financial theory that define risk quantitatively and relate that risk to the expected return. These models are called *asset pricing models*

Total Risk

The first major step in the development of asset pricing models was to show how to think about and quantify risk in general. Harry Markowitz explained that the risk of an individual stock should be quantified by using a measure from probability theory called the standard deviation or variance.[1] Specifically, risk can be measured by the standard deviation or variance of the stock's return. This measure of risk is referred to as *total risk* and we will see why it bears this label shortly. Thus, according to financial theory, the total risk that an investor faces from investing in a stock is measured using the standard deviation or variance of the stock's return.

Markowitz then went on to show that the total risk of a portfolio of assets is *not* found by simply adding up the total risk of the individual assets included in the portfolio. Rather, the total risk of a portfolio as measured by the variance of the portfolio's return depends on the correlation (or covariance) between the returns for each pair of assets in the portfolio. The lower the correlation, the lower the total risk of the portfolio. The procedure for diversification is then to combine assets in a portfolio giving recognition to the correlation between stocks. Markowitz then went on to show how an efficient portfolio can be created. An *efficient portfolio* is a portfolio where for a given level of expected return, the portfolio's total risk will be the smallest of all possible portfolios that can be created.

Systematic Risks and Unsystematic Risk

Subsequent analysis of risk developed two principles. The first is that in a reasonably efficient stock market, investors are only rewarded for accepting risks that cannot be diversified away by an investor. The second principle is that total risk as measured by the variance of an asset's return can be decomposed into two general categories of risk—risks that can be diversified away and risk that cannot be diversified away.

Risks that an investor cannot diversify away are called *nondiversifiable risks* or *systematic risks*. Any remaining risk is called *unsystematic risk* or *residual risk*. It is the systematic risks that the first principle asserts investors should be compensated for, not unsystematic risk.

---

[1] Harry Markowitz, "Portfolio Selection," *Journal of Finance* (March 1952), pp. 77–91.

ASSET PRICING MODEL

Now the problem becomes one of identifying systematic risks. Such risks are referred to as *factors* or *risk factors*. Asset pricing models show the relationship between the expected return for a stock and risk factors. The two dominant asset pricing models are the capital asset pricing model and the arbitrage pricing theory model.

Capital Asset Pricing Model

Let's look at a popular asset pricing model, the capital asset pricing model (CAPM). Based on certain assumptions, CAPM says that there is only one form of systematic risk. This systematic risk is the movement of the market in general. Mathematically, the CAPM is expressed as follows:

$$E(R_i) = R_F + \beta_i \, [E(R_M) - R_F]$$

where

$E(R_i)$ = expected return for asset i
R_F = risk-free rate
$E(R_M)$ = expected return for the market
β_i = a measure of the systematic risk of asset i

In theory, the market is defined as all assets. However, in practice, in the application of the CAPM, the market is defined as a broad-based equity market index such as the Standard & Poor's 500.

The β_i is referred to as the asset's beta. It is defined as the ratio of the covariance of the asset's return with the market to the total risk (variance) of the market. It is a measure of systematic risk because it quantifies how the asset's return systematically varies with the market's return. The CAPM asserts that the expected (or required) return on an individual asset is a positive linear function of its index of systematic risk as measured by beta. The higher the beta, the higher the expected return. Notice that it is only an asset's beta that determines its expected return—which is what we noted earlier that the CAPM assumes only one form of systematic risk.

We have demonstrated how to use the CAPM to obtain the expected return in Chapter 7 where we used it to obtain the required return.

Beta is estimated statistically. There are two approaches used to estimate beta. The first is to use a time series of monthly or weekly returns to estimate the following relationship between the return on the stock and the return on the market:

$$R_{i,t} = \alpha_i + \beta_i R_{M,t} + e_t$$

where

$R_{i,t}$ = return for stock i in period t
$R_{M,t}$ = return for the market in period t
β_i = beta for stock i
e_t = error term in period t

The α_i and β_i are the parameters to be estimated and the latter is the estimate used for the beta of stock i in the CAPM. The regression relationship above is called the *market model* and the estimated beta is sometimes referred to as the *historical beta*.

The problem with using historical beta is that beta captures fundamental attributes of a company such as leverage, size, earnings growth, and liquidity, and these attributes change over time. What is important is that the analyst use the future beta in estimating the expected return when employing the CAPM. Because company attributes change, historical beta may not be a good predictor of future beta.

This problem leads to the second approach to estimating beta. The approach involves first calculating historical beta for all firms using the market model. Suppose there are N firms and therefore N estimated betas denoted by β_i. Then suppose that there are K fundamental attributes that have been found to affect the beta of firms. We will denote these attributes at a given point in time as $X_1 \ldots X_K$. Then the following cross-sectional multiple regression is estimated:

$$\beta_i = a_0 + a_1 X_{1,i} + a_2 X_{2,i} + \ldots + a_K X_{K,i} + e_i$$

where the as are the parameters to be estimated and the $X_{k,i}$ is the observed fundamental attribute k for firm i.

Given the estimates for the parameters, we estimate a company's beta by substituting its fundamental attributes into the previous equation. The resulting estimated beta is called a *fundamental beta*.[2] The assumption in using this procedure is that for all companies the fundamental beta is affected in the same way for each fundamental attribute. For example, it assumes that an increase in the leverage ratio by a certain amount affects the fundamental beta of Microsoft in the same way it affects Kmart.

---

[2] The term fundamental beta was first coined by Barr Rosenberg and Vinay Marthe in "The Prediction of Investment Risk: Systematic and Residual Risk," *Proceedings of the Seminar of the Analysis of Security Prices*, University of Chicago, November 1975, pp. 85–225.

Consider an application of this to the analysis of a single company. Suppose we have the estimates for the coefficients in the fundamental beta equation. If the company we are analyzing is acquiring another company and its liquidity, returns, leverage, and other fundamental factors are expected to change, the analyst can use this equation and the estimated coefficients to estimate the company's new beta.

The research into the fundamental factors of beta indicates that operating leverage and financial leverage are drivers of a company's systematic risk.[3] In addition, researchers have found that companies in industries that are more cyclical have higher betas.[4] In their analysis of the drivers of betas of value and growth stocks, John Campbell, Christopher Polk, and Tuomo Vuoteenaho find that betas are driven, in large part, by the cash-flow characteristics of the companies.[5]

Arbitrage Pricing Theory Model

In 1976, Stephen Ross developed an alternative equilibrium asset pricing model He derived this model based purely on arbitrage arguments, and hence he called it the *arbitrage pricing theory* (APT) model.[6] In its simple form, arbitrage is the simultaneous buying and selling of an asset at two different prices in two different markets. The arbitrageur profits without risk by buying cheap in one market and simultaneously selling at the higher price in the other market.

The APT model says that there may be more than one systematic risk. In contrast, the CAPM asserts that there is only one systematic risk. However, the APT model does not specify what the factors are. Following is the APT model:

---

[3] See, for example, Baruch Lev, "On the Association Between Operating and Risk," *Journal of Financial and Quantitative Analysis* (September 1974), pp. 627–642; and Stewart Myers, "The Relationship Between Real and Financial Measures of Risk and Return," in *Risk and Return in Finance*, Irwin Friend and James Bicksler (eds.), (Cambridge, MA: Ballinger, 1977).

[4] Myers, "The Relationship Between Real and Financial Measures of Risk and Return."

[5] John Y. Campbell, Christopher Polk, and Tuomo Vuolteenaho, "Growth or Glamour? Fundamentals and Systematic Risk in Stock Returns," NBER working paper 11389, May 2005. In their analysis, they break betas into two parts: that which is driven by changes in cash flow estimates and that which is driven by discount rate changes. The authors explain the differences in betas for value and growth stocks with these drivers. For example, they find that the growth stock's higher betas are attributed to the higher cash-flow uncertainty of these companies.

[6] Stephen A. Ross, "The Arbitrage Theory of Capital Asset Pricing," *Journal of Economic Theory* (December 1976), pp. 343–362.

$$E(R_i) = R_F + \beta_{i,M} [E(R_M) - R_F] + \beta_{i,F1} [E(R_{F1}) - R_F]$$
$$+ \beta_{i,F2} [E(R_{F2}) - R_F] + \ldots + \beta_{i,FK} [E(R_{FK}) - R_F]$$

where

$\beta_{i,Fj}$ = the sensitivity of asset i to the jth factor

$E(R_{Fj}) - R_F$ = the excess return of the jth systematic factor over the risk-free rate, and can be thought of as the price (or risk premium) for the jth systematic risk

The APT model states that investors want to be compensated for all the factors that *systematically* affect the return of a asset. The compensation is the sum of the products of the each factor's systematic risk ($\beta_{i,Fh}$), and the risk premium assigned to it by the market [$E(R_{Fh} - R_F)$]. As in the case of the CAPM, an investor is not compensated for accepting unsystematic risk.

Examining the APT and CAPM, we can see that the latter is actually a special case of the former. If the only factor in the APT is market risk, the APT model reduces to the CAPM.

Supporters of the APT model argue that it has several major advantages over the CAPM. First, it makes less restrictive assumptions about investor preferences toward risk and return.[7] Second, no assumptions are made about the distribution of security returns.

FACTOR MODELS

CAPM and APT are equilibrium models that tell us the relationship between risk and expected return. Factor models are empirically derived models that seek to identify the risk factors that explain stock returns. There are three types of factor models: statistical factor models, macroeconomic factor models, and fundamental factor models. We briefly describe the first two models below and then provide more detail on the model of principal interest to us, fundamental factor models.

A major difficulty in the application of factor models to equity valuation is that of identifying the risk factors. In a *statistical factor model,* historical and cross-sectional data on stock returns are tossed into a statistical model. Using a statistical technique called *principal components analysis*

---

[7] Specifically, CAPM assumes investors trade off between risk and return solely on the basis of the expected returns and standard deviations of prospective investments. The APT, on the other hand, simply requires some rather unobtrusive bounds be placed on potential investor utility functions.

"factors" are derived that best explain the variance of the observed stock returns. For example, suppose that monthly returns for 3,000 companies for 10 years are computed. The goal of principal components analysis is to produce "factors" that best explain the observed stock returns. Suppose that there are six "factors" that do this. These "factors" are statistical artifacts. The objective in a statistical factor model then becomes to determine the economic meaning of each of these statistically derived factors.

Because of the problem of interpretation, it is difficult to use the factors from a statistical factor model for valuation and risk control. Instead, practitioners prefer the two other models described below, which allow them to prespecify meaningful factors, and thus produce a more intuitive model.

In a *macroeconomic factor model*, the inputs to the model are historical stock returns and observable macroeconomic variables. These variables are called *raw descriptors*. The goal is to determine which macroeconomic variables are pervasive in explaining historical stock returns. Those variables that are pervasive in explaining the returns are then the factors and included in the model. The responsiveness of a stock's return to these factors is estimated using historical time series data.

FUNDAMENTAL FACTOR MODELS

Fundamental factor models use company and industry attributes and market data as the basic inputs to the model. Examples of the basic inputs are price/earnings ratios, book/price ratios, earnings momentum, and financial burden measures. The fundamental factor model uses stock returns and the basic inputs about a company and tries to identify those basic inputs that are pervasive in explaining stock returns. Those basic inputs about a company that are found to be important in explaining stock returns are called *raw descriptor*s and used in a fundamental factor model.

In practice, an investor can either develop a fundamental factor model or purchase one from a commercial vendor. Here we discuss a popular commercially available factor models—the MSCI Barra model. We also look at a factor model developed by two academic researchers.

The model developers begin with raw descriptors. Then using a proprietary statistical process, the raw descriptors are combined to produce risk factors to capture related company attributes. In the MSCI Barra E3 model these risk factors are referred to as *risk indices*.[8] The model

---

[8] For purposes of illustrating a fundamental factor model, we will discuss the E3 version of the MSCI Barra. There firm updates its fundamental factor model periodically.

has 13 risk indices and 52 industries/13 sectors. The 13 risk factors are (1) volatility, (2) momentum, (3) size, (4) size nonlinearity, (5) trading activity, (6) growth, (7) earnings yield, (8) value, (9) earnings variability, (10) leverage, (11) currency sensitivity, (12) dividend yield, and (13) nonestimation universe indicators.

Exhibit 9.1 gives the definitions of the 13 risk indices. Exhibit 9.2 lists the 52 industries in the model. Exhibit 9.3 shows the six risk indices that include raw descriptors using the measures or variants of measures discussed in earlier chapters.

EXHIBIT 9.1   MSCI Barra E3 Model Risk Index Definitions

---

1. *Volatility*
This risk index captures relative volatility using measures of both long-term historical volatility (such as historical residual standard deviation) and near-term volatility (such as high-low price ratio, daily standard deviation, and cumulative range over the last 12 months). Other proxies for volatility (log of stock price), corrections for thin trading (serial dependence), and changes in volatility (volume beta) are also included in this descriptor.

2. *Momentum*
This risk index captures common variation in returns related to recent stock price behavior. Stocks that had positive excess returns in the recent past are grouped separately from those that displayed negative excess returns.

3. *Size*
This risk index captures differences in stock returns due to differences in the market capitalization of companies.

4. *Size Nonlinearity*
This risk index captures deviations from linearity in the relationship between returns and log of market capitalization.

5. *Trading Activity*
This risk index measures the amount of relative trading in each stock. Stocks that are highly traded are likely to be those with greater institutional interest. Such stocks may display different returns behavior compared with those that are not widely held by institutions.

6. *Growth*
This risk index uses historical growth and profitability measures to predict future earnings growth.

7. *Earnings Yield*
This risk index combines current and historical earnings-to-price ratios with a measure of analyst-predicted earnings-to-price. Stocks with similar values of earnings yield behave in a similar fashion with respect to their returns.

8. *Value*
This risk index distinguishes between value stocks and growth stocks using the ratio of book value of equity to market capitalization.

EXHIBIT 9.1 (Continued)

> 9. *Earnings Variability*
> This risk index measures the variability in earnings and cash flows using both historical measures and analyst predictions.
>
> 10. *Leverage*
> This risk index measures the financial leverage of a company.
>
> 11. *Currency Sensitivity*
> This risk index measures the sensitivity of a company's stock return to the return on a basket of foreign currencies.
>
> 12. *Dividend Yield*
> This risk index computes a measure of predicted dividend yield using the past history of dividends and the market price behavior of the stock.
>
> 13. *Nonestimation Universe Indicator*
> This risk index flags companies outside the estimation universe. It allows the linear factor model to be extended to stocks outside the US-E3 estimation universe.

Source: United States Equity Risk Model Handbook: Version 3 (E3) (Berkeley, CA: Barra, 1998), pp. 74–76.

EXHIBIT 9.2 MSCI Barra E3 Industries and Sectors

Sector	US-E3 Industry
Basic Materials	Mining & Metals
	Gold
	Forest Products & Paper
	Chemicals
Energy	Energy Reserves & Production
	Oil Refining
	Oil Services
Consumer Noncyclicals	Food & Beverages
	Alcohol
	Tobacco
	Home Products
	Grocery Stores
Consumer Cyclicals	Consumer Durables
	Motor Vehicles & Parts
	Apparel & Textiles
	Clothing Stores
	Specialty Retail
	Department Stores
	Construction & Real Property

EXHIBIT 9.2 (Continued)

Sector	US-E3 Industry
Consumer Services	Publishing
	Media
	Hotels
	Restaurants
	Entertainment
	Leisure
Industrials	Environmental Services
	Heavy Electrical Equipment
	Heavy Machinery
	Industrial Parts
Utility	Electrical Utilities
	Gas Utilities
Transport	Railroads
	Airlines
	Trucking, Shipping, Air Freight
Health Care	Medical Providers & Services
	Medical Products
	Drugs
Technology	Electronic Equipment
	Semiconductors
	Computer Hardware & Office Equipment
	Computer Software
	Defense & Aerospace
Telecommunications	Telephones
	Wireless Telecommunications
Commercial Services	Information Services
	Industrial Services
Financial	Life & Health Insurance
	Property & Casualty Insurance
	Banks
	Thrifts
	Securities & Asset Management
	Financial Services

Source: United States Equity Risk Model Handbook: Version 3 (E3) (Berkeley, CA: Barra, 1998), pp. 83–84

Three of the risk indices include at least one of the measures of earnings, earnings forecast, or price-to-earnings ratio described in Chapter 5—the growth risk index, the earnings yield risk index, and the earnings variability risk index. The the growth index and the dividend yield risk index have raw descriptors using one of the dividend measures described in Chapter 5. The raw descriptors for the leverage index are those discussed in Chapters 4 and 8.

EXHIBIT 9.3 MSCI Barra E3 Risk Indices that Include Measures Covered in this Book as Raw Descriptors

Risk Index	Raw Descriptor
Growth	Payout ratio over five years
	Variability in capital structure
	Growth rate in total assets
	Earnings growth over the last five years
	Analyst-predicted earnings growth
	Recent earnings change
Earnings yield	Analysts-predicted earnings-to-price
	Trailing annual earnings-to-price
	Historical earnings-to-price
Value	Book-to-price ratio
Earnings variability	Variability in earnings
	Variability in cash flows
	Extraordinary items in earnings
	Standard deviation of analyst-predicted earnings-to-price
Leverage	Market leverage
	Book leverage
	Debt to total assets
	Senior debt rating
Dividend yield	Predicted dividend yield

Source: Extracted from *United States Equity Risk Model Handbook: Version 3 (E3)* (Berkeley, CA: Barra, 1998), pp. 71–73.

Now look at the factor models suggested by Eugene Fama and Kenneth French in their 1992 and 1993 studies.[9] They examine the relationship between stock returns, beta, and several fundamental factors, including the earnings-price ratio, leverage, size, and book-to-market value of equity. They observe that in addition to the market index, stock returns can be explained by size (market capitalization) and the book-to-market value of equity ratio. In general, smaller capitalization firms have greater returns than larger capitalization firms. Further, firms with high book-to-market ratios have higher returns than firms with lower

---

[9] Eugene F. Fama and Kenneth R. French, "The Cross-Section of Expected Stock Returns," *Journal of Finance* (June 1992), pp. 427–465; and Eugene F. Fama and Kenneth R. French, "Common Risk Factors in the Returns on Stocks and Bonds," *Journal of Financial Economics* (February 1993), pp. 3–56.

book-to-market ratios. This model has come to be referred to as the *Fama-French 3-factor model.*[10]

APPLICATIONS OF FUNDAMENTAL FACTOR MODELS

The output of a fundamental factor model is the expected return for a stock after adjusting for all of the risk factors. This return is called the *expected excess return.* From the expected excess return for each stock, an expected excess return for a portfolio comprised of stocks can be computed. This is the weighted average of the expected excess return for each stock in the portfolio. The weights are the percentage of a stock's value in the portfolio relative to the market value of the portfolio. Similarly, a portfolio's sensitivity to a given factor risk is a weighted average of the factor sensitivity of the stocks in the portfolio. The set of factor sensitivities is then the portfolio's risk exposure profile. Consequently, the expected excess return and the risk exposure profile can be obtained from the stocks comprising the portfolio.

With respect to applying the fundamental factor model to evaluate the risks of a company, consider that a company is simply a portfolio of assets. If the financial analyst understands and can forecast the fundamental factors that affect risks and returns for the segments, products, or divisions of the company, this can then be used once we view the company as a portfolio of investments. It is often easier to forecast the performance and condition of a component of a company. The analyst can then assemble these parts into the portfolio that is the company, thereby developing a better forecast of the company's risks and returns.

Since a stock market index or benchmark is nothing more than a portfolio that includes the universe of stocks making up the index, an expected excess return and risk exposure profile can be determined for an index. This allows a manager to compare the expected excess return and the risk profile of a stock and/or a portfolio to that of a market index whose performance the portfolio manager is measured against.

---

[10] Additionally, Fama and French provide evidence that suggests that many observed "anomalous" asset pricing relationships can be explained using this 3-factor model. See Eugene F. Fama and Kenneth R. French, "Multifactor Explanations of Asset Pricing Anomalies," *Journal of Finance* (March 1996), pp. 55–84. While there is further support for the role of the three factors in explaining stock returns, as pointed out by James L. Davis, Eugene F. Fama and Kenneth R. French, this model is incomplete—the three factors explain some, but not all of the variation in stocks' returns ("Characteristics, Covariances, and Average Returns: 1929 to 1997," *Journal of Finance* 55, no. 1 (February 2000) pp. 389–406).

Portfolios can be constructed by managers so as to have the desired exposure to the fundamental factors. To understand what this means, it is necessary to understand what the manager is attempting to do. A client specifies a benchmark for a manager. The goal of the manager is to outperform the benchmark. A common benchmark is the S&P 500. The benchmark has the risk exposures as defined by the fundamental model. The distinction between active money management and passive management is that the latter tries to match the performance of the benchmark while the former seeks to outperform the benchmark. In terms of fundamental factor models, a money manager who follows a passive strategy known as indexing will seek to construct a portfolio to match the factor exposures of the benchmark. Of course, the manager can do this by buying all the stocks in the benchmark. Alternatively, the manager can use an optimization program to construct a portfolio whose exposure to the factors is such that the portfolio constructed has minimal risk of not matching the performance of the benchmark. That is, the constructed portfolio has minimal "tracking error."

Active money management involves the money manager making bets. In terms of fundamental factor models, the bets are in the form of departures of the constructed portfolios exposure to the factors from the exposure of the factors in the benchmark.

SUMMARY

The total risk of a stock can be measured by the variance or standard deviation of the stock's return. The total risk of a portfolio depends on the correlation of returns of the stocks in the portfolio. The total risk of a stock can be divided into systematic risks and unsystematic risk. Investors should be reward only for accepting systematic risks. An asset pricing model shows the relationship between the systematic risks and expected return. The key is to determine the systematic risks. The capital asset pricing model asserts that there is only one systematic risk. Factor models assume that there may be more than one systematic risk.

There are three types of factor models: statistical factor models, macroeconomic factor models, and fundamental factor models. The factors in a statistical factor models are statistical artifacts and are therefore difficult to interpret and such models are rarely used by practitioners. The more common factor models are the macroeconomic factor model and the fundamental factor model. The raw descriptors in a macroeconomic factor model are macroeconomic variables; in a fundamental factor model the raw descriptors are fundamental variables for a company. In a factor model, the sensitivity of a stock's return to a factor is estimated. The risk exposure profile of a stock is identified by the set of factor sensitivities. The risk exposure profile of a portfolio is the weighted average of the risk exposure profile of the stocks in the portfolio. The power of a factor model is that given the risk factors and the factor sensitivities, a portfolio's risk exposure profile can be quantified and controlled.

CHAPTER 10

The Lessons We Learn

Financial analysis involves gathering the information about a company, its industry, and the economy, and developing an evaluation of the company's future financial condition and operating performance. The financial scandals of recent years have increased the awareness of the need for more transparency in financial disclosures and more analysis of the available information.

Former Chairman of the Securities and Exchange Commission, Harvey Pitt, summed up this era in his March 20, 2002 testimony before the Committee on Financial Services, U.S. House of Representatives:

> In recent years, corporate leaders have been under increasing pressure from the investment community, including individual investors, to meet elevated expectations. They also have been operating under a system that can misalign the incentives of investors and those of management. Our culture over the past decade has fostered a short-term perspective of corporate performance. Corporate leaders and directors have been rewarded for short-term performance, sometimes at the expense of long-term fundamental value. Investors have purchased stock not because they believed in the business or its strategy as an investment over the long-term, but simply under the assumption that stock prices would only go up.

As a result of these problems, we have seen many new laws and regulations, including the Sarbanes-Oxley Act of 2002.

Our focus in this book has been on fundamental value. Key to a company's fundamental value is its future financial condition and operating performance. In our analysis of a company, however, we rely upon information supplied by others; in particular, the company's own financial disclosures.

One of the buzzwords of recent years is transparency. *Transparency* in financial reporting means that companies provide information to owners and other stakeholders in an understandable manner. This requires that financial disclosures be clear, reliable, and comparable. Transparency is important in financial disclosures to insure the ability of stakeholders to evaluate the financial condition and performance of companies. Transparency is viewed as important for the efficient functioning of financial markets.[1]

We have focused on the interpretation of required financial disclosures that companies make, as prescribed by regulatory requirements. But in addition to the wealth of information available through these disclosures, many companies choose to disclose information above and beyond these required disclosures. In its Business Reporting Research Project, the Financial Accounting Standard Board (FASB) analyzed voluntary disclosures of companies. The FASB classified these disclosures into six categories:

1. Business data about the company's sales, products, and financial performance
2. Management analysis of business data, including goals, trends, impact of strikes, and benchmarking against competitors
3. Forward-looking information about products and operations, including patent expirations, growth targets for products or regions, expected growth
4. Information about management and shareholders
5. Background about the company, including a discussions of key legislation, industry trends, facilities, and strategies
6. Information about intangible assets, such as information about research and development, customer relations, and innovations

These voluntary disclosures should be used to supplement the required disclosures because they provide management's perspective of what drives the company's financial results.

In a perfect world, the system of financial disclosure would provide information that is:

---

[1] For a discussion of the issues of transparency in the telecommunications industry, see the testimony of John M. Morrissey before the Subcommittee on Oversight and Investigations Committee on Financial Services, March 21, 2002.

- *Relevant* to the determination of fundamental value
- *Reflective* of the true economics of the transactions
- *Verifiable*, such that estimates and assumptions are reasonable and understood
- *Neutral* with respect to any predetermined result, such as analysts' forecasts
- *Comparable*, enabling the analyst to compare information among companies and over time
- *Complete*, providing sufficient information to understand a company's past, current, and future performance
- *Understandable* to all stakeholders

Of course, we do not live in a perfect world. The improvements in financial disclosures and the audit function, as well as enhanced penalties for misdeeds, will result in better quality financial disclosures. The financial analyst must, however, still be diligent in looking at this information critically.

One of the signs of an increasing awareness and importance of the accuracy of financial statement has been the increased number of companies restating their financial disclosures for "accounting irregularities." Restatements occur when companies correct errors in previously reported financial statement information, with revenue recognition being the most frequent basis for restatements.

EXHIBIT 10.1   Number of Restatements of NYSE, AMSE, and NASDAQ-Listed Companies, 1997–2002

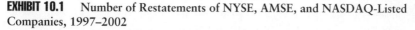

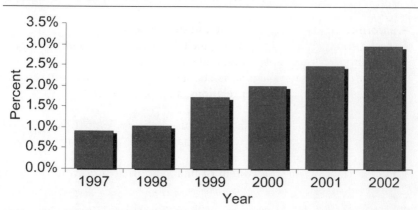

Source: Financial Statement Restatements: Trends, Market Impacts, Regulatory Responses, and Remaining Challenges, General Accounting Office, Report to Chairman, Committee on Banking, Housing, and Urban Affairs, U.S. Senate, (October 2002).

In a study of restatements, the General Accounting Office (GAO) reported the frequency of restatements. Using the data from this study, we show the trend of restatements in Exhibit 10.1.[2] As you can see, though the proportion of companies restating results is small, the number of restatements has increased, coinciding with the revelation of corporate scandals. In terms of who is initiating the restatements, the company itself is the most frequent initiator, initiating 49% of these restatements. What this tells us is that companies are aware of the increased scrutiny of financial disclosures and they are taking measures to insure that their disclosures are accurate.[3]

THE LESSONS

Throughout this book, we have offered tools and techniques that the analyst may apply in performing a financial analysis. We have also pointed out some of the things that analysts missed along the way, which were eventually brought to light in the financial scandals of recent years. From all of this, you should take along with you a number of lessons regarding financial analysis.

Lesson 1: Understand What You Are Looking At

The financial analyst must be aware of the type of disclosure that he or she is looking at.

- Is this a disclosure that is prepared according to generally accepted accounting principles, or is this pro forma information?
- If the disclosure is earnings, specifically what earnings are these? Before or after the effects of an accounting change? Before or after the effects of discontinued items? Before or after extraordinary items? Before or after special items?

The analyst must have a thorough understanding of accounting principles, as well as understand the source of the information.

Consider the issue of a company's earnings. Within generally accepted accounting principles, the company's management has some discretion with regard to how it classifies some income and expenses on the income

---

[2] *Financial Statement Restatements: Trends, Market Impacts, Regulatory Responses, and Remaining Challenges*, General Accounting Office, Report to Chairman, Committee on Banking, Housing, and Urban Affairs, U.S. Senate, (October 2002).

[3] This also tells us that a financial analyst should try to understand the reasons that companies restate their financial numbers. It is often the case that there are accounting irregularities.

statement. Researchers have observed that investors give less weight to transitory items on the income statement than to permanent items.[4] With that in mind, we can see why companies have wanted to separate transitory from permanent items. But this introduces an element of confusion because there are now many earnings figures to sort through, for example:

- Earnings before interest, taxes, depreciation, and amortization (EBITDA)
- Operating income
- Income before income taxes
- Income from continuing operations
- Income before extraordinary items
- Income before effect of changes in accounting principles
- Net income

In addition, companies may develop their own measures that they present alongside the GAAP figures. Consider TXU, which is an energy holding company. For 2004, it reported income that

> Operational earnings, which exclude special items, for the fourth quarter of 2004 were $183 million, $0.67 per share of common stock, compared to $34 million, $0.11 per share for 2003, a 509 percent increase in per share earnings.

This statement by the company's management suggests that the company did well on a continuing basis, producing an increase in earnings. We get a slightly different picture of company performance when we look at GAAP earnings over time, as we see in Exhibit 10.2, Panel A. The net income declined from $582 million in the 2003 fiscal year to $485 million, whereas net income to common shareholders declined from $560 million to a loss of $386 million.

Why the different financial pictures? It is the terminology: the company's introduction of the term "operational earnings" muddies the waters. The definition provided in the footnote to the company's press release indicates that this is income adjusted for special items, discontinued operations, and the cumulative effect of accounting change. The special items, detailed in its 10-K filings for 2004, include employee severance costs, asset

---

[4] See, for example, Mark T. Bradshaw, Matthew Moberg, and Richard G. Sloan, "GAAP Versus the Street: An Empirical Assessment of Two Alternative Definitions of Earnings," *Journal of Accounting Research* 40 (2002), pp. 41–65; or David Burgstahler, James Jiambalvo, and Terry Shevlin, "Do Stock Prices Fully Reflect the Implications of Special Items for Future Earnings?" *Journal of Accounting Research* 40 (2002), pp. 585–612.

EXHIBIT 10.2   TXU Corporation's 2004 Earnings
Panel A. Trends in GAAP Earnings, 1994–2004

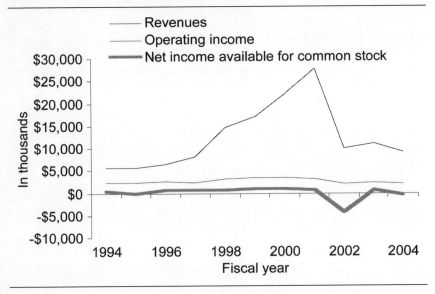

Panel B. TXU and its Operational Earnings

Net loss to common	–$386
Less: Income from discontinued operations	378
Less: Extraordinary gain	16
Less: Cumulative effect of changes in accounting principles	10
Add: Premium on exchange preferred membership interests	849
Income from continuing operations	$59
Add: Special items	828
Operational earnings	$887

Source: 10-K filings, various years, and TXU News Release, February 2, 2005.

impairments, software write-offs, changes on leased equipment, and consulting and professional fees. Many companies do not consider these items
"special," so for comparability purposes, we would want to take a close
look at the company's adjustments to arrive at "operational earnings."

So what earnings should the financial analyst use in the analysis of
TXU? Probably a number somewhere between the loss of $386 million
and income of $887 million. The analyst must delve into the footnotes
and explanations of the extraordinary gains and losses, the special items,
and discontinued items to determine how much, if any, of these items are

likely to recur in the future. For example, in the case of TXU, there is an $849 million charge to arrive at net income for common stockholders for the buyback of exchangeable preferred membership interests. From a review of footnote 9 of TXU's 2004 10-K filing, we see that this is a repurchase of preferred stock that reduces paid-in capital, similar to a repurchase of common stock. We would not expect to see this in the future and therefore it is reasonable to back out this charge in using the income for 2004 to help forecast future income to common shareholders.

Lesson 2: Read the Fine Print

The information that companies provide in their balance sheet, income statement, and statement of cash flows is informative; but there is so much more that we can learn from footnotes, the management discussion and analysis, and other disclosures.

The trend in regulation and accounting pertaining to financial reporting is requiring companies to disclosure more information in the management discussion and analysis and footnotes. In fact, these items should be the starting place in the examination of financial statements—understanding what is behind the numbers that appear in the balance sheet, income statement, and statement of cash flows. The challenge is that footnotes may be neither concise nor clear. Companies are required to provide these footnotes, but there is no standard for the format or readability. For example, the convoluted nature of the "special purposes entities" of Enron Corporation was evident in the company's own footnotes and the publicly available filings of the special purpose entities. Though it may not have been possible to unravel all the financial threads in this case, there was enough to raise questions.

Many of the companies involved in financial scandals in the past provided information that should have been a red flag (or at least a caution flag) regarding the management of earnings. Consider the case of Waste Management. Waste Management used many different devices, including extending depreciable lives and altering salvage values on depreciable assets, to meet analysts' earnings expectations. Hints of this were offered in its footnotes. For example, in a footnote in its 1995 10-K filing (p. 27), Waste Management disclosed the following:[5]

> In 1995, depreciation and amortization decreased due to the change in the estimated useful life of excess cost over net assets of acquired businesses related to certain acquisitions from 25 to 40 years, effective January 1, 1995,

---

[5] Formerly USA Waste.

which resulted in decreased amortization expense of
approximately $1,488,000 for the year. This change in
accounting policy substantially offset the normal increase
in depreciation and amortization of property and equipment used to generate increased operating revenues.

In other words, operating earnings were enhanced from the change
in the estimated lives of depreciable assets. In 1998, Waste Management
restated its earnings for this and other irregularities, becoming at the
time the largest restatement of earnings in corporate history.

Lesson 3: If It's Too Good To Be True, It May Be

There are many corporate success stories, such as Microsoft and Wal-
Mart Stores, and we enjoy watching these successes. But each of these
successes can be explained by the company's comparative or competitive
advantage. Value is not created from the proverbial thin air, but rather
must come from some advantage the company is able to exploit.

In a study of a large number of U.S. companies, Chan, Karceski, and
Lakonishok examine the level and persistence of earnings growth rates.[6]
They find that in the period from 1951–1998:

- The median growth rate of earnings is 10% per year.
- After removing dividends, the growth rate of earnings mirrors that of
  the gross domestic product, between 3% and 3.5%.
- Only 5% of companies have growth rates that exceed 29% per year
  over 10 years, with most of these highest-growth companies being
  smaller companies.
- Persistence in sales growth does not always translate to persistence in
  earnings growth.
- On average, only 3% of companies have growth consistently above
  the median for five years running.

If we look at the growth in revenues of Enron Corporation from
1986 through 2000, we see that revenues grew at an average annual rate
of 20.29% and earnings grew at a rate of 22.43% per year. You can see
the growth in revenues in Exhibit 10.3, Panel A. In fact, Enron's revenues more than doubled from fiscal year 1999 to 2000.

But this growth was not without its problems, as we saw with the
eventual scandal and bankruptcy that followed fiscal year 2000. Enron
relied heavily on accounting gimmicks and debt financing to fuel its rev-

---

[6] Louis K. C. Chan, Jason Karceski, and Josef Lakonishok, "The Level of Persistence
of Growth Rates," *Journal of Finance* 58, no. 2 (2003), pp. 634–684.

EXHIBIT 10.3   Enron Corporation, Revenues and Capital Structure, 1986 through 2000

Panel A. Enron Corporation Revenues, 1986–2000

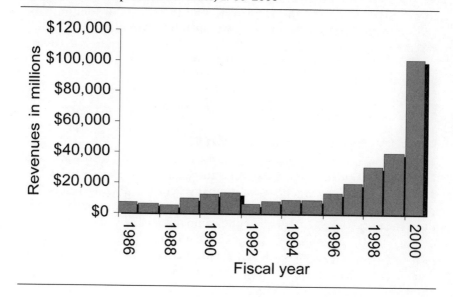

Panel B. Enron Corporation Liabilities and Equity, 1986–2000

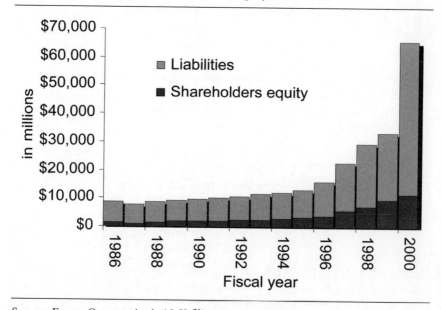

Source: Enron Corporation's 10-K filings, various years, and www.enron.com.

enue growth. By 2000, Enron reported that over 82% of its assets were financed with debt—and this does not consider the debt that was shifted off the balance sheet through the special purpose entities. We have graphed the reported liabilities and equity of Enron Corporation from 1986 through 2000 in Panel B of this figure. The growth in Enron was based largely on debt financing, which is difficult to sustain over time.

Lesson 4: Follow the Money

An analysis of a company must include an analysis of its cash flows. Alongside the typical financial ratios, a financial analyst should also be looking closely at cash flows—the trends in these flows, as well as how cash flows compare to income. Cash flow information is generally more reliable than earnings information because earnings may include non-cash income and expenses items that are arbitrary.

We can see some of the problems of Enron by looking beyond the annual figures to see the patterns emerging on a quarterly basis. Many companies experience seasonal fluctuations in their business, which affects revenues and net income. We often see a difference between a company's cash flow from operations and its operating income, which is resolved over time; in other words, the differences between operating income and cash flow from operations are generally zero, when considered over time.

In the case of the Enron Corporation, whose cash flows we depict in Exhibit 10.4, Panels A and B, the relation between cash flows and earnings was not as expected. On a quarterly basis, as shown in Panel A, cash flows from operations were largely negative in many quarters in which operating income was positive. In Panel B, we can see how the growth in operating income far exceeded that of cash flows from operations, suggesting that there may have been some management of earnings.

The question arises as to why financial analysts did not see these problems as they occurred. First, hindsight is 50–50 and it is not easy to detect fraudulent acts that distort publicly available financial information. Second, some analysts did point out some problems with Enron Corporation prior to the scandal, but it is difficult for nay-sayers to get attention with a stock that was rising and a company that has investment grade ratings.[7]

---

[7] And still a third issue is that there is a tendency for analysts to be overly optimistic in the near-term in the case of companies issuing debt. See Mark T. Bradshaw, "Playing Favorites: Financing Options Sway Analysts' Thinking," *Investor Relations Quarterly* (June 2004). There is harsh criticism of analysts who missed the problems with Enron. See, for example, "The Watchdogs Didn't Bark: Enron and the Wall Street Analysts," Hearing Before the Senate Governmental Affairs Committee, 107th Cong., Senate Hearing 107-385 (February 27, 2002).

EXHIBIT 10.4   Enron Corporation's Operating Income versus Cash Flow from Operations

Panel A. Quarterly Operating Income and Cash Flow from Operations, 1997–2001

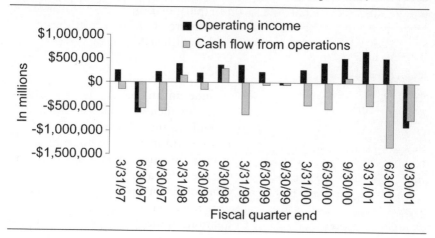

Panel B. Annual Operating Income and Cash Flow from Operations, 1986–2001

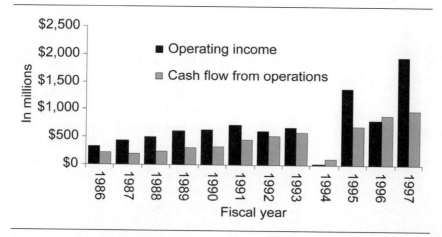

Source: Enron Corporation's 10-K filings, various years, and www.enron.com.

Lesson 5: Understand the Risks

There are many risks that a company faces and the types and extent of these risks vary from company to company, even within the same industry. For example, if you consider airlines and their problem with a high degree of business risk, you can see differences in how these airlines manage these risks, as we show in Exhibit 10.5. The ratio of debt to

EXHIBIT 10.5   Long-Term Debt to Equity Ratios of Companies in the Airline Industry

Airline	Ratio of Long-Term Debt to Equity
AMR Corporation	nmf
Delta Air Lines	nmf
Jet Blue Airways	1.846
Midwest Air Group	0.794
Southwest Airlines	0.308

Note: nmf is undefined because shareholders' equity is negative.
Source: 10-K filings for fiscal year 2004.

equity is wide ranging in this industry, suggesting different willingness to add financial risk to the already substantial business risk. Therefore, there are two dimensions to understand risks: (1) understanding what they are, and (2) understanding how companies deal with these risks.

Types of Risk

The types of risks that a company faces are varied. We can use financial analysis to get an idea of the company's sales, operating, and financial risk. However, there are more specific risks that companies face. We can get an idea of these risks by looking at the company's market risk disclosure (Item 7A in the company's 10-K filing).

Consider the risks disclosed in IBM's *2004 Annual Report* (p. 33–34):

■ Interest rate risk
■ Foreign currency exchange rate risk with respect to debt and non-U.S. dollar-denominated assets and liabilities
■ Collectibility of accounts receivable
■ Recoverability of residual values on leased assets

These risks are different, say, from a company that relies on raw materials, such as a manufacturer of food products. For example, Kellogg lists three risks in its *2004 Annual Report* (pp. 28–29):

■ Foreign exchange risk
■ Interest rate risk
■ Price risk with respect to commodities and energy

An analyst may derive information about a company's other risks from the company's disclosure about contingencies (e.g., lawsuits) and segment disclosures.

Management of Risks

Though most companies are exposed to interest rate risk, foreign currency exchange risk, credit risk, and other risks, the analyst must examine how companies manage these risks. For example, many companies use derivatives to affect the magnitude or the direction of such risks.[8] Analyst need to understand the actions and transactions that companies take to manage risks. For example, who are the counterparties in a swap transaction? Is the company hedging their interest rate risk? If so, what means are they using to do so?

Many companies, for example, hedge some of their risk using derivatives, such as forward, futures, and swaps. A company's use of derivatives will be disclosed according to Statement of Financial Accounting Standards No. 133, *Accounting for Derivative Instruments and Hedging Activities*.[9] When a company uses derivatives, it must determine at the outset how this derivative is being used.

- If the derivative is being used to hedge exposure to changes in the value an asset or liability, the extent to which the hedge is not effective is recognized in the income statement.
- If the derivative is being used to hedge exposure to variable cash flows (such as future cash flows from a forecasted transaction), the effective portion of the derivative's gain or loss goes into comprehensive income (and hence directly to shareholders' equity, bypassing the income statement), and then is recognized as a part of a gain or loss when the forecasted transaction affects earnings.
- If the derivative is being used to hedge a foreign currency exposure of an investment in a foreign corporation, any gain or loss is a part of comprehensive income (and shareholders' equity, bypassing the income statement).

Actually, the accounting for derivatives is much more complicated than this simple description and results in a rather obtuse disclosure.

---

[8] Warren Buffett, in the 2004 Annual Report of Berkshire Hathaway, remarks on companies' use of derivatives (p. 11), "Like Hell, derivative trading is easy to enter but difficult to leave."

[9] This SFAS is amended by SFAS No. 149, Amendment of Statement 133 on *Derivative Instruments and Hedging Acti*vities, which clarifies some of the more confusing aspects of No. 133.

Warren Buffett, in the 2003 Berkshire Hathaway Annual Report (p. 15) sums up this reporting:

> If our derivatives experience—and the Freddie Mac she-
> nanigans of mind-blowing size and audacity that were
> revealed last year—makes you suspicious of accounting in
> this arena, consider yourself wised up. No matter how
> financially sophisticated you are, you can't possibly learn
> from reading the disclosure documents of a derivatives-
> intensive company what risks lurk in its positions. Indeed,
> the more you know about derivatives, the less you will feel
> you can learn from the disclosures normally proffered you.
> In Darwin's words, "Ignorance more frequently begets
> confidence than does knowledge."

And the true test of a company's use of derivatives, according to Warren Buffett, is what it does over a period of time in which there is no growth, because everyone does well in a bull market. As he cleverly points out, "You only learn who has been swimming naked when the tide goes out."[10]

THE FUTURE OF FINANCIAL ANALYSIS IN THE POST-SOX ERA

There is no doubt that the financial scandals of the past few years and the resulting legislation, regulation, and rule-making have changed financial analysis. The Sarbanes-Oxley Act of 2002 (SOX) is the single-most important legislation affecting financial reporting since the Securities Act of 1933 and the Securities Exchange Act of 1934. SOX provides for more oversight of the auditing function, increased corporate financial disclosures, and improved corporate governance.

There are many implications of SOX to financial analysis. Examples include the following:

1. The management discussion and analysis section of the 10-K filing is more informative. In particular, this section will provide information about off-balance sheet arrangements.
2. A larger number of events trigger an 8-K filing. The financial analyst therefore has more information about more events related to a company. The additional triggering events include the entry or termination

---

[10] *Berkshire Hathaway 2004 Annual Report.*

of a material definitive agreement, the completion or asset acquisition or disposition, creation of a financial obligation (direct or off-balance sheet), and changes in the certifying accountant.

3. An adverse opinion with respect to a weakness in internal controls should at least get the attention of the analyst. When SOX's internal control requirement (section 404) is first implemented, we expect a number of companies to have some type of ineffective internal control or weakness. However, beyond the law's initial implementation, a weakness or ineffective control should be a red flag to the financial analyst.

Additionally, there are many provisions in SOX, such as those to seek to reduce conflicts of interest, which provide more confidence in the data reported by companies.

One of the themes of SOX is the responsibility of the "gatekeepers" to our financial markets. Along with auditors, boards of directors, and lawyers, financial analysts are important gatekeepers, with a responsibility to the capital markets. As gatekeepers, financial analysts have a responsibility to interpret financial disclosures, along with other available information, to provide useful information to stakeholders with regard to the company's financial condition and operating performance in the future.

CONCLUSION

Financial analysis requires using all available information to assess a company's current financial condition and performance and to predict its future condition and performance. In this book, we have introduced you to a number of tools and techniques that you can apply in your analysis of a business enterprise. You may want to explore the resources mentioned in this book, which include:

EDGAR, Electronic Data Gathering, Analysis, and Retrieval system, U.S. Securities and Exchange Commission, www.sec.gov/edgar.shtml. Complete filings for all publicly traded companies in the United States.

Federal securities laws, U.S. Securities and Exchange Commission, www.sec.gov/about/laws.shtml. Includes the Securities Exchange Act of 1934 and the Sarbanes-Oxley Act of 2002

Financial Accounting Standards Board, www.fasb.org/. Exposure drafts and adopted rules, research, and staff positions.

Information for accountants and auditors, Office of the Chief Accountant, Securities and Exchange Commission, www.sec.gov/about/offices/oca.htm. Accounting rules and requirements for compliance with SEC filing requirements.

International Financial Reporting Standards, www.iasb.org/standards/index.asp. Standards, interpretations, and summaries of international accounting standards.

Regulatory actions and rules, U.S. Securities and Exchange Commission, www.sec.gov/rules.shtml. Includes policy statements, proposed rules, and final rules.

The CFA Institute, www.cfainstitute.org. A global organization that advocates transparency in capital markets.

To expand your knowledge in this area even further, you may want to continue your study of financial analysis with these further readings:

CFA Institute, *Analyzing, Researching and Valuing Equity Investments*, CFA Institute Conference Proceedings (Charlottesville, VA: CFA Institute, June 2005).

CFA Institute, *Equity Analysis Issues, Lessons, and Techniniques*, CFA Institute Conference Proceedings (Charlottesville, VA: CFA Institute, April 2004).

Coggin, T. Daniel, and Frank J. Fabozzi, *Applied Equity Valuation* (New York: John Wiley & Sons, 2001).

Copeland, Tom, Tim Koller, and Jack Murrin, *Valuation: Measuring and Managing the Value of Companies*, 3rd edition (New York: John Wiley & Sons, 2000).

Damodaran, Aswath. *Investment Philosophies: Successful Strategies and the Investors Who Made Them Work* (New York: John Wiley & Sons, 2003).

Dechow, Patricia M, and Catherine M. Schrand. *Earnings Quality* (Charlottesville, VA: The CFA Institute: The Research Foundation of CFA Institute, July 2004).

Fridson, Martin S., Fernando Alvarez, and Marc A. Rubin, *Financial Statement Analysis* (New York: John Wiley & Sons, 2006).

Penman, Stephen H., *Financial Statement Analysis and Security Valuation*, 2nd ed. (New York: McGraw-Hill Irwin, 2004).

Stowe, John D., Thomas R. Robinson, Jerald E. Pinto, and Dennis McLeavey. *Analysis of Equity Investments: Valuation* (Charlottesville, VA: CFA Institute, 2002).